18.95

D1008228

Colorado Springs
Dec 1983

The
Executive
Mind

*New Insights on Managerial
Thought and Action*

Suresh Srivastva and Associates

The
Executive
Mind

 Jossey-Bass Publishers

San Francisco • Washington • London • 1983

THE EXECUTIVE MIND
New Insights on Managerial Thought and Action
by Suresh Srivastva and Associates

Copyright © 1983 by: Jossey-Bass Inc., Publishers
433 California Street
San Francisco, California 94104
&
Jossey-Bass Limited
28 Banner Street
London EC1Y 8QE

Library of Congress Cataloging in Publication Data

Srivastva, Suresh (date)
    The executive mind.

    Based on a symposium held at Case Western Reserve
University in 1982.
    Bibliography: p. 311
    Includes index.
    1. Organizational behavior—Congresses. 2. Executives
—Congresses. 3. Thought and thinking—Congresses.
I. Title.
HD58.7.S7   1983   658.4'09   83-48165
ISBN 0-87589-584-0

Manufactured in the United States of America

The paper in this book meets the guidelines for
permanence and durability of the Committee on
Production Guidelines for Book Longevity of the
Council on Library Resources.

JACKET DESIGN BY WILLI BAUM

FIRST EDITION

Code 8331

A joint publication in
The Jossey-Bass Management Series
and
The Jossey-Bass Social
and Behavioral Science Series

Consulting Editors

Organizations and Their Management

Warren Bennis
University of Southern California

Richard O. Mason
University of Arizona

Ian I. Mitroff
Universtiy of Southern California

Preface

In 1982 an event took place at Case Western Reserve University
in the form of a symposium that shared the title of this volume.
This book is the final culmination of ideas developed and
shaped during that symposium. The chapters have been re-
written and revised to provide an integrated view of the topic of
executive mind, as inquiry into this area has been only partly
understood and largely avoided owing to its innate complexity.
Its exploration requires a rekindling of a quality of intellect too
long dormant in the social sciences, a reunion of rationalism and
intuition, and a mindful rather than mindless exchange of ideas.

The choice of topics has been guided by a recognition
that executives are powerful actors in and shapers of the environment in which all of us live and those of us in academia pur-
port to understand. By failing to address the quality of executive
thought processes, we have too often characterized executives
as master politicians or supreme logicians and tacticians and
have viewed their actions as rational responses to stimuli about
them that they somehow were able to perceive more closely

than others of lesser caliber. The works contained in this volume attempt to rehumanize the concept of executive mind and to capture both its essence and its unique variability in a holistic, empathic fashion. Moreover, the choices here are influenced by a desire to distinguish these contributions from others that have maintained the strict academic walls of psychology, sociology, and other academic disciplines. The contributors to this volume are distinguished by their efforts to meld theory and practice and on their heavy reliance on a theory-building approach through innovative processes of inquiry. Historically, most of their solid works have been characterized by an activist approach to organizational change and by implicit normative assumptions about human behavior in their methods of inquiry. Thus, their major efforts in understanding organizations have been process-oriented, problem-centered, and developmental. These contributors as professionals and scholars have not taken a hands-off attitude toward their subject of inquiry; rather, they have taken advocacy positions for organizational change. In this sense they have assumed that research itself is an intervention for the better within the organizations. These assumptions have served to support the research action and action research strategies.

    The theme of executive mind is pertinent for deliberations because much of the holistic research and knowledge in the field has emphasized both the primary and secondary mental processes involved in understanding executive behavior. The primary processes involving explorations of feelings, affect, and subjective states have led to the understanding of beliefs, values, attitudes, mental states, symbols, emotions, and a whole range of topics not easily dealt with through the arguments of rationality. While this emphasis has opened up new avenues of inquiry, the studies of secondary processes such as decision making, learning styles, problem solving, and leadership have enhanced knowledge by establishing causal connections among sets of variables in an attempt to explain executive behavior. In studying primary and secondary processes, the works included here move the subject of inquiry away from its conventional status as a behavioral science toward a new position as a combined *cognitive* and behavioral science. More thought will be given *to* thought and more effort devoted to understanding both unique and collective experiences. Such movement will necessarily require new research methods and strategies, as some authors of the chapters included here point out; in addition, this movement will require an appreciation of the subjects of our research heretofore espoused but not carried out in practice. Certainly this volume will throw down a gauntlet of humanistic challenge to those who would think and write about the behavior of executives as well as others in organizational settings.

The volume contains eleven original chapters in addition to an introductory and final chapter. The original chapters represent views developed by leaders in the field of organizational behavior. Executives themselves should find this volume refreshingly descriptive rather than prescriptive. None of the chapters will provide simple lists for gaining influence or winning long-term success. Rather, executives should read the volume introspectively, reflecting time and again on its lucid explications of processes and feelings that they may previously have guessed could never be shared, let alone discussed, with others. It is a book that executives should find to be as exceedingly complex and undeniably captivating as their own lives, because these seminal thinkers have shared not only their lives' work but the work of their lives. The authors have risked to share openly, through their words and meanings, heartfelt experiences of themselves and others; the work of each is an expression of his own executive mind in action.

The book should appeal to both the academic and executive worlds. It would provide suitable material for advanced graduate courses but more likely will become one of the standard reference works that will help us formulate our research and action ideas. It is a book that is timely given the current level of interest in discovering more effective means of managing organizations, but it is timeless in that the basic processes and dilemmas described will always have relevance to those in executive positions and those who study them.

The spirit behind the preparation of this volume needs special notice. In addition to maintaining exacting standards of

excellence in writing individual chapters, the participants exhibited many resourceful characteristics that made the book a
gathering of ideas from colleagues who are inclined to celebrate
a learning festival. The authors' use of appreciative modes of
interaction, ability to learn from the ideas of others, keenness
to observe the deeper meaning of human processes, and avuncu-
lar instinct to contribute to the development of others are
extraordinarily rich.

My colleagues who have prepared the original papers and
those who have participated in the endeavor to prepare this volume deserve cheers and gratitude.

During the nascent phase I was supported most ably by
all my faculty colleagues in the Department of Organizational
Behavior at Case Western Reserve University in the idea formulation and design development of this book. My faculty colleagues included Frank Friedlander, Ronald Fry, Gregory
Gaertner, Karen Gaertner, David Kolb, Eric Neilsen, William
Pasmore, Michelle Spain, and Donald Wolfe. All our graduate
students acted as genuine colleagues and worked with me at
every step on the way. David Cooperrider and Dennis O'Connor
stand out as most valuable, as they were directly involved in
helping and working with me in making this book an actuality.
I am grateful to colleagues from other disciplines, the group of
participants who were members of our alumni group, senior
managers from organizations, and colleagues from other universities, who have assisted me in this effort. Warren Bennis, Richard O. Mason, and Ian I. Mitroff, who are consulting editors of
the series, have been continuously supportive, thoughtful, and
generous with their ideas and time. I am grateful to many human beings, and I cherish their assistance, support, and encouragement. All intellectual and human efforts require some administrative underpinnings, and in that endeavor the work and
untiring efforts of Retta Holdorf are a model for other administrators.

Cleveland, Ohio   Suresh Srivastva
August 1983

Contents

Contents

The Authors

Chris Argyris is the James Bryant Conant Professor of Education and Organizational Behavior in the Graduate School of Education at Harvard University. He received his Ph.D. degree in industrial and organizational psychology from Cornell University (1951).

Argyris received the 1977 American Board of Professional Psychology Distinguished Contribution Award. His books include *Increasing Leadership Effectiveness, Behind the Front Page, The Applicability of Organizational Sociology, Personality and Organization,* and *Reasoning, Learning, and Action.*

Warren Bennis is Joseph Deubell Distinguished Professor of Management at the University of Southern California. He received his Ph.D. degree in industrial economics and social science from the Massachusetts Institute of Technology (1955).

Bennis and his colleagues revolutionized the ideas of management on the most effective means of motivating employees and thereby increasing productivity. He has published over 300 articles and twenty books. The coveted McKinsey award for the best book on management was awarded to two of his books.

Bennis has been provost and executive vice-president at the State University of New York at Buffalo and president of the University of Cincinnati.

Frank Friedlander is a member of the faculty at the Fielding Institute in California. He received his Ph.D. degree in psychology from Western Reserve University (1962). He spent sixteen years on the faculty of the Department of Organizational Behavior at Case Western Reserve University before moving to California.

Friedlander has published many articles in well-known journals. He has been elected to serve as chairman of the Division of Organization Development, Academy of Management; representative to the council of the American Psychological Association; a member of the executive committee, Division of Industrial and Organizational Psychology, American Psychological Association; and a member of the executive committee, board of directors, Ohio Psychological Association. He has been on the editorial board of the *Journal of Applied Psychology* and has served as a part-time reviewer for *Administrative Science Quarterly, Psychological Bulletin,* and *Contemporary Psychology.*

Ronald E. Fry is assistant professor of organizational behavior, Weatherhead School of Management, at Case Western Reserve University. He received his Ph.D. degree in management from the Massachusetts Institute of Technology (1978).

Fry's research interests include the application of the "learning environment" framework to the study of groups and multiple group relations in organizations. He has coauthored several books: *Managing Health Care Delivery: A Training Program for Primary Care Physicians; Managing Human Resources in Health Care Organizations: An Applied Approach;* and *Improving the Coordination of Care: A Program for Health Team Development.*

David A. Kolb is professor of organizational behavior and management in the Department of Organizational Behavior, Weatherhead School of Management, at Case Western Reserve University. He received his Ph.D. degree in social psychology from Harvard University (1967).

Recently Kolb has been engaged in a major research project concerning experiential learning and adult career development that focuses on, among other issues, the impact of mid-career changes on managers. He has coauthored an innovative textbook, *Organizational Psychology: An Experiential Approach,* which is used in many leading schools of business throughout the world. He is also coauthor of *Organizational Psychology: A Book of Readings* and *Changing Human Behavior: Principles of Planned Intervention.*

Richard O. Mason is professor of management and management information systems, School of Business and Public Administration, University of Arizona. He received his Ph.D. degree in management from the University of California, Berkeley (1968).

Mason has been involved in research and consulting in the fields of information systems, strategy, and organizational behavior with a number of public, private, and not-for-profit organizations. His current interests include organizational strategy, the behavioral side of information systems, and the ethics of information. He is a coauthor of *The 1980 Census: Policymaking amid Turbulence, Challenging Strategic Planning Assumptions, Creating a Dialectical Social Science, Measurement for Management Decision,* and *Strategic Management and Business Policy,* as well as other books and publications.

Fred Massarik is professor and chairman, behavioral and organizational science faculty, at the University of California, Los Angeles (UCLA). He received his Ph.D. degree in psychology from UCLA (1957).

He is codirector of the Ojai Leadership and Organization Development Laboratories, UCLA Extension, Division of Applied Behavioral Science, which is the longest continuing human relations training, team-building, and organization development program of its kind in the western United States.

He is author/editor of numerous articles and books in the application of behavioral science and psychological knowledge, including *Leadership and Organization, The Course of Human Life,* and *Social Psychological Approaches in Genetic Disease Control.*

Henry Mintzberg is Bronfman Professor of Management, Faculty of Management, McGill University. He received his Ph.D. degree in management policy from the Massachusetts Institute of Technology (1969).

Mintzberg is known for his research on managerial work, strategic decision making, and strategy formation. He has written numerous articles in the management field, including the McKinsey prize winner as the best article in the 1975 *Harvard Business Review.* He has recently completed *The Structuring of Organizations,* the first of a series of five books by Mintzberg to be published under the title "The Theory of Management Policy Series."

Ian I. Mitroff is Harold Quinton Distinguished Professor of Business Policy, Department of Management and Policy Sciences, University of Southern California. He received his Ph.D. degree in engineering science from the University of California, Berkeley (1967).

Mitroff's research is especially concerned with the development of methods that are both theoretically sound and practically effective to aid decision makers in coping with messy, ill-defined problems. He has published a number of papers and books on such topics as the decision and problem-solving styles of managers and scientists; the philosophy, psychology, and sociology of science; knowledge acquisition and use; the design of management information systems; management and strategic planning; and organizational psychology. His most recent book is *Stakeholders of the Organizational Mind.*

He is a faculty participant in the consulting organization Management Analysis Center and for the year 1980–81 was president of the Planner's League, an association of practicing corporate planners.

William A. Pasmore is associate professor of organizational behavior, Weatherhead School of Management, at Case Western Reserve University. He received his Ph.D. degree in administrative sciences from Purdue University (1976).

Pasmore is author of numerous articles on work redesign and organizational change. He is also coauthor of *Sociotechnical Systems: A Sourcebook* and is currently working on two additional volumes: *Sociotechnical Systems: An Action Research Perspective* and *Parallel Groups in Organizations*.

Louis R. Pondy is professor of organizational behavior and head of the Department of Business Administration at the University of Illinois, Urbana-Champaign. He received his Ph.D. degree in industrial administration from Carnegie-Mellon University (1966).

Pondy has written numerous articles on organizational conflict, behavioral aspects of budgeting and resource allocation, health systems research and other public policy issues, organization structure and design, and phenomenological approaches to organization. He was chairman of the Organizational Behavior Division of the Academy of Management and associate editor of *Administrative Science Quarterly*.

Suresh Srivastva is professor and chairman, Department of Organizational Behavior, Weatherhead School of Management, Case Western Reserve University. He received his Ph.D. degree in social psychology from the University of Michigan (1960).

Srivastva has been involved in research and consulting with a number of industrial enterprises and health care systems in the field of organization development. His present interests are in teaching professional managers in the field of social and managerial policy and consulting with organizations developing policies in the context of environmental and social change. He is the coauthor of *Job Satisfaction and Productivity* and *The Management of Work* as well as author of numerous other publications and articles in the field of organizational behavior.

William R. Torbert is associate dean in the Graduate School of Management at Boston College. He received his Ph.D. degree in administrative sciences from Yale University (1971).

In addition to articles and reviews, Torbert has published three research books: *Being for the Most Part Puppets: Interactions Among Men's Labor, Leisure, and Politics; Learning from Experience: Toward Consciousness;* and *Creating a Community of Inquiry: Conflict, Collaboration, Transformation.*

His administrative roles have included associate director, Yale Summer High School; director, Yale Upward Bound; and president, the Theatre of Inquiry, Inc.

James A. Waters is associate professor of management, Faculty of Management, at McGill University. He received his Ph.D. degree in organizational behavior from Case Western Reserve University (1976).

Waters's research interests include strategy formulation and organizational change. Before receiving his Ph.D., he was director of planning for SOHIO, where he directed a study of the economic and sociological impact of the trans-Alaska pipeline.

Karl E. Weick is Nicholas H. Noyes Professor of Organizational Behavior and professor of psychology at Cornell University. He received his Ph.D. degree in social psychology from Ohio State University (1962).

Weick is editor of *Administrative Science Quarterly,* advisory editor, *Contemporary Psychology,* and advisory editor, *Journal for the Theory of Social Behavior.* He has coauthored several books: *The Social Psychology of Organizing; Managerial Behavior, Performance, and Effectiveness;* and *Productivity in Organizations: A Metatherapy of Work and Its Assessment.* He has also written numerous chapters in edited volumes, book reviews, and articles.

The
Executive
Mind

*New Insights on Managerial
Thought and Action*

Introduction:
Common Themes in
Executive Thought
and Action

Suresh Srivastva

The authors who have contributed to this volume are widely recognized as leaders in the study of organizations. For most, writing about the functioning of the executive mind was a logical extension of their previous work; others had already begun to explore the topic before the symposium. The ideas expressed are of the same quality and provocative nature as those that helped to define the field of organizational behavior; the new ideas these boundary setters offer will have impact on the frontier of inquiry for some time to come. The goal of this introduction is to highlight some of the intriguing insights the reader will encounter in this volume.

The chapters here have been organized into four sections representing the most significant common themes which run throughout the chapters and which respond to the issue of executive mind as the center for tacit knowledge. These processes and themes are (1) the process of envisioning, (2) processes of experiencing and sense-making, (3) processes of knowing and enacting, and (4) processes for developing the executive mind. Each of these areas represents a function of the executive mind that sets its thinking apart from other, more mundane cognitions. Each is written about by every author, although some authors address themselves more to one area than another. Each area also represents a challenging line of inquiry that the authors here have just begun. Finally, each area describes processes that are basic to organizational success. For all these reasons, we expect that scholars and managers alike will find the chapters in each section to be consistently stimulating and useful.

The Process of Envisioning

Life at the workplace is like a pendulum, moving between flashbacks and fantasies, recollections and predictions, memories and dreams, historical events and science fiction scenarios. In all such movements one is engaged in responding to the present. The envisioning process thus involves concepts of time and space. In envisioning, one thinks about the future as though it were already present and remembers the past as though it had not disappeared. By *envisioning* we mean creating in one's mind an image of a desired future organizational state that can serve as a guide to interim strategies, decisions, and behavior. The authors who contributed to this section view the process of envisioning as the most basic precursor of effective executive leadership. Without the ability to define a desired future state, the executive would be rudderless in a sea of conflicting demands, contradictory data, and environmental uncertainty. Everyone dreams of a better life; but the executive's dream must be one that simultaneously challenges perceptions of what is possible, what can be realized; motivates others to set aside their misgivings to pursue it; and fits with the forces in the environment that can drive the organization toward higher states of development.

The process of envisioning is at present enigmatic. No one can say exactly how executives learn this skill or whether envi-

sioning is a native ability that can be developed in those who
have the potential for it. At the same time, the process of envisioning is anything but haphazard. The executive mind functions thoughtfully, not whimsically. Experience, insight, creativity, and the disciplined study of possible alternatives produce a
vision that may appear whimsical at first to others but in fact is
not. The vision is invested with the executive's own ego and,
therefore, is carefully devised by the executive to be successful.
Quite often failure of the vision represents a personal failure for
the executive; success, in contrast, produces an organization
that is very nearly a hologram of the executive mind.

The authors whose papers are included in this section are
Warren Bennis, Chris Argyris, and Henry Mintzberg and James
A. Waters. Each chapter, like the vision created by the execu-
tive, represents the culmination of years of work by the authors.

Warren Bennis captures the dialectic of the artform of
leadership as the tension between the need to create a compelling vision to guide others and simultaneously create opportunities within that vision for others to operate in ways that maximize the chances of their success. He defines leadership as the
skills of translating intention into reality and sustaining it.
These skills include the ability to create visions that have the
potential to inspire others to act; facility at communicating that
vision to others and, in so doing, gaining the support of multiple
constituencies; persistence under less-than-ideal circumstances;
empowerment, which is the ability to create social architectures
that sustain energy toward desired results; and organizational
learning, which allows for the monitoring of performance and
adjustments of actions to stay on course in the pursuit of objectives.

Through in-depth interviews and observations of executives at work and at home, Bennis has pieced together a fascinating portrayal of life at the top in American corporations. His
search to understand the common characteristics among these
leaders has produced conclusions that could well influence the
study of organizations and also the educational processes used
to develop executives in this country and elsewhere. For example, he concludes that to be successful enactors of visions, exec-

utives must have virtually no fear of failure. Instead, they must be prepared to view the decisions they make about their organizations and lives as experimental. In this light, failures produce as much data as successes, and it is the data, not the outcome, that are crucial to obtain.

Together the abilities of the executive allow him or her to literally transform reality as others experience it. Hence the title of Bennis's chapter, "The Artform of Leadership."

Indicative of a developing paradigm, conflicts have already begun to surface about the functioning of the executive mind. The chapter by Chris Argyris elaborates on the process of envisioning. Argyris is not at all certain that executives are aware of inconsistencies between their stated visions or beliefs and their actual behaviors. Through analysis of executives' reactions to a series of hypothetical situations, he explores differences between the theories executives say they hold regarding human behavior and the theories they actually use in dealing with others. He analyzes how, particularly when trying to solve difficult problems, executives can become trapped in patterns of behavior that they themselves recognize as counterproductive. He hypothesizes that this may occur for two reasons. First, the abstract theories in actual use help the executive deal with a world that is significantly more complex than the human mind can comprehend at any given moment and are therefore efficient; however, the economy of explanation provided by the theories may cause the executive to interpret events in ways that confirm the theories rather than allowing the executive to make valid observations that might call for new theories. Second, processes of executive thinking are themselves rarely thought about; consequently, executives may be unaware of their thought processes unless they encounter significant failures that cause them to reconsider their theories-in-use. Hence, although Argyris agrees with Bennis about the power of the executive to transform reality, he is concerned that, in the act of doing so, executives may blind themselves to critical errors in strategy.

Strategy formulation is likewise the envisioning process considered by Mintzberg and Waters. For them, strategy as a vision of the future is developed out of interplay between forces enacted by the environment, the organization, and executives themselves. Also indicative of a developing paradigm is the movement away from universal statements to contingency theories; Mintzberg and Waters offer a contingency theory of the envisioning process based on the nature of the particular organization.

Organizations that have been developed and continue to be owned and influenced most significantly by their chief executive are termed "entrepreneurial." In these organizations, the envisioning, strategy-formulating process is mostly a function of the leader. In this respect, Mintzberg and Waters would agree with the previous authors in this section that the executive in entrepreneurial organizations holds tremendous power to influence others' experiences of reality within the organization.

In more highly developed organizations, more characteristic of what Mintzberg and Waters call "machine bureaucracies," the pattern of envisioning is different. Here the transformative power of the executive is more limited by organizational constraints. Rules, procedures, historical decisions, contracts among parties, and other features of bureaucracies limit the executive's freedom to act. Envisioning in the bureaucratic context requires more attention to what is organizationally feasible, rather than being merely an expression of the executive's dreams.

In a third type of organization, the "adhocracy," the environment is the key influence in the envisioning process, owing to its profound and unpredictable impact on organizational functioning. Here patterns of events must be linked together to create a somewhat hazy vision of the future. Without recognition of environmental forces and patterns, executive decisions would at best be random. Success under such conditions requires attention to external factors rather than simply to the desires of the executive.

Mintzberg and Waters support their assertions with case-study data from eleven organizations that they studied historically. The major decisions that shaped the success of the various organizations were of different origin and produced quite different visions for each of the three types of firms. Together the

cases provide important insights into the role of executives in
different organizational settings and help clarify the variables
that influence our understanding of the functioning of the
executive mind.

The three chapters in this section set the stage for the
study of what executives actually do and how they do it, which
are the concerns of the authors who contributed chapters in the
next section of the book. Key to answering such questions are
inquiries into the processes of experiencing and sense-making by
executives.

Processes of Experiencing and Sense-Making

Executives, like all other human beings, use their sensory
receptors as basic resources for understanding the environment.
They talk and eat through their mouths, breathe and smell
through their noses, hear and listen through their ears, see and
observe through their eyes, touch and feel through their skin. In
addition, although they make sense out of talking and listening,
observing and feeling, initiating and responding while making
sense of the environment, they thereby become part of it. Experiencing and sense-making, therefore, are processes that give
meaning to the environment and that make all human beings a
part of the environment simultaneously. This interchange with
the environment provides opportunities of interaction among
experiencing human beings who are engaged in sense-making.
The envisioning process provides the executive with a sense of
purpose and direction that is embodied in the leadership function. When one thinks of charismatic leaders, one tends to focus
on the key decisions or actions they took to inspire their followers to achieve what appeared to be impossible objectives.
The envisioning process alone is not what separates great leaders from lesser ones, however. Also needed are skills in processing information, experiencing the effect of the world on one's
actions and the effect of one's actions on the world, and making
sense of the data and experiences that together portray the
complexity of reality. The executive's visions collide with the
tangible through the sense-making process. The executive must

first formulate plans and later revise them as necessary in light
of data that indicate whether or not the initial plans are working. But where do such data come from? And which data, both
solicited and unsolicited, should the executive heed? When
should the present course be maintained (a vital component of
successful envisioning transformation), and when should it be
altered or abandoned? These are questions addressed by the
authors of chapters in this section. Their answers provide fascinating glimpses of the executive mind in action. Here the analogy of the mind as a computer, albeit an emotional, sometimes
irrational one, fits most closely with the processes described.
Gathering data, sorting through them, making decisions, solving
problems, recasting frameworks for viewing the world, and
working toward more complete understanding are only a few of
the executive behaviors addressed by William R. Torbert, David
A. Kolb, Ian I. Mitroff and Richard O. Mason, and Louis R.
Pondy.

Torbert argues that the executive mind can be distinguished from the ordinary mind by its ability to cultivate timely
actions—that is, actions that effectively transform physical and
social realities in the direction of desired purposes and ideals.
The experience of executive mind is possible, according to Torbert, only when the executive is fully aware of three separate
but interpenetrating scales of time—one's own lifetime calling,
the rhythms of one's enterprise, and world historical events.
Torbert illustrates the functioning of the executive mind
through various examples of executive behavior and discusses
the dilemma of entering the executive role, the dilemma of
executive succession, and the creation of executive teams. He
takes the additional step of suggesting a theory to support activities for social scientists that would cultivate an understanding of the executive mind.

Further, Torbert adds his own insights about the ability
of executives to maintain their conviction of the value of their
dreams, discussed by authors in the preceding section. He views
optimism as an essential driving force for executives and points
out that executives, more than others, have the capability of remaining optimistic at what seem′ to be the darkest moments,

persevering until they are able to make their dreams come true. This optimism is derived from passionate motivation fired by desires to accomplish the improbable. Amid the multiple demands and distractions of the executive environment, the executive stays on course by controlling time in rhythm with his or her lifetime calling, with the temporal pace of the enterprise, and with world historical currents. Torbert notes that such qualities in individuals are unlikely to manifest themselves before the second half of life, when success is no longer defined in others' terms. He also notes that the executive is a vision creator but seldom a vision executor and that, consequently, to retain the participation of others in their dreams, executives must constantly balance their own initiatives against others'. Presumably, this necessity carries over into the way they make sense of the world; executives must therefore be committed to their own sense of purpose, timing, and order of things while being open to influence of these views from others.

Finally, Torbert suggests a useful approach to understanding the mind when he asserts that maximum understanding follows study of the mind by the executive himself or herself rather than others. Such a study would by necessity be existential, increasing awareness of thought processes as they relate to the executive's experience of his or her actions and the timing of decisions.

David Kolb explores the processes that executives use to manage problems. The dialectical nature of the problem-solving process requires a constant interplay between what Kolb calls grasping the problem through apprehension and through comprehension and between transforming it through extension and through intention. He borrows from Hilgard the differentiation of "red" from "green" mind sets to characterize the learning/problem-management process; the red mode facilitates analysis, criticism, logical thinking, and active coping, while the green mode facilitates valuing, information gathering, idea getting, and participation. Both the red and green modes are essential to the problem-management process, although organizations tend to reward logical, red-mode thinking more frequently than emotional, green-mode thinking, making it safer for executives to be critical than to be creative.

The dialectics of situation analysis through these modes of sense-making involve the successive articulation of possible goal states and the exploration of current realities in order to create a menu of problems and opportunities in the situation, from which the most urgent can be chosen. Urgency is determined largely by the emotion the executive attaches to alternative end states through a process that Kolb calls "valuing." Valuing assists not only in priority setting but in providing the energy for problem solving that mobilizes others to pursue directions specified by the executive.

Kolb highlights the social nature of the executive problem-management process in noting that what distinguishes the way executives think and solve problems from the way other adults do is the particular social system they live and work in. According to Kolb, the structure of the organization itself creates problem-management heuristics that tend to sort problems into categories that can be dealt with using predetermined solutions. Interpersonal communication, influence, and other social dynamics then affect the outcome of particular decisions that fall within the predefined framework.

Ian Mitroff and Richard Mason attempt to explain the development of organizational strategy by executives as a process of dealing with their myths about the environment they face and the relevant stakeholders who characterize that environment. Stakeholders are all the individuals, groups, and institutions, past, present, and future, that both affect and are affected by any proposed policy or strategy in dealing with a problem. These stakeholders provide stimuli for executive strategy formulation, based on both rational and intuitive assumptions that executives make about their individual and collective behaviors. How these assumptions form and affect executives, groups, and organizations through the telling of stories, myths, fairy tales, and eventually unifying themes is the focus of this chapter.

Mitroff and Mason point out that the most important problems in organizations involve the *whole* organization and are therefore complex. Such problems, they argue, require similarly complex thinking, most probably of a dialectical nature. At the same time, they recognize that different personality types will tend to see problems differently, so that complex realities are molded to match individual preferences. This is important because finding/defining is as important as problem solving in that the initial construction of the problem usually limits what solutions will eventually be considered acceptable. Thus, differences in personality types that lead to different assumptions about what is important to be attended to will lead to different solutions and eventually different courses of action by the executive and the organization. Their personality-influenced assumptions about stakeholders lead Mitroff and Mason to conclude that conscious plans are more affected by the unconscious than most executives would dare acknowledge and that planning and depth psychology need each other more than they probably recognize.

Louis Pondy argues for viewing the executive mind through a framework of logical incrementalism, as this approach allows a union of rational and intuitive modes of inquiry over time. He conceives the intuitive and rational approaches to sense-making as a dialectical process in that logic is incrementally derived from a set of seemingly intuitive actions or decisions that is later interpreted "as if" rationality had been in use at the time the actions or decisions took place. He stresses that executives live amid an ongoing stream of organizational events that require that they respond to behaviors, not intentions or preconceptions. To do so effectively, he concludes, requires that the executive perfect the art of joining the rational and intuitive modes of thinking.

Pondy maintains that the intuition of executives creates imaginative interpretations of events or data that gradually give meaning to new images of the world. The new images are then used by others as theories on which to base observations and test assumptions guiding action. In this way, intuitive responses to local anomalies become clarified, elaborated, and enlarged until eventually they become fully developed strategies for the firm. In this sojourn of strategy development executives invent words, phrases, and symbols to draw attention to these strategic possibilities and decisions tend to gather momentum when coalitions form in organizations that tend to support those in power and, therefore, the status quo.

The processes of information processing, experiencing, and sense-making described by these authors help us understand how executives make choices in reacting to the world around them. At a still deeper level, underlying those choices and guiding executive behaviors are fundamental, epistemological processes of knowing. Ontological knowledge of self and others accumulates over time as executives learn how they learn, think how they think, and look deeply into themselves to find their guiding spiritual core. These processes of knowing and acting are the topic of the final section of this book.

Processes of Knowing and Enacting

Frank Friedlander, Karl E. Weick, and Fred Massarik have chosen in their chapters to grapple with some of the most elusive but essential aspects of the functioning of the executive mind. Processes of knowing and acting are elusive because they are often unconscious and always in flux, changing with each new experience or encounter of the executive. Each new data point represents a possible revision of internal theories that help executives make sense of their world. It is essential to discover these theories and to understand when they are subject to change, for only in so doing can we understand executive actions as meaningful, thoughtful expressions of internal hypotheses. Once identified and understood, these theories and hypotheses from which actions spring can be challenged to create basic paradigm shifts in thinking that facilitate more successful encounters with reality.

Frank Friedlander looks directly at the learning process, paying particular attention to the conditions that facilitate and hinder executive learning. He notes that the continual and overpowering interaction of components in the executive's environment leads to massive uncertainty, to which the executive must respond with continual on-line learning at a personal level. This learning occurs at the interface between desire and reality that forces the executive to reconstruct his or her understanding of the world to account for the discrepancy. Friedlander notes that learning occurs only when the discrepancy is acknowledged and that many opportunities for learning are overlooked when

differences are suppressed rather than explored. He points out
that learning depends on the successful incorporation of a new
set of dimensions for understanding the environment and on the
resolution of inconsistencies, which results in the attainment of
a higher developmental state. The opposing forces of differentiation and integration created by organizational structures both
provide energy for learning and make contact difficult at organizational interfaces where learning could occur. Power differences diminish heterogeneity and contact, thereby reducing
learning; contact with past events as experiences enhances learning. Conflict, tension, and negative feedback can produce learning, but only under conditions of trust and support. The act of
planning for the future enhances learning, provided that the implied modification of behavior is allowed to occur; changes in
identity are threatening and can inhibit the learning process. Importantly, strategic change can be delayed or avoided because
pursuing past strategies produces managerial values and philosophies consistent with those strategies that make consideration
of alternative approaches difficult. Finally, transitions representing the learning process must occur in the context of one's
need to be learningful rather than productive and competent;
the former mode implies risk taking and mistake making, whereas the latter mode implies commitment to an already-learned set
of behaviors.

Karl Weick questions the traditional notion that executives need more time for reflection in their work to allow them
an opportunity to think; instead, he proposes that executives
think through acting and that successful executives can be distinguished from less successful ones by how thinkingly they perform their various activities. He argues that since most outcomes are sufficiently overdetermined, thought and deliberation
are unlikely to improve those outcomes. Instead, by acting
thinkingly, executives can help to create situations from which
positive outcomes may follow. When people act thinkingly, according to Weick, they pay close attention to what is happening, try to impose order on the setting and their actions in it,
and correct their performance when it strays from reference
standards. Weick discusses how one can communicate thinkingly

by referring to group frameworks, persuade by assertion, and generalize quickly and freely. He also explains why managers choose to impose order and logic on situations where order and logic do not exist so that they can draw consistent interpretations of organizational acts. Finally, he proposes a model that demonstrates how managers, once having imposed an arbitrary logic on a situation, take action based on that logic and then interpret the results achieved in light of their original theory. He concludes that "fighting fires, which managers do all the time, is not necessarily thick-headed or slow-witted. . . . Thinking well is wise; planning well, wiser; doing well, wisest and best of all."

Fred Massarik addresses the issue of needing to develop a new research methodology for understanding the complex and intimately personal nature of the executive mind. His dialectic is the fundamental conflict between self and other; to know others we must use ourselves as research instruments, but in so doing we always color with our own biases what we know of the other. The resolution to this dialectic, for Massarik, is to embrace it rather than deny it, by making the self and other as close to each other in the relationship as possible so that barriers to knowing and sharing by both are minimized.

Massarik suggests a phenomenological methodology in which the researcher takes an active part in developing the data by sharing as much about himself or herself as the subject does, thereby creating a climate for inquiry in which basic emotional processes can be revealed and explored. In this process, "interviewer and interviewee respond to each other as total persons, ready to actively examine and disclose both remote and accessible aspects of their lives." Massarik also provides tantalizing insights based on the results of some preliminary phenomenological observations of executives.

Processes for Developing Executive Mind

The chapter by Ronald E. Fry and William A. Pasmore is a clarion call for looking into our educational efforts in the context of discussions of the functioning of the executive mind. It posits that our educational processes need revitalization if they claim to be in the business of mind building. The ideas were developed from a review of the preceding chapters in this book.

The concluding chapter develops a set of guidelines for experimenting with new ideas for developing executive mind and action. The basic theme suggests that executives manage ideas and discover that managerial action is related to the processes of the mind as envisioned in this volume.

1

The Artform
of Leadership

Warren Bennis

To understand the artform of leadership the following question
must be addressed: What are the components of an organization
that can translate intention into reality and sustain it? The question itself contains a complexity and depth as well as a chronic
elusiveness. The question, probably because of just those characteristics, tends to be avoided—although it addresses the essence
of organizational leadership. And even when it is obliquely
touched on, writers tend to avoid the orchestral richness that in-
heres in the question for the doctrinal, predictable, and prosaic
clichés. Between the blur produced by trying to say too much
at once and the banality produced by dismissing mysteries,
there remains the possibility of articulating just what it is that

This is a part of a larger study that will appear as a book, *The
Chief*, to be published by William Morris, Inc., New York, January 1984.

enables some organizations to translate an intention into reality and sustain it. This is the starting point for an examination of what I am calling transformative power.

The Environment of Leadership in the 1980s

This much can be said about leadership for the 1980s: Those responsible for governing the enterprise will be spending more and more of their time managing external relations. All organizations are surrounded by an increasingly active, incessant environment, one that is becoming more and more influential—the senior partner, as it were—in all kinds of decisions that affect the institution.

Leadership (and its companion, decision making) will become an increasingly intricate process of multilateral brokerage, including constituencies both within and without the organization. More and more decisions made will be public decisions; that is, the people they affect will insist on being heard. Leaders will have to reckon with the growing role of the media as a "fourth branch" of government available for use by the people who oppose or support a particular decision. The idea of a relatively small group of "movers and shakers" who get things done is obsolete. Increasing numbers of citizens and stakeholders, and even those who are only indirectly involved in an issue, have interested themselves in its outcome—and when the decision goes the "wrong way," very noisily so. This state of affairs has led one writer to describe the organization of today as a "jungle of closed decisions, openly arrived at."

The bigger the problem to be tackled, the more power is diffused and the greater the number of people who have to be involved. Thus, decisions become more and more complex, more ill defined, affecting more and more different (and sometimes conflicting) constituencies.

Inevitably there will be frustration, not only among leaders but among followers who ask, "Who's in charge here?" as more and more people/groups have to be consulted. Leaders ask, "How do you get everybody in the act and still get some action?"

Ambiguity and surprise are ubiquitous. Leaders have to lead under uncertain, risky conditions in which it is virtually impossible to get ready for *something* when you have to get ready for *anything*. Just as effective leaders know about, and are becoming more competent at coping with, the politicization of our institutions—by which I mean that institutions are becoming the focus for a new kind of politics, that is, mobilizing public opinion and working more closely with state and federal legislative bodies and with other key constituencies—they are also learning more about an enlarged concept of the "management team."

No longer can "managing external relations" be left in the hands of the public relations department. Top leadership must be involved—directly. In short, the political role of the organization leadership's responsibility must be reconceived. These trends, these changing characteristics of the organizational/managerial environment that we are now living with, will become even more pronounced and problematic over the next ten or so years.

The Three Components of Transformative Power

Leader. Some important clues about the nature of effective leadership have come out of my recently completed study of eighty chief executive officers (CEOs) plus ten in-depth interviews conducted over the past few months with ten successful, "innovative" leaders. These studies provide a basis for making some generalizations about those leaders who successfully achieved mastery over the noisy, incessant environment—rather than simply reacting, throwing up their hands, and living in a perpetual state of "present shock." In short, the study I am about to summarize was able to illuminate some of the darkness around the question earlier posed: How do organizations translate intention into reality and sustain it? Leadership is the first component, although, as we shall see later, leadership must be held within a context of other interacting factors.

What all these effective CEOs shared and embodied was directly related to how they construed their role. To use a popular distinction, they viewed themselves as *leaders,* not *managers,* which is to say that they were concerned with their organization's basic purposes, why it exists, its general direction. They did not spend their time on the "how to," the proverbial "nuts and bolts," but on purpose, on paradigms of action. In short, they were concerned not with "doing things right" (the overriding concern of managers) but with "doing the right thing." They were capable of transforming doubts into the psychological grounds of common purpose.

The question that guided my study was what common set of characteristics, if any, those leaders possessed who were capable of translating intention into reality. The answer clarifies the role of the effective leader. In varying degrees, it seemed that all the CEOs possessed the following competencies:

1. *Vision:* The capacity to create and communicate a compelling vision of a desired state of affairs—to impart clarity to this vision (or paradigm, context, frame—all those words serve) and induce commitment to it.
2. *Communication and alignment:* The capacity to communicate their vision in order to gain the support of their multiple constituencies.
3. *Persistence, consistency, focus:* The capacity to maintain the organization's direction, especially when the going gets rough.
4. *Empowerment:* The capacity to create environments—the appropriate social architecture—that can tap and harness the energies and abilities necessary to bring about the desired results.
5. *Organizational learning:* The capacity to find ways for the organization to monitor its own performance, compare results with established objectives, have access to a continuously evolving data base on which to review past actions and base future ones, and decide how, if necessary, the organizational structure and key personnel must be abandoned or rearranged when faced with new conditions.

In short, nothing serves an organization better—especially during these times of agonizing doubts and paralyzing ambigui-

ties—than leadership that knows what it wants, communicates those intentions successfully, empowers others, and
knows when and how to stay on course and when to change.

Intention. The second element is the "compelling vision"
mentioned earlier, what will now be called "the intention." The
expression of an intention is the capacity to take an organization to a place it has never been before, the unknown. The characteristics of the intentions that successful leaders use include
the following:

• *Simplicity.* This characteristic is akin to Occam's razor,
the law of parsimony. It implies that each assumption or element is independent. The word *simple* derives from the notion
of one or unity.

• *Completeness.* This criterion requires that all the available facts be included. In most organizations the bulk of the
major tasks to be accomplished are easily and readily incorpo-
rated within almost any kind of organizational structure. It is
those few remaining tasks that test or prove the adequacy of the
organization. Not only should the organization be capable of
incorporating tasks that need to be performed at the time it is
set up, it should also be capable of adjusting to and assimilating
new tasks as they arise.

• *Workability.* Does the intention deliver the goods?
Does the context achieve the organizational goals or contribute
to them? William James, as usual, says it well: "By their fruits
ye shall know them, not by their roots."

• *Communicability.* The last criterion for judging intentions, communicability, contains two components. The more obvious one is the ease with which the context is understood by
the organization. The robustness of the organization, in terms
of its empowerment, depends to a large extent on the degree to
which the context is clear and understood. The other meaning I
give to this criterion is what in *est* terms, I believe, would be
called "alignment"—not alignment of organizational members,
though, but alignment with other contexts indigenous to the
particular organization. In other words, the effectiveness of organizational structure depends partly on the mutual relatedness
of its various contexts.

The problem with the forgoing characteristics is betrayed

by application of one of them, "completeness." The list is not complete. Originality, muting of ego, subtlety, and an esthetic are all important, but space limitations preclude anything but their mention now. The one exception is "an esthetic," an exception based both on its significance and on its neglect. Indeed, I believe that the esthetic of the intention plays an important—perhaps the key—role in understanding how intention can lead to implementation. That is, after all, the whole point of leadership (more about that later).

Organization. Transformative power implies a transaction between the leader and the led, between the leadership and some sort of participative response. If the leadership expresses the characteristics noted earlier and if the vehicle of this expression, the intention(s), is effectively expressed, the organization becomes a blending of each individual's uniqueness into collective action.

Such an organization is similar to something observed in healthy individuals; in fact, it is isomorphic with a healthy identity in an individual. More technically, we can assume that an organization possesses a healthy identity—organizational integrity—when it has a clear sense of who it is and what it is to do; and that is a way of defining *organizational integrity.*

Achieving organizational integrity is easier said than done. Part of the problem is the lack of understanding of the various substructures that all organizations, no matter how small, contain. One block to our understanding is perpetuated by the myth of organization-as-monolith, a myth reinforced almost daily by the media and the temptation of simplicity. The myth is not only grossly inaccurate but dangerous as well. When the evening paper, for example, announces that the Defense Department or the University of California or IBM (or any corporate body, for that matter) will pursue this or that course of action, the said action is typically ascribed to a single, composite body, *the* administration. This "administration," whose parts vibrate in harmony and whose acts, because we are denied a look at the human drama that leads up to them, take on an air of superhuman detachment, is as mythical as the griffin. Into every step taken by *"the* administration" goes a complicated pattern of meetings, disagreements, conversations, personalities, emotions, and missed connections. This very human process is bureaucratic politics. Parallel processes are responsible for our foreign policy, the quality of our public schools, and the scope and treatment of the news that the media choose to deliver to us each day.

Our perceptions of organizational decision making, based on such reports and other sources of information, tend to emphasize the *product* of decision making, never (or rarely) the *process*. The result, of course, is false—at times, destructively so. The elements of chance, ignorance, stupidity, recklessness, and amiable confusion are simply not reckoned with; they are selectively ignored, it seems. Thus, the public rarely sees the hundreds of small tableaux, the little dramas, that result in a policy statement or a bit of strategy. It sees only the move or hears only the statement, and it not unreasonably assumes that such an action is the result of a dispassionate, mechanistic process in which problems are perceived, alternative solutions weighed, and rational decisions made. Given human nature, that is almost never so.

For an organization to have integrity, it must have an identity—that is, a sense of who it is and what it is to do. In personality theory, analogously, every person is a summation of various "selves." If those units of the person are not in communication, then the person cannot maintain valid communications with others. The problem of integrity, which is central to much of the contemporary literature in the mental health field, can in organizations be examined by understanding the various "organizational selves" or structures that exist.

Every organization incorporates four concepts of organization, often at odds with one another or existing in some strained coherence: (1) the *manifest* organization, or the one seen on the organization chart and formally displayed. (2) The *assumed* organization, or the one that individuals perceive as the organization (what they would produce were they asked to draw their view of the way things work, much like the legendary New Yorker's view of the United States in which the Hudson River abuts Los Angeles). (3) The *extant* organization, or

the organization as revealed through systematic investigation—
say, by an outside consultant. (4) The *requisite* organization, or
the organization as it would be if it were in accord with the reality of the situation within which it exists.

The ideal, but never realized, situation is that in which
the manifest, the assumed, the extant, and the requisite are
aligned as closely as possible. Wherever these four organizational
concepts are in contradiction, the organizational climate is such
that the organization's identity is confused and its integrity difficult to achieve.

Another useful analogy with mental health can be drawn
here. Many, if not all, psychotherapeutic schools base their notions of mental health on the degree to which the individual
brings into harmony the various "selves" that make up his or
her personality. The healthy person will be much the same person as he or she is known to others.

Virtually the same criterion can be used to establish organizational integrity—that is, the degree to which the organization maintains harmony among, and knowledge about, the manifest, assumed, extant, and requisite concepts. All four concepts
need not be identical. Rather, all four types should be recognized
and allowance made for all the tensions created by imbalances. It
is doubtful that an organization can (or even should) achieve total
congruence. The important factor is recognition, a heightened
consciousness of the confusions and contradictions.

To achieve organizational openness and, through it, integrity, each individual within the organization—particularly the
leader—must strive to be open. From its embodiment in the individual, openness moves to the group level and, through individual and group interaction, infuses the organizational culture
that sustains openness. The process is as slow as the building of
a pyramid, and far more complex.

The Artform of Leadership

We have gone only partway in understanding leadership
(and transformative power) by decomposing the three key elements at the political center of a complexly organized aggregate—

that is, an organization—into (1) a leader or governing elite or strategic core, (2) a set of symbolic forms expressing a tapestry of intentions, and (3) those constituent groups and individuals who make up the membership of the organization. The intention and its expression—crowns and coronations, limousines and conferences—give what goes on in organizations its aura of being not merely important but in some odd fashion connected with the way the world is built. The gravity of organizational leadership and the solemnity of high worship spring from impulses more alike than might first appear.

The extent to which leadership is truly effective is based on the extent to which individuals place symbolic value on the intentions and their expression—the esthetic I mentioned earlier. What makes the difference between transformative power and other forms is the relationship of the governed to the active centers of the social order. Such centers have nothing to do with geometry and little with geography. They have nothing to do with "humanizing the workplace," Theory X or Theory Y, with "quality of worklife" or "participative management." What is important is that the organization and its members are essentially concentrated on what appear to be *serious acts.* Active centers consist in the point or points in a society where its leading ideas come together with its leading institutions to create an arena in which the events that most vitally affect members' lives take place. The artform of leadership means involvement, even oppositional involvement, with such arenas and with the momentous events that occur in them that translates intention into reality and sustains it. I have in mind a sign not of popular appeal or inventive craziness, but of being near the heart of things.

It is crucial, necessary, that leaders use a set of symbolic forms expressing the fact that they are, in truth, *leading.* Whether the symbolic expression of context, its symbolization, takes the form of stories, ceremonies, insignia, formalities, and appurtenances that have been inherited or, in more revolutionary times, invented makes no difference. Whatever the expression, the crowns and coronations, limousines and conferences serve to mark the center and give what goes on there its aura of being not merely important but in some fashion connected with the way the world is built.

It is not, after all, standing outside the social order in some excited state of self-regard that makes a leader numinous. It is not a "System 4" or a "Theory Y" or a grid score of "9,9" that makes a leader effective. It is a deep, intimate involvement near or at the heart of things that motivates and empowers.

Where the vision/intention is esthetically and compellingly presented, the space within can be ambiguous and oblique. When I began to realize that the relationship between the expression of the intention, the context, is clear and the space within as ambiguous and roomy, I then began to see how *the dialectic of the oblique to the specific is the artform of leadership*. The precise tension between them is the difference between *proceeding*, which is what the "compelling vision" propels, and *deciding*, which goes on within the space generated by the vision.

Without spelling out the details, the relationship between the vision and the space it generates and holds reveals why transformative leadership, which is what I have been talking about, is genuinely participative and noncoercive. This relationship also provides some clues to why Japanese managers have surpassed their earlier masters.

2

Productive and Counterproductive Reasoning Processes

Chris Argyris

Human beings are socialized during early life to reason and act in ways that are counterproductive to solving difficult, threatening problems and to be unaware that this is the case. The same human beings will therefore create conditions within their organization that inhibit effective problem solving of threatening issues and an organizational culture to reinforce these limitations. People come to accept the idea that organizations are not a place for learning and the self-sealing loop is closed.

It is the responsibility of top executives to help their organizations be effective in solving difficult underlying issues. Without that competence, organizations may get the everyday job done but only with increasing cost and rigidity.

Reprinted, by permission of the publisher, from *Organizational Dynamics*, Autumn 1982. © 1982 by AMACOM Periodicals Division, American Management Associations. All rights reserved.

During the past decade I have been studying executives' reasoning processes while they are solving difficult human and technical problems. The executive mind seems to work in bewildering ways, a few of which I discuss in this chapter.

I have identified a pattern of three nested paradoxes embedded in executive reasoning.

First, the reasoning that executives use to manage people and technical issues leads simultaneously to productive and to counterproductive consequences.

Second, executives are unaware of this feature because they are disconnected from their own reasoning processes while making tough decisions.

Third, they are disconnected from their reasoning processes because of the skills they have mastered to solve tough problems. The skills that lead to success will also lead to failure (Argyris, 1976b).

How can the same reasoning necessarily lead to productive and counterproductive consequences? How can people act and at the same time be disconnected from their reasoning processes? Why must they be disconnected from their reasoning processes in order to solve difficult problems? And what impact do these features have on executive problem solving and on the organization?

These nested paradoxes indicate that we are dealing with some deeply embedded features of the human mind. And it is the executive mind that concerns us because it is executives who are most often held responsible for dealing with the difficult issues in organizations and in society at large.

By *executive mind* I mean the way executives create premises, make inferences, and arrive at conclusions. Surprisingly, executives (or anyone else, for that matter) are usually unaware of their reasoning processes. There are two reasons for this. First, they have great reasoning skill—the activity is second nature to them, and they are rarely aware of it while doing it. Indeed, as is true of most skilled behavior, they rarely focus on it unless they make an error. Second, when they do make errors, other people—especially subordinates—may feel it is safest to play down the error or may ease in the correct information so subtly that the executive will probably not even realize that he or she did make an error.

These actions at the upper levels are especially detrimental to the organization's capacity to detect and correct errors, to innovate, to take risks, and to know when it is unable to detect and correct error. Such consequences can lead to difficulties in getting the everyday job done correctly. But worse, lack of attention to the underlying policy issues can lead to the organization's losing control of its destiny.

In a previous article (Argyris, 1976a) I gave an example in which individuals at all levels of management "rounded out" sentences in reports so that the top would not become too upset and simultaneously the subordinates could cover themselves. The result was a multi-million-dollar error that led to the closing of major facilities. The error was known and the consequences predictable by the managers at the lower levels several years before the crisis exploded into the open.

Our research indicates that when executives deal with difficult, threatening underlying issues, they use reasoning processes that, at best, simultaneously lead to immediate success and long-range problems. Often the problems are not solved and the long-range difficulties compound. Much of this occurs without executives realizing it. Or if they do realize it, many believe that no other outcome is possible. They are correct if they are willing to accept the world as it is, without seeking alternatives (Argyris, 1982). According to the Pentagon Papers, this is what happened at the upper levels in the defense department as well as in the state department.

To illustrate how we arrived at these conclusions, I want to present data from a case we have given to many executives. The case concerns one of the most difficult problems that executives face—namely, how to help fellow executives realize that their performance is deteriorating when they believe otherwise. Later I will show how the results from this case apply to other common and difficult leadership problems. (Readers may wish to try their hand at solving this case and compare responses with those of our sample.)

Correcting Poor Performance: A Diagnostic Case

Y, a senior executive, must communicate to X, an older officer, that his performance during the past five years has fallen below standard. Y knows that the difficulty of his task is compounded by the fact that X believes his performance has topped off because of the way the firm has dealt with him.

We give the executives in the seminar a transcript of several key sentences that Y used in talking with X, sentences that represent the range of meanings that Y communicated to X during their session:

1. X, your performance is not up to standard (and moreover . . .)
2. You seem to be carrying a chip on your shoulder.
3. It appears to me that this has affected your performance in a number of ways. I have heard words like *lethargy, uncommitted,* and *disinterested* used by others in describing your recent performance.
4. Our senior professionals cannot have those characteristics.
5. Let's discuss your feelings about your performance.
6. X, I know you want to talk about the injustices that you believe have been perpetrated on you in the past. The problem is that I am not discussing something that happened several years ago. Nothing constructive will come from it. It's behind us.
7. I want to talk about you today and about your future in our system.

We then ask the executives to answer three questions:

1. How effective do you believe Y was in dealing with X?
2. What advice would you give Y?
3. Assume that Y asked you for your evaluation of his effectiveness in dealing with X. Write your response using the following format, for two or three double-spaced pages.

Your Thoughts and Feelings	*What You and Y Said*
(Give in this column any thoughts and feelings which you had during the session but which you did not communicate.)	I: (Write what you would say) Y: (Write what you expect Y's response would be) I: (Write your response to this) Y: (Write Y's response)

. . .

The responses to be presented were made by the fifteen top senior officers, including the CEO, of a $5 billion corporation. If your answers do not vary significantly from those in our sample, then the consequences that followed for the executives will more than likely occur for you. (If your answers are different, please mail them to me. It will help us better understand the gaps in our research.)

Executives' Evaluations of Y's Effectiveness. Exhibit 1 is a collage of the executives' answers to Question 1. Briefly, the results are:

- The executives evaluated Y as being ineffective in his dealings with X.

By the way, the reader may be interested to know that line executives were as compassionate about X as were governmental executives and organizational development professionals. Indeed, the line executives were slightly more concerned than the two other groups that Y was too power-oriented, an "uncaring executioner of company policies."

- The executives organized their responses by inventing what might be called a miniature causal theory of human behavior:
  If Y (or anyone else) communicates meanings of the kind that Y communicated to X,
  then the recipient will feel defensive, and
  then learning will be blunted.

If you agree with this explanation, then you are using an explanation that, strictly speaking, does not come from the data. For example, why should telling Y that his performance is poor and unacceptable make him defensive? "That is obvious," you may respond, "because such statements are probably experienced as punishing and unjust, an attack on the person's competence. Such acts are threatening." To arrive at this conclusion—which is probably correct—you must hold a tacit theory of threat.

- Therefore, embedded in the first miniature causal theory is another one, a theory about what makes people defensive.

Exhibit 1. Summary of Responses to the X and Y Case
by Line Executives.

Y's Action Strategies

Y's comments have a strong power tone to them; they smell of
conspiratorial knowledge.

Y gives no sign of interest or compassion.

Y set up X to give only answers Y wants to hear.

Y comes across as a blunt, uncaring executioner of the firm's policy decision about X.

Y makes it abundantly clear that he does not want to be bothered
with X.

Y is insensitive to X's feelings.

Y waits too long to listen to X.

Y does not give X a chance to respond. He pays lip service to hearing X's side.

Y is too blunt, direct, one-sided.

Y cuts off X.

Y communicates the seriousness of the situation from the company's point of view.

At no time does he appear to communicate that he and the firm
genuinely want X to have a second chance.

Impact on Y

Makes X feel defensive, rejected.

Makes X defend his past performance aggressively.

Y will feel prejudged, "loaded deck."

X is not likely to relax and learn.

X is left with no room for constructive exploration.

Totally demoralizes X; makes X feel inferior.

X is placed in a no-win situation.

Impact on Learning

Inhibits learning on the part of both persons.

X will probably look for another job.

- All the explanations that the executives produced have a
  taken-for-granted quality because they have been absorbed
  and learned in the experience of everyday life. In my jargon,
  people are socialized to believe this theory of defense because they have been taught from an early age that such an
  act—telling someone his performance is poor—can be counterproductive.

Some Puzzles and Surprises. First, two puzzles: (1) If everyone has learned these causal explanations early in life, why have we not also eventually learned not to create situations that make people defensive? Why, for example, did Y behave the way he did toward X? (2) If Y had asked these executives what they thought of the way he dealt with X, and if the line executives had told Y what is in Exhibit 1, they would be using the same causal theory with Y that they were criticizing Y for using with X. For example, to tell Y that he is insensitive and blunt is to be blunt and insensitive.

When the executives were confronted with the first puzzle, they were quick to reply that Y was either not very competent or maybe even a bit flustered and that he tried to cover this up by being directive. Notice the reasoning: The executives dealt with the first puzzle (of why Y behaved thusly) by saying that Y lacked some skill or was upset. That places the responsibility on Y. It also means that the executives do not have to question the validity of their diagnoses.

How accurate are their diagnoses? Let us ask Y.

When the executive said that Y . . .	Y could have responded that he . . .
1. Blamed X completely.	1. Blamed X justly or only partly.
2. Resisted hearing X's views.	2. Only resisted getting into a past history that was a can of worms.
3. Discounted X's feelings.	3. Understood X's feelings, but he did not want to get mired in them for X's sake; that he was trying to think positively and look toward the future.

When the executives were confronted with the second puzzle (that they were using the same approach as Y), their initial response was surprise and disbelief. A few tried to prove that this was not an inconsistency on their part, but fellow executives disagreed. When the defensive reactions wore thin, there was a momentary silence. Then someone said, "Yes, you are right, there is the inconsistency. But what you fail to realize is that none of us would say to Y what we have written down." "No," added another with a smile, "we're too smart to say what we think."

Note the difference between the executives' reactions to the first and second puzzles. Their response to the first puzzle was to place the blame on Y. In the second, unable to explain away their own inconsistency, they decided they would not say what they thought. They accepted as natural their being surprised about and unaware of their impact on Y. But they never suggested that Y might have been unaware of his impact on X.

Once the executives made a diagnosis, they assumed it was true, and they countered questioning of it in such a way as to keep their diagnosis intact.

Executives' Advice to Y. Recall that the executives tried to evade the second puzzle (that they were using the same causal theory as Y) by asserting that they would not tell Y their diagnosis.

We collected two kinds of data to test their assertion. First, the executives were asked to write scenarios of a conversation they might have with Y about Y's handling of X. They were at liberty to mold Y's reactions as they wished.

The executives used three basic strategies in their scenarios. The first strategy (used by five executives) was direct. In effect, they told Y their diagnosis. But many who used a direct approach communicated with Y in such a way that they neglected important features of their own advice. For example, most of them were "up front" with Y but were unable to create an "open process," a "receptive mood," a process for Y's "growth and development."

Here are examples of how three of the executives using the direct approach began their scenarios with hypothesized reactions that Y might have had but did not disclose.

Executive Said	According to Executive, Y Could Have Thought
Executive 1: To tell the truth, I don't think you accomplished what you wanted to.	1. He is telling me not only that I failed but that I was blind to that fact.
Executive 2: Some of your comments were bound to hit X pretty hard and force a defensive reaction.	2. I had to be straight with him. Speaking of hitting pretty hard, you're not doing badly yourself!
Executive 3: Well, you started off pretty hard on his performance, his defensive reaction. The poor bastard almost had to defend his record to set you straight.	3. Somebody had to be straight with him. We had been pulling punches for five years. He didn't have much to defend, and he knew it. I feel I have to set you straight about me!

A more lengthy example from one scenario indicates the flow of conversation and the possible buildup of Y's reactions.

Executive Said	According to Executive, Y Could Have Thought
Nobody believes the judgment about his own poor performance is accurate unless he can balance it against a number of successes.	If this is true, I really was doomed to failure, because this guy has no successes.
	Are you also thinking the same about me? If so, how about a few successes?
Did you get a defensive reaction from X?	Of course I did, just as you predicted from what you just said.
Well, my only point is that you probably were guaranteed to get some defensiveness.	Just like you are guaranteed to do with me. Let's begin to end this diplomatically. ("Thanks for the advice.")
Don't be afraid to be honest.	I'm not afraid to be honest except with people like you.

To summarize the findings from the scenarios:

The Executives	*The Executives Advised Y*
1. Were in unilateral control.	1. Not to unilaterally control X.
2. Evaluated Y unilaterally and negatively.	2. Not to evaluate X.
3. Failed to hear Y's pent-up feelings.	3. To listen to X's pent-up feelings.
4. Failed to solicit Y's participation.	4. To solicit X's participation.

So a third puzzle was that the executives created the very conditions that they advised Y not to create with X *and* they appeared to be unaware of doing so.

The Easing-In Approach. Ten executives used another approach, which we might call an easing-in approach, or a combination of a beginning easing-in approach and a final direct approach. The easing-in approach basically asked Y questions in order to get him to see his errors.

Executive Said	*Y Could Have Thought*
1. It's hard to say from just reading your notes. I guess I would like to hear a little about how X reacted.	1. What is he driving at? Why does he want to focus on X's reaction?
2. What do you think he was thinking?	2. How do I know what X was thinking? I told him that X didn't say much. What is he driving at?
3. Do you suppose there might have been a way to let him know you mean it?	3. I did let him know that I meant it. If he didn't believe me, that's more his problem than mine. I think this guy has an agenda.

Executive Said	*Y Could Have Thought*
4. You mean his attitude wasn't any better in the meeting?	4. Couldn't you tell that he was pretty unresponsive? Again, what is he driving at? Does he believe that X's attitude was better?
5. Perhaps if you could persuade him to open up about it, he might get it off his chest.	5. Maybe this is what he is driving at. If so, he is wrong. The last thing I want to do is open up past wounds . . . oh, these bleeding hearts!

Although the executives asked Y questions, if our interpretations about the impact on Y are valid, they were acting in ways that placed them in control of Y.

To summarize:

The Executives	*The Executives Advised Y*
1. Were in unilateral control.	1. Not to unilaterally control X.
2. Evaluated Y as ineffective.	2. Not to prejudge X as being ineffective.
3. Made attributions about Y's motives.	3. Not to make attributions about X's motives.

The executives again created the very conditions that they advised Y not to create with X, *and* they appeared unaware of doing so.

We conclude that when the executives tried to communicate information that they believed was threatening, they unknowingly created conditions of miscommunication, misunderstanding, and inconsistency. None of them tested their views openly. Self-fulfilling prophecies resulted, because every comment that Y made in his defense, they saw as validating their diagnosis. This made Y even more defensive, which "proved" to the executives that their diagnosis was correct. Since the executives never publicly tested their views, they did not know they had created a self-fulfilling prophecy. So we have not only a self-fulfilling prophecy but one that is self-sealing as well.

We have obtained these results with twenty-seven groups —slightly under 1,000 subjects of varying ages, positions, roles, and cultures and of both sexes. In all cases we have taped the discussions. Many different views were expressed, as well as feelings of bewilderment and frustration. We analyzed the tape recordings of these discussions. They too illustrate that when the participants disagreed with each other, they did so by using the same counterproductive reasoning and strategies just described.

How Do We Explain These Results? Briefly, people acquire through socialization two kinds of skills and values for dealing with other people. The first are those values and skills which they espouse and of which they are aware. I call these *espoused* theories of action.

Often when people are dealing with difficult and threatening problems, their behavior is inconsistent with their espoused theories. "Do as I say, not as I do" illustrates the point— and proves that the point is not new.

What is new is the idea that all behavior is designed consistently with a theory that we actually use. Moreover, we are rarely aware of this type of theory of action, because it is ingrained in us from early childhood. I call it the *theory-in-use*. We use it without thinking about it. When we do think about it, we see that the results are often at odds with what we espouse. For example, the executives espoused theories advocated dealing with Y in such a way that he did not become defensive. Many followed an easing-in approach, and the theory-in-use for easing in is: Ask Y questions that, if he answers correctly, will enable him to discover what we are hiding. As we have seen, this strategy can be counterproductive, and in fact, the other person may imitate this approach by not saying what he or she really feels.

Although each person said something different when using an easing-in approach, there was almost no variance in people's theory-in-use. We have observed the same theory-in-use among rich or poor, white or black, male or female, young or old, and powerful or powerless and in several cultures.

We have created a model of the theory and call it *Model I* (Figure 1). It is composed of governing values (or variables), action strategies, and consequences.

Now we can return to the question of why we get such consistent results in the X and Y case.

Evaluations and attributions that the executives made about Y's motives were not self-evident. They required several layers of inference. For example, Y's statement to X "Your performance is below standard" is on the first rung of a ladder of inference (Figure 2). The second rung is the culturally understood meaning of such a sentence: "X, your performance is unacceptable." The third rung up consists of the meanings that the executives imposed. Here is where their theory-in-use came into play. They explained Y's actions by describing him as insensitive, blunt, and not listening.

Why do people use concepts at such a high level of inference? Because the environment in which we operate is significantly more complex than what the human mind can process at a given moment. In order for the human mind to deal with reality, we must abstract from the buzzing confusion of everyday life (rung 1) by using more abstract concepts.

Such concepts have two key features. First, they can be used to cover many meanings. For example, "blunt" and "insensitive" can cover many different sentences. A second feature is that they are usually learned at an early age. Hence, most of us learn to use the same concepts in similar ways. Soon we take them for granted. They become obvious and concrete, not abstract and questionable. Recall that there was a high degree of consistency and agreement in the way the executives diagnosed Y's actions toward X. It was "obvious" to most of the executives that Y had behaved counterproductively.

But the features of the human mind that make it efficient may also lead to counterproductive consequences. Why? Because, as we have seen, there can be differences between the executives' views and Y's. But so what? Cannot human beings

Figure 1. Model I Theory-in-Use.

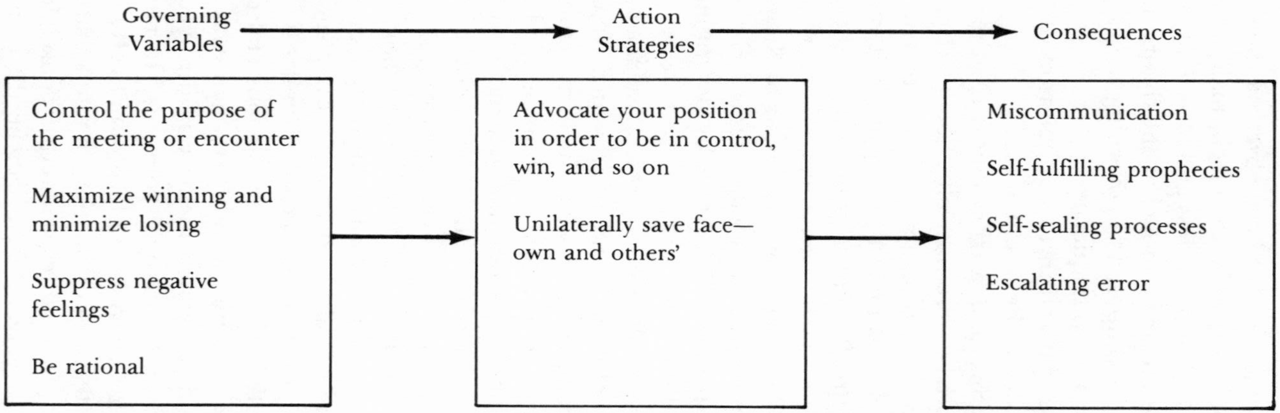

Governing Variables	Action Strategies	Consequences
Control the purpose of the meeting or encounter	Advocate your position in order to be in control, win, and so on	Miscommunication
Maximize winning and minimize losing	Unilaterally save face—own and others'	Self-fulfilling prophecies
Suppress negative feelings		Self-sealing processes
Be rational		Escalating error

Figure 2. Ladder of Inference.

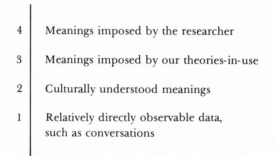

4	Meanings imposed by the researcher
3	Meanings imposed by our theories-in-use
2	Culturally understood meanings
1	Relatively directly observable data, such as conversations

differ in their views? Of course. But if they wish to reduce the number of misunderstandings when they do differ, they should test the validity of their reasoning.

Why do people choose not to test the validity of their reasoning? First, because they believe their reasoning is obvious and correct. Second, because they hold a theory of human defensiveness that tells them that the recipient will probably not listen or, if he or she does, will probably become defensive. And it makes little sense for them to test their views with someone who they believe will be defensive.

Third, in a Model I world, testing makes the testers vulnerable. They could discover that they are wrong, lose unilateral control, or generate negative feelings—consequences that would violate their Model I governing values.

The same counterproductive reasoning and consequences have been shown to occur when executives deal with technical and organizational problems, provided that the problems are threatening to some of the key players involved. Once the players diagnose the problem as threatening, they use the reasoning described in the X-Y case.

Other Examples of the Consequences of Model I Reasoning. People programmed to be in unilateral control and to maximize winning tend to have difficulties in dealing with paradoxes. Paradoxes contain contradictions, and holding contradictory views makes the actor vulnerable to criticisms of being vague or self-contradictory. It is not surprising to learn from Barnes's

(1981) insightful descriptions that the way executives deal with paradoxes may be counterproductive.

Barnes's Observations	*Theory-of-Action Explanation*
Often we fail to go beyond our initial reactions in order to look at deeper levels of the issues.	Do not run the risk of losing control and making yourself vulnerable—that is, losing.
Issues fall in opposing camps; hard data and facts are better than soft ideas and speculation.	Create win/lose dynamics. Seek hard data to win, to prevent losing. Abhor speculation lest you become vulnerable.

Turning to organizational consequences, recall that people who use Model I tend to create misunderstanding, self-fulfilling prophecies, self-sealing processes, and escalating error. These consequences drive people to be even more Model I in an attempt to maintain control, to win. They also create competitive win/lose group and intergroup dynamics with many protective games that are undiscussable. And that undiscussability is itself undiscussable. The Model I world is, as the executives reported to Barnes, "an unsafe place where nice guys finish last."

An excellent illustration of these consequences at the group, intergroup, and interagency level can be found in a recently published story of the interaction among Secretaries Califano and Marshall and President Carter and his aides regarding welfare reform (Lynn and Whitman, 1981). The players acted toward one another in Model I ways. Califano kept secret for a long time his doubts of genuine welfare reform at zero cost increase. The president sensed his doubts but apparently never explored them directly with Califano. When Califano said that he was working hard on a plan that Carter might possibly be able to call his own, the president asked Califano for a plan that he would gladly call "the Califano plan." Califano's policy analysts were frustrated by his actions. They never said so, but they built up strategies to protect themselves. These strategies got them in trouble with Califano and a competing group of analysts in Secretary Marshall's office (Department of Labor).

This led to interagency warfare, a state in which positions harden and everybody looks out for Number One.

Reich's recent article (1981) suggests that an entire industry is rising as a result of the self-fulfilling prophecies, self-sealing processes, and escalating error between private and governmental sectors. The new industry is composed of experts who deal with difficult relationships of private business and government by—

- Seeking to achieve clear controversies in which the client's position can be sharply differentiated from that of its regulatory opponent.
- Exaggerating the danger of the opponent's activities.
- Prolonging and intensifying conflict.
- Keeping business executives and regulatory officials apart.

Remember that regulatory agencies are also administered by Model I reasoning processes. That means the regulators will probably deal with difficult, threatening issues that are undiscussable by translating them into discussable, nonthreatening issues. For example, I have found that if regulators do not trust builders, instead of dealing with that issue, they create piles of regulations in an effort to prevent cheating by dishonest builders. These regulations may drive out the honest builders and may lead the dishonest ones to new heights of creative dishonesty.

To summarize: Holding a Model I theory-in-use makes it highly likely that the reasoning used for any difficult, threatening issues, whether technical or personal, whether at the individual, group, intergroup, organizational, or interorganizational level, will have counterproductive features that lead to self-fulfilling, self-sealing, error-escalating processes.

The reasoning is the same because it is individuals who deal with the substantive or human problems—who act as agents for groups, intergroups, organizations, and interorganizations. Programmed with Model I, they seek to win and not lose, to be in unilateral control, to suppress negative feelings. Thus, whether the issue being dealt with is helping Y realize his error or dealing with a group that the executive believes is recommending the wrong investment strategy, in both cases the executives will try to communicate their views in such a way that they cannot be held responsible for upsetting Y or the group members. The executive strives to evade responsibility for the defensiveness of others so that they cannot attack the executive and ignore the validity of his or her views. As we have seen, however, the strategies that executives use to minimize being accused of making others defensive actually do make others defensive, but in a way that makes it difficult or unlikely for them to say so. We then have the appearance of agreement.

We not only find these same consequences at all levels of the organization; we also find that managerial policies and practices are designed to take these consequences into account. For example:

1. To reduce the probability that individuals will be able to blame the superior's evaluation of their performance, have them list and sign ahead of time a set of specific goals that are objectively measurable if possible.
2. To reduce the probability of groupthink, have several competing groups deal with the same problem.
3. To reduce miscommunication about difficult issues, have people send each other detailed position statements, backed up with hard numbers.
4. To reduce misunderstanding between regulators and regulatees, have the regulators define in detailed, unambiguous terms the standards of acceptable performance.

The first policy requires a technocracy of MBO experts and trainers. The second duplicates efforts. The third requires staff groups that may "pencil-and-paper an issue to death." The fourth requires mountains of specifications, including specifications on how to understand the specifications.

What Can Be Done

What can interested readers do to begin to learn more about the effectiveness of their reasoning processes and their actions?

First, may I remind the reader of the two most fundamental findings: that the executives' responses were highly automatic and skillful and that the executives were programmed to be unaware of their faulty reasoning as well as of the counterproductive impact. To change highly skilled action is not easy; to do so hampered by programmed unawareness is difficult indeed. Since the basis for the programmed unawareness is what we have been taught since early childhood, the task is formidable. It requires double-loop learning.

In order to define *double-loop learning,* let us first define *learning.* Learning is defined as occurring under two conditions. First, learning occurs when an individual or an organization achieves what it intended; that is, there is a *match* between the design for action and the actuality or outcome. Second, learning occurs when a *mismatch* between intentions and outcomes is identified and corrected; that is, a mismatch is turned into a match. Learning has not occurred until a match or mismatch is produced. From our perspective, therefore, learning *cannot* be said to occur if someone acting for the organization merely discovers a new problem or invents a solution to a problem. Learning occurs when the invented solution is actually produced.

Whenever an error is detected and corrected without questioning or altering the underlying values of the system (be it individual, group, intergroup, organizational, or interorganizational), the learning is single-loop. The term is borrowed from electrical engineering or cybernetics, where, for example, a thermostat is defined as a single-loop learner. The thermostat is programmed to detect states of "too cold" or "too hot" and to correct the situation by turning the heat on or off. If the thermostat asked itself such questions as why it was set at 68 degrees or why it was programmed as it was, then it would be a double-loop learner.

Single-loop and double-loop learning are diagrammed in Figure 3. Single-loop learning occurs when matches are created or when mismatches are corrected by changing actions. Double-loop learning occurs when mismatches are corrected by examining and altering first the governing variables and then the actions. Governing variables are the preferred states that individ-

Figure 3. Single- and Double-Loop Learning.

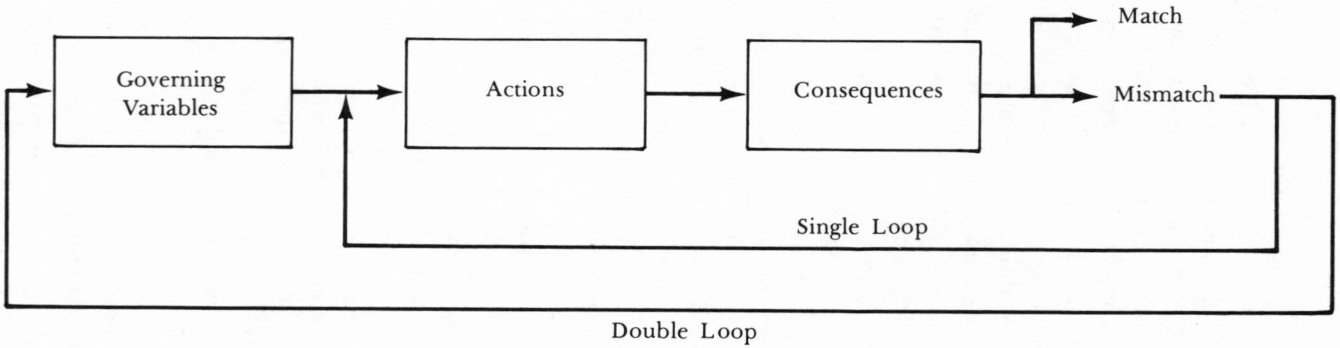

uals strive to satisfice when they are acting. These governing variables are *not* the underlying beliefs or values that people espouse. They are the variables that can be inferred, by observation, to drive and guide the actions of individuals acting as agents for the organization.

Learning new reasoning processes, like learning to play tennis or golf, requires plenty of practice. Herein lies an advantage, because most of us are constantly in situations where we must use reasoning processes. There is plenty of opportunity to practice in everyday life.

The nature of the practice will be different at different stages of learning. During the early stages you should be able to make errors without high cost to you or to the organization, and you should have plenty of time to get feedback and to redesign your actions. These two features, when combined, suggest that the best kind of learning environment during the early stages is one that allows for slowdown of the action and decomposition of the problem. This means creating a learning environment separate from everyday pressures.

For example, select a double-loop issue that is important to you, one that you must deal with others in order to solve. Using the X-Y-case format, write, in one paragraph, how you define the issue. In a second paragraph, write how you tried to solve it (or might try to solve it if it is a future problem). Next, write an actual scenario of several pages describing the conversation as you can best recall it (or, if it is a future problem, what you would expect the conversation to be). Include thoughts and feelings that you might not communicate for whatever reason.

By the way, do not worry about how accurately you recall the incident or how well you plan the future dialogue. If our theory is correct, you cannot write down anything except what is consistent with your theory-in-use.

Now put the case away for at least a week. When you reread it, analyze it as if you were trying to help a friend. Here are some of the questions you can ask yourself about the dialogue:

- Do the sentences indicate advocating a position in order to be in control and to win and not lose? Or is the advocacy of the position combined with encouraging the other person to inquire? Is there an easing-in or forthright strategy? How aware is the writer of the possible interpretations by the receiver?

- Are the evaluations or attributions made illustrated with examples or unillustrated? Are they tested publicly, or do they go untested?
- What kind of information is on the left-hand side of the paper (thoughts and feelings)? Does it include information that would better enable the other person to understand your intentions? If so, what prevented you from communicating this information?
- If the feelings and thoughts in the left-hand column would predictably upset others, then what change would be necessary so that they could be effectively communicated?

More important, why does the writer think and feel about other people in ways that are not directly communicable? True, it may be that the other people are SOBs. But it may also be that the writer is unknowingly creating self-fulfilling prophecies and self-sealing processes.

The next step is to try to redesign some part of the dialogue, especially the sentences that you find difficult to deal with.

- Read the sentence(s) several times and write down the (culturally acceptable) meaning that you infer (rung 2 on the ladder of inference).
- Write down the meaning that you would impose on the cultural meaning (rung 3).
- Invent a possible solution to deal with such meanings.
- Write an actual conversation that produces the invention you just made.

Feel free to make all the changes you wish during the exercise. Every change is a sign of learning and another opportunity for practice. This is not a win/lose competitive situation with yourself or with others.

Again, put your written work away, this time for at least a day, before rereading it. Or, if you prefer not to wait, show your efforts to someone else. It is best to do this with persons who are also interested in learning about themselves and who might reciprocate by showing you a case they have written in this format. The set is then one in which both of you are learning.

Another step is to make exercises like those just described part of the firm's executive development activities. For example, you and your group members could each write a case. One of these could be the subject of discussion during a seminar. (I recommend at least an hour and a half and some trained professional help for each of the early sessions.)

Another possibility is for all individuals to write a case about an organizational problem that plagued, or continues to plague, the organization. It is then possible not only to see how each player conceptualizes the problem but how he or she has tried (or would try) to solve it.

During these discussions the players soon generate lots of data about the organization, its culture, and the way decisions are made. Grouping the cases provides a new data source for diagnosing organizational features that inhibit or facilitate organizational learning. For example, in a large professional firm, the top management realized that if the partners were going to be successful at dealing with mediocre performance, they would have to become much more candid and forthright. They also realized that such candor ran counter to the firm's culture and hence the partners had to learn new skills. They also realized that if the partners learned to confront constructively, and if it worked well with the subordinate professionals, the latter would probably take them up on their challenge and start confronting the partners and the firm's policies. The top management believed this would lead to constructive dialogue and possibly a new culture. All the top executives agreed with this espoused policy. However, as they examined their scenarios and the self-initiated censorship (what they placed on the left side of the page), they became aware that their theory-in-use was quite different. About half of them were trying to act in ways that were consistent with the new policy. About half were easing in but denying that they were. One senior executive said: "Let's assume for the moment that our subordinates will be watching not only what we espouse but how we act. If that is so, then many of them should be aware of the bipolar nature of our actions. Yet to my knowledge this is never discussed. They give much lip service to our policies. This means in the name of candor we must be (unknowingly) helping them to identify what is undiscussable, to keep it undiscussable, and to act as if they were not doing so!"

The next phase is to use the new skills in everyday situations. For example, in one firm the professionals at all levels had gone through the X-Y experience. When the officers had to evaluate their professionals in the normal review process, they used the opportunity to practice their new skills. Often the officers asked me to meet with them ahead of time to help them prepare for the session. The number and length of the preparatory sessions were greatly reduced once the officers felt secure in their new skills.

Since the bewilderment, bafflement, and frustration of the X-Y case had been experienced by all, subordinates who came to a review session knew how difficult it would be for the officer to behave in line with the new model. It was easy for the officers to say that the evaluation was going to be a learning experience for them as well as for the subordinates. If the subordinate agreed, I participated in the evaluation sessions. The subordinate and the superior often listened to the tape of the session, reporting that doing so was an eye opener for them.

Another type of intervention is illustrated by the officer who asked his project team to reflect on a job it had recently completed. Although all involved evaluated the project as a success, he felt that they could have done better, since they were exceptionally talented professionals. In the first session team members reflected on their experience of the project. They identified ten factors that had led the team to be less creative than it could have been. For example, they admitted that, as senior professionals, they had all acted as chiefs, each in his own bailiwick, and admitted that they often recognized a lack of coordination and integration throughout the project. Their conclusion was that the team could have gained by stronger leadership.

The second session was held to dig into the reasoning that the team had used during the first meeting. For example, I noted that the team had recognized the lack of coordination early in the project. "Do you recall what prevented you from surfacing these views?" Their replies cluster around (1) the fear that they would step on someone's toes, (2) the fact that they were all very busy, and (3) the assumption that team coordination was the officer's responsibility. The officer mentioned that he had reduced his time with the team because he had been asked by top management to take on additional and unexpected work. He had agreed to the extra work in part because the team members were so senior that he believed they could administer themselves.

I asked what cues or data the members got that led them to believe they would be stepping on other people's toes. The responses ranged from cues individuals gave each other to informal policies of the firm that made them hesitate to speak out. Their theory-in-use was to cover up their views and to cover up the cover-up in order to get the job done. This deeper analysis pointed to a different change target. If they could change the need for the cover-up, if they could learn to generate more effective cooperative relationships (including being able to make the heretofore undiscussable issues discussable), then the need for a strong leader might be greatly reduced. If so, the firm could use its senior officers more flexibly.

An episode in another firm involved design of a new organizational structure. Sides were taken; subgroups began to view each other as conservatives and liberals. In X-Y-case terminology, each side held untested and often unillustrated attributions that led to divisive intergroup dynamics. Instead of reenacting their history of intergroup warfare, several executives pointed out the connection between the reasoning they had used in the X-Y case and the reasoning they were using now. A meeting was held with the key players on both sides present. Several executives presented their analysis of the situation and asked, "If this makes sense to you, would you all be willing to

join us in reflecting on what we are doing?" Most agreed spon-
taneously; a few agreed but were concerned. As one said, "This
could lead to blows." It never did. They were able to map the
attributions and evaluations that people were making and not
testing, the games being played, and the possible negative consequences of all this for their final decision and for the firm. The
result was a jointly developed plan on how to reduce counterproductive factors. The participants agreed that the result was a
greater degree of internal commitment to make the new design
work, as evidenced by their willingness to monitor it actively
and to design and implement changes that would make it more
effective.

   Another important consequence of the exercise was not
learned until several months later. Many of the executives at the
middle or near-top level—especially those who tended to play it
safe—were baffled by the degree of commitment and especially
by the near absence of undiscussable issues among the top people. Many had predicted that it would take years to implement
the plan. They told their subordinates not to become too anxious because top management would probably be changed before the new scheme had an important impact on their levels.
The middle executives, accordingly, reduced their vigilance and
concern about implementation. However, in contrast to previous occasions, not only did the implementation move faster,
but the space for hiding was greatly reduced. This taught the
middle and lower levels a more vivid lesson about the change in
the firm than could have occurred in the usual information and
exhortation exchanges.

Model II Theory-in-Use

   Embedded in the forgoing advice is a different theory-in-
use, which we shall call Model II (see Figure 4). Its governing
variables are valid information, free and informed choice, and
an internal commitment to that choice in order to monitor the
effectiveness of the implementation of the action. Model II is a
theory of action that combines learning and inquiry with advocating one's views. It is not a nondirective model (such a model

Figure 4. Model II Theory-in-Use.

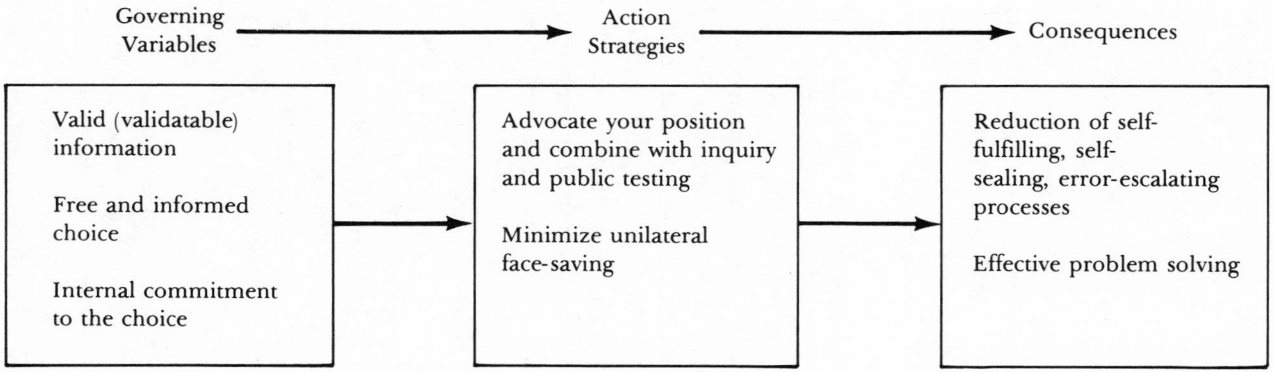

Governing Variables → Action Strategies → Consequences

Governing Variables	Action Strategies	Consequences
Valid (validatable) information	Advocate your position and combine with inquiry and public testing	Reduction of self-fulfilling, self-sealing, error-escalating processes
Free and informed choice	Minimize unilateral face-saving	Effective problem solving
Internal commitment to the choice		

would simply be the opposite of Model I). Model II action strategies are to combine advocacy with inquiry, to minimize face-saving, and to encourage the acceptance of personal responsibility.

Let us now consider the X-Y case with a view to redesigning it to be more consistent with Model II. Recall that the meanings the executives produced were high on the ladder of inference, unillustrated, and untested. However, the executives believed that their evaluations and attributions were *low* on the ladder of inference—that is, they were concrete and obvious inferences—and that it was therefore unnecessary to test them.

An outstanding feature of the participants' evaluations of Y was their negativeness. The most probable explanation for this negativeness was that Y's actions *were* negative. What is ineffective about communicating negative judgments if they are valid? The answer, from this perspective, is "Nothing." The problem is that negative evaluations should not be communicated by using the same features that the actors believe it is ineffective for someone else to use. To the extent that meanings are communicated in a way that follows the same causal theory the sender has told the recipient is counterproductive, the recipient will experience the sender as behaving inconsistently and unjustly.

The participants' attributions had two major features. First, they explained Y's actions by attributing motives "in" Y. For example, Y was protecting himself, was seeking to frighten X, intended to intimidate X, and was insecure. Second, the attributions placed the cause in the role or the position that Y held. For example, Y was acting like a company man, like an authoritarian boss, like a superior identifying with the hierarchy.

The attributions not only contain negative evaluations, but they imply that Y intended to make X defensive in order to protect himself or the organization.

If we combine the features of the evaluations and attributions just described, and if we keep in mind that the receiver is also programmed with Model I, then we have the basis for the predictions of self-fulfilling prophecies, self-sealing processes, and escalating error that were illustrated.

To invent and produce a different way of dealing with X, let us first identify the key features of an intervention that contains negative or threatening meanings although the intention is to facilitate learning.

Messages should be designed so that they are experienced as credible by the recipients. Recipients must have access to the data and to the reasoning the sender used to arrive at his or her evaluation or attribution. Hence, the evaluations or attributions should be illustrated and the reasoning made explicit.

The message should be communicated in ways that will minimize individuals' automatic response of defending themselves. This means that senders should state their messages in such a way as to encourage inquiry into or confrontation of their reasoning and meanings.

From the preceding it is possible to infer several rules for producing such messages:

1. Provide the (relatively) directly observable data (first rung on the ladder) that you use to infer your evaluations or attributions, and check to see whether the recipient agrees with your data.
2. Make explicit the cultural meanings that you inferred from the data and seek confirmation or disconfirmation from the other person.
3. Make explicit your judgments and opinions in ways that permit you to show why the consequences of the actor's action were inevitable, but without implying intentions to produce such consequences.
4. Encourage others to express feelings or ideas that they may have about the process.

The reader might ask, "How efficient can such rules be? Can we get anything done under real-time constraints?" First, recall that these rules are for dealing with double-loop issues. Second, how much is actually accomplished in the present modes of communication? Research suggests that present modes actually take longer and, worse, they generate a social pollution of misunderstanding and mistrust that gives people a sense of helpless hopelessness. As our world becomes saturated with this pollution, even a small incremental error can be the straw that breaks the camel's back. The process of designing and implementing meanings in accordance with Model II does not take much longer. When we have clocked Model I and Model II roleplay, Model II (when produced by actors who are moderately competent) usually requires the same amount of time as the Model I roleplay, or even less.

We now turn to an illustration of how the interventionist might deal with Y. Remember the ladder of inference and Y's statement that led us to infer the meaning "X, your performance is unacceptable." Remember, too, that inferences are subject to error and hence should be put to public test. Every move up or down the ladder necessarily means that inferences are made; the higher up the ladder of inference and the more abstract the ideas, the greater the chance of error, and therefore the greater the importance of public testing. Whatever theory one uses, it should make public testing as easy as possible.

To test an inference with someone else, it is necessary to make explicit both the premise and the conclusions drawn from the premise. The inference "Your performance is unacceptable" in the X-Y case is based on the premise of Y's words to X. One can test the inference by asking Y: "When you said, 'X, your performance is not up to standard,' did you mean that his performance was unacceptable?" or "When you said, 'You seem to be carrying a chip on your shoulder,' did you intend to attribute to him unacceptable attitudes?" If Y responds yes, then the meanings have been affirmed, and it is possible to proceed to the next rung on the ladder.

If a participant in an X-Y seminar wanted to reveal his diagnostic frame, it is at this point that he would have to say something like "Well, I infer from these data that you prejudged X" or "You were too blunt" or "You were insensitive." Such a response is likely to produce defensiveness in Y for several reasons. First, Y may not agree with the evaluations/attributions. Y may believe that he had to be blunt or insensitive in order to get through to X. Or he may believe that he did not prejudge X, that X generated years of data that led to the present judgment.

Second, the evaluations not only attribute errors to Y but imply that he intended to be blunt and insensitive. Since no one knowingly produces error, if Y knew what he was doing, then he knew he was being blunt and insensitive. An explicit negative evaluation is coupled with an implicit attribution that Y intended to have the encounter with X produce these negative consequences.

Under these conditions the interventionist's testing is more of a trick than a helpful strategy. He or she may have tested the first two levels of inference only in order to nail Y with his or her third-level evaluations and attributions, themselves difficult to test. Indeed, in our experience not only is it difficult for the interventionist to see and agree with the logic of inference between successive levels of inference, but the participants also have difficulty. Recall how often the participants either were unable to illustrate their inferences or illustrated them with further inferences. If inferences are to be tested, then no matter how high on the ladder of inference they occur, it should be possible to proceed down the ladder and explicitly connect them with the first and second levels.

To summarize, whatever the concepts being used, one should be able to order them on a ladder of inference, advancing from relatively directly observable data to the culturally acceptable meaning and then up to the concepts used to organize the previous two rungs. It is at this point that interventionists are introducing their own (usually tacit) theory of help.

Let us return to the interventionist's two questions to Y. Recall that Y confirmed the meanings. But let us assume that Y said yes but was showing signs of impatience: "Of course I meant his performance was unacceptable!" or "Naturally I think X's attitudes are wrong! What are you driving at?" At this point the interventionist, using our theory of action, could say:

> I'll be glad to tell you what I am driving at.
> First I want to make sure that I understood you correctly.
> I have a way of understanding the effectiveness of the kinds of comments that you made to X. Your first comment [repeats it] I call an "unillus-

trated evaluation." It tells the person he is wrong,
but it does not include the data and logic of how
you arrived at that conclusion.

People tend to react to such unillustrated
evaluations and attributions by feeling bewildered
and/or misunderstood. Depending on how free
they feel, they may confront you, or they may imitate your style and make their own unillustrated
evaluations and attributions about you. If they do
the latter, it upsets the receiver, just as X was upset by your comments. Now, if X reacted on inferences that he is keeping secret, you would probably
sense that secrecy because you would not see
clearly the reasoning he used to come to his stated
conclusions.

Let's stop for a moment. What is your reaction? Does this make sense? [or] Am I communicating?

Several features of this response should be highlighted.
First, not only do the concepts of "unillustrated evaluation"
and "unillustrated attribution" provide insight into a problem,
but the insight is in the form of a causal theory.

- If someone produces unillustrated evaluations, whoever
  receives the evaluations or attributions will not know the
  basis of them unless they are illustrated.
- The receiver will feel bewildered and misunderstood. He
  may therefore react defensively (unless he is afraid or prefers to be dependent on you).

The causal theory in these propositions is true for anyone, not
only for Y. Therefore, framing it as we do provides Y with a
degree of distancing from the problem that may help him to
understand it better. We are not saying "Y, *you* are wrong." We
are saying that anyone who behaves as Y did will produce the
unintended consequences described.

When people observe the redesign that shows what they
could have said to Y, they are often impressed with its simplicity and obviousness. Many report that they expected the answer
to be more surprising. The redesign may be unsurprising because
the ideas behind it are self-evident and not new. Another reason

is that many people report that they had considered some of these intervention ideas, but they did not know how to design responses that made sense.

Both these reasons show how crucial is the distinction between being aware of a possible action and being able to produce that action. In our terms, the roleplay may not seem surprising because it fits many individuals' espoused theories. But the difficulty is evident when people try to produce such redesign and are unable to. They are surprised that they have difficulty redesigning their own interventions. The reason for their difficulty is that they still hold a Model I theory-in-use. When they are listening or advising, people use their espoused Model II theories. When they try to produce action, their Model I theory-in-use is activated.

The governing values of the theory are especially important. It is possible to make Model II statements to Y and yet fail because the actor still holds, and subtly conveys, Model I governing values such as "Win, don't lose" or "Maintain unilateral control." Indeed, some people initially react to the Model II redesign as if they were using a new and more subtle form of Model I. Their disguised Model I approach is usually revealed when they try to defend their views with fellow learners.

To close, the skills and competencies that executives learn for dealing with an X-Y type of problem can be used for dealing with any double-loop problem. The key is to learn the new skills *and* to acquire a new set of governing values. If executives learn the new skills—such as advocating their position and encouraging inquiry—but use them to maintain unilateral control and to maximize winning, they will be using new skills in the service of Model I values. They remain within a Model I mode; they hide their views about the gimmickiness of the new behavior and yet act as if they were not hiding anything. As a result, others may interpret their newly acquired skills as gimmicks or as new ways to manipulate people.

Luckily, people judge the credibility of human skills by evaluating what values they serve. This means that those who learn the new skills as gimmicks and tricks will be discovered. It also means that those who wish to gain credibility not only must learn the new skills but must internalize a new set of values.

3

The Mind of the Strategist(s)

Henry Mintzberg
James A. Waters

Trying to understand the functioning of the executive mind strikes us as a tall order. Our more cynical side doubts that anyone understands the functioning of any mind. But that is the problem of the psychologist, and we, at least in the context of this paper, are organization theorists. That is to say, we study the behavior of collections of people called organizations. More specifically, for a number of years now we have been tracking the strategies of organizations to understand how these collections of people end up in certain positions in their environments and how they go about changing those positions. Among the conceptual themes we have been focusing on is one about the role of leadership in strategy formation, or, more exactly, the interplay of the three forces of environment, leadership, and organization in the development of strategies. Since this is the closest we come to the functioning of the executive mind, we shall focus our attention on this theme in our chapter.

A preliminary word on our research and its data base is in order. First, what is strategy? Let us suggest four definitions:

1. *Strategy is a plan.* To most people, not just laypersons but writers of dictionaries, military theorists, management practitioners, and even most management theorists, a strategy is a plan, a set of guidelines intended to influence behavior in the future. Chandler's definition is typical: ". . . the determination of the basic long-term goals and objectives of an enterprise, and the adoption of courses of action and the allocation of resources necessary for carrying out these goals" (1962, p. 13). Most people, we maintain, *define* strategy this way, although many, as we shall discuss below, do not necessarily so *use* the term.

2. *Strategy is a position.* Not inconsistent with the first definition (although not supportive of it, either) is the definition of strategy as a position—for example, a niche in a particular market. Under this definition strategy is the means to define or at least to identify an organization in an environment.

3. *Strategy is a perception.* The Germans say *Weltanschauung* ("world view"), behavioral scientists who have read Kuhn (1970) say "paradigm," we prefer to say "perception" or "concept." Under this definition an organizational strategy is, therefore, how the members of an organization view their world.

4. *Strategy is a pattern.* Although most people, as noted earlier, define strategy as a plan, many of them often use the term in reference to a pattern, specifically a pattern in a stream of organizational decisions or actions. The press infers the U.S. President's strategy by finding a pattern in his behavior. Competitors do the same thing, as do subordinates, to try to understand the strategies of senior executives in a company. Strategy by this definition is synonymous with consistency. Of course, this definition of strategy relates not to intention but to realization, or enactment—what actually happens in the organization. Hence, we can combine our first definition with our fourth to generate three other definitions, as shown in Figure 1—

Figure 1. Types of Strategies.

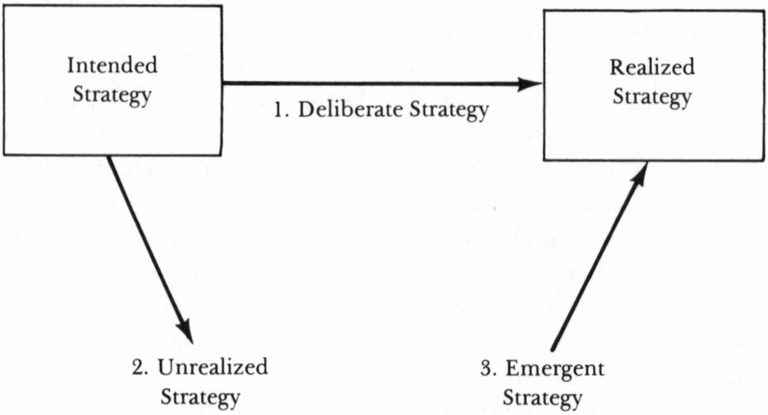

namely, *deliberate* strategies (intended and then realized), *unrealized* strategies (intended but not realized), and *emergent* strategies (patterns realized although never specifically intended).

There is the comment in the Introduction to *Winnie-the-Pooh* that "there are some people who begin the Zoo at the beginning, called WAYIN, and walk as quickly as they can past every cage until they get to the one called WAYOUT, but the nicest people go straight to the animal they love the most, and stay there." We are not sure that we are the nicest people, but we do know which definition we love the most, and we went straight to it to design our research methodology and have stayed there for some years.

Defining strategy as a pattern in a stream of decisions or actions almost dictates a research methodology to study strategy formation in organizations: (1) isolate streams of organizational decisions or actions in various critical areas, (2) infer strategies as consistencies in three streams, (3) infer periods in the history of the organization by considering stabilities and changes in the various strategies, (4) investigate the critical turning points from one period to another, and (5) then brainstorm with the findings around some key theoretical issues. Chief among these issues are the pattern of strategic change; the interplay of environment, leadership, and organization; and the relationship between deliberate and emergent strategies.

This methodology demands a good deal of time in each organization in order to trace its strategies across very long periods, with the result that the size of the research sample must be severely restricted. In fact, since 1971 we have conducted eleven intensive studies (aside from a number of others that have been carried out by students writing theses). These covered U.S. strategy in Vietnam, 1950-1973; Volkswagenwerk, 1934-1974; Steinberg (a retail chain), 1917-1974; Canadelle (a women's undergarment manufacturer), 1939-1976; the *Sherbrooke Record* (a newspaper), 1946-1976; Arcop (an architectural firm), 1953-1978; the National Film Board of Canada, 1939-1976; Air Canada, 1937-1976; *Saturday Night* magazine, 1928-1971; Asbestos Corporation, 1912-1975; and McGill University, 1921-1981. The first three of these studies have been published (Mintzberg, 1978; Mintzberg and Waters, 1982), the fourth is in press (Mintzberg and Waters, 1983), and by the time of this publication most of the others should be in press. Our specific intention in this chapter is to draw together some of the conclusions about the interplay of environment, leadership, and organization in a number of these studies.

In "Strategy Making in Three Modes" (Mintzberg, 1973b), an article first written just as this research was getting underway, three approaches to the making of strategy were described as depicted in the conceptual—not the empirical—literature. Table 1 summarizes the dimensions of each. In another publication (Mintzberg, 1979), written several years later, a typology of five "configurations" of structure and situation was proposed, in this case based on a reading of largely empirical literature. These were labeled simple structure, machine bureaucracy, divisionalized form, professional bureaucracy, and adhocracy. As a rough guide, the entrepreneurial mode would seem to fit with simple structure, the planning mode with machine bureaucracy, and the adaptive mode with adhocracy. A number of the organizations we have studied seem to fall rather close in characteristics to these three configurations (at least during certain periods in their histories), and each of these three groupings of organizations appears to exhibit its own distinct interplay of the forces of environment, leadership, and organization. Notably, a different one of these forces tends to take the lead in

Table 1. Characteristics and Conditions of the
Three Modes of Strategy Making.

Characteristic	Entrepreneurial Mode	Adaptive Mode	Planning Mode
Motive for decisions	Proactive	Reactive	Proactive and reactive
Goals of organization	Growth	Indeterminate	Efficiency and growth
Evaluation of proposals	Judgmental	Judgmental	Analytical
Choices made by	Entrepreneur	Bargaining	Management
Decision horizon	Long term	Short term	Long term
Preferred environment	Uncertainty	Certainty	Risk
Decision linkages	Loosely coupled	Disjointed	Integrated
Flexibility of mode	Flexible	Adaptive	Constrained
Size of moves	Bold decisions	Incremental steps	Global strategies
Vision of direction	General	None	Specific
Condition for Use			
Source of power	Entrepreneur	Divided	Management
Objectives of organization	Operational	Nonoperational	Operational
Organizational environment	Yielding	Complex, dynamic	Predictable, stable
Status of organization	Young, small, or strong leadership	Established	Large

From Mintzberg (1973b, p. 49).

each grouping. The body of this chapter discusses these various
relationships.

Leadership Taking the Lead:
Entrepreneurship in the Simple Structure

Steinberg and Canadelle, at least for a good part of their
histories, exhibited strong characteristics of the simple structure. By this we mean that their structures tended to be simple
and fluid, with relatively little hierarchy, minimal reliance on

technocratic staff groups or the formalization of behavior, and above all, the lodging of power firmly in the hands of the chief executive officer, who exercised it in a personal way—one typically described as entrepreneurial.

The entrepreneurial mode was characterized as follows in the article cited earlier: power centralized in the hands of the chief executive, whose behavior is dominated by the active search for opportunities, by the pursuit of the goal of growth above all, and by the taking of dramatic leaps forward in the face of uncertainty. That, as noted, is the view in the conceptual literature. What about entrepreneurship in our empirical studies?

Steinberg is a Canadian retail chain that began with a tiny food store in Montreal in 1917 and grew to a sales volume of over \$1 billion by the end of our study period in 1974. Most of that growth came from supermarket operations, although the firm did diversify (primarily into other retailing activities) after 1960. In many ways, Steinberg fits the entrepreneurial mode rather well. Sam Steinberg, who joined his mother in the first store at the age of eleven and personally made a quick decision to expand it two years later, maintained complete formal control of the firm (that is, every single voting share; public stock was never voting) to the day of his death in 1978. He also exercised close managerial control over all major decisions, at least until the firm began to diversify.

As for the "bold stroke" of the entrepreneur (Cole, 1959), we certainly saw evidence of some rather dramatic changes in the company—for example, a plunge into self-service in the 1930s or into the shopping center business in the 1950s. But for the most part, Sam Steinberg did not plunge until he had tested the water. The story of the move into self-service is indicative. To paraphrase from our report (Mintzberg and Waters, 1982), in 1933 one of the company's eight stores "struck it bad," in the chief executive's words, incurring "unacceptable" losses (\$125/week). Sam Steinberg closed the store one Friday night, changed its name from "Steinberg's Service Stores" to "Wholesale Groceteria," slashed prices by 15–20 percent, instituted a form of self-service, printed handbills, stuffed them into neighborhood mailboxes, and reopened on Monday morning! From that point on, after turning that store around and converting the others, in his words, "We grew like Topsy."

This anecdote tells us something about the bold stroke of the entrepreneur; the term we use in the article is *controlled boldness*. And it also tells us something about the proaction of the entrepreneur. Sam Steinberg was solving a problem, not searching out an opportunity. Indeed, he viewed it more as a crisis than as a problem. It was this kind of perception that distinguished his treatment of problems: getting more excited about them than other people. Most others would have viewed this situation as a problem to be solved, likely by doing the obvious—closing the store. By making it into a crisis, Sam Steinberg turned it into an opportunity. That was his way of getting energy behind action and of keeping ahead of his competition. He "oversolved" the problem and remade his company. We refer to this behavior as the "proactive reaction."

Another point about the entrepreneurial mode that came out in this study is that strategy, for the entrepreneur, is not a formal, detailed plan on paper. It is a personal vision in a brain, a concept of the business. That vision may sometimes get partially articulated, but for the most part it remains locked inside the brain. So long as the entrepreneur is able to make the key decisions for the organization, this poses no problem. Indeed, the great advantage of strategy as personal vision is that it can be changed rather easily. A formal plan, in contrast, tends to get widely disseminated in an organization and so cannot easily be changed.

A further point that emerged clearly in this study is that the key to generating such a vision, and to changing it at the right time, is intimate, detailed knowledge of the business. In discussing his firm's competitive advantage, Sam Steinberg told us: "Nobody knew the grocery business like we did. Everything has to do with your knowledge." He added, "I knew merchandise, I knew cost, I knew selling, I knew customers, I knew everything . . . and I passed on all my knowledge; I kept teaching my people. That's the advantage we had. They couldn't touch us."

This study indicates how effective such knowledge can be when it is concentrated in one person who is fully in charge (having no need to sell others with different views and different levels of knowledge, neither subordinates below nor superiors at some distant headquarters) and who retains a strong, long-term commitment to the organization. So long as the business is simple and concentrated enough to be comprehended in one brain —and this one was before it diversified—the entrepreneurial mode is powerful; indeed, unexcelled. No other mode of strategy making can provide the same degree of deliberateness and of integration of strategies with one another and with the environment. None can provide so clear and complete a vision of direction, yet also allow the flexibility to elaborate and rework that vision. The conception of a novel strategy is an exercise in synthesis, which is typically best carried out in a single, informed brain. That is why the entrepreneurial mode is at the center of the most glorious corporate successes.

The genius of Sam Steinberg, in our view, was that he could pursue one vision for twenty years (from the change to self-service in 1933 until the early 1950s) and then change it when he had to. After spending years in the 1930s and 1940s worrying about fluorescent lighting and new ways to use cellophane to package meat for self-service, he was able to shift his thoughts in the 1950s to the impact of shopping centers on overall retailing habits, realizing that he had to redefine the nature of his business. We believe such a Gestalt shift—from cellophane to shopping centers—requires a high degree of sophistication. How does the executive mind function when such a shift becomes necessary?

Let us turn to our study of Canadelle for some hints at the answer. Canadelle produces women's undergarments. It too was a highly successful organization, though hardly on the same scale as Steinberg. Things were going very well for the company in the late 1960s, under the personal leadership of the son of its founder. Suddenly everything changed. To draw from our report (Mintzberg and Waters, 1983): A sexual revolution of sorts was brewing. In contrast to the pointed look that had been so popular for a decade, women wished to appear more natural.

"Bra burning" was a major symbol of the social upheaval of the times, and for a manufacturer of brassières, the threat was obvious. The miniskirt dominated the fashion scene, making the girdle obsolete and leading to the development of pantyhose. Moreover, the girdle itself was threatened by the same social trend that was demanding increased freedom, comfort, and naturalness. As the executives of Canadelle put it, "The bottom fell out of the girdle business." Sales dropped by 30 percent per year, eventually stabilizing at about 5 percent of the firm's total business. Essentially, it appeared that the whole environment, long so receptive to the company's strategies, had suddenly turned rejective.

We had the good fortune to be able not only to interview the chief executive at length on his response to these changes but also to include him on our brainstorming team that dealt with these issues in a conceptual way. Let us first describe the events as we saw them in our report and then present our conceptual interpretation of them.

At the time, a French company was promoting a light, sexy, molded garment called "Huit" with the theme "Just like not wearing a bra." Their target market was 15–20-year-olds. Though expensive when it landed in Quebec, and not well fitting, the product sold well. The chief executive flew to France in an attempt to license the product for manufacture in Canada. The French firm refused, but he claimed that what he learned in "that one hour in their offices made the trip worthwhile." He learned that the ostensibly no-bra movement was going to manifest itself primarily as a less-bra movement. What women seemed to want was a more natural look. He also found that the product was being target-marketed to younger women.

The second event, shortly after, was a trip to a sister firm in the United States. There the CEO realized the importance of market segmentation by age and life-style. The company then sponsored market research to better understand what women wanted from a brassière. The results indicated that, for the more mature customer, the brassière was a cosmetic, which she wore to look and feel more attractive. The product had an important sex-appeal dimension for these customers. Moreover, it was found that the company's brand had high recognition among these consumers. In contrast, the younger customer wanted to look and feel natural; the sex-appeal dimension was considerably less important. Also, in the minds of these consumers, Canadelle's brand name was associated with older women. On the basis of these distinctions, the CEO became convinced that some major product-line differentiation was required.

These two events led to a major shift in strategy. The CEO described it as a kind of revelation—the confluence of different ideas to create a new mental set. In his words, "All of a sudden the idea forms." His groping had led to two new major concepts in the firm's strategy. On the marketing side was market segmentation—specifically, the division of market into older and younger customers. And on the technology and manufacturing side was the use of molding to produce seamless brassière cups.

Canadelle initiated an intensive technology development program to produce its own molded brassière, stimulated by the recent introduction of new fabrics. The firm introduced a molded garment made of tricot under its existing brand name for older customers and a stretch garment of Lycra for the younger market.

On a conceptual level we can draw on Lewin's (1951) notion of unfreezing, changing, and refreezing to explain this Gestalt shift in vision. The process of unfreezing is essentially one of overcoming the natural defense mechanisms to realize that the environment has in fact changed. Effective managers are supposed to scan their environments continually; indeed, effective *strategic* managers are supposed to be especially in touch with changing trends. One danger of strategic management is that it may encourage managers to be *too* in touch. Managers may be so busy managing strategic change—the big issues—that they may fail to do well what usually matters, namely, to function effectively with a given, viable strategy. Or, equally dangerous (and perhaps more likely), they may give so much attention to strategic monitoring when nothing important is changing that when something finally does change, they do not even notice it. The trick, of course, is to pick out the discontinuities that count. Many changes are temporary or simply unimportant. Some are consequential and a few revolutionary. For Canadelle, the changes in the late 1960s were of the latter category.

A second step in unfreezing is to be willing to step into the void, so to speak: The leader must shed his or her conventional notions of how the business is supposed to function (the industry recipe, as Grinyer and Spender, 1979, have termed it) and really open his or her mind to what is happening. It is critical to avoid premature closure—not to seize on a new thrust before it is clear what the signals really mean. This takes a special kind of management, one able to live with a good deal of uncertainty and discomfort. The president of Canadelle was able to articulate his feelings at the time: "There is a period of confusion before you know what to do about it. . . . You sleep on it . . . start looking for patterns . . . become an information hound, searching for [explanations] everywhere." This stage may be painful, but in our view it is critical to successful resolution.

Strategic change of this magnitude seems to involve mind set before strategy and seems to be essentially conceptual in nature. In other words, the concepts of the strategist—his or her *Weltanschauung*—must change before anything else can change. If this study gives any indication, then although problems and threats in the environment may provoke the unfreezing, it is opportunities that stimulate the process of change. With some idea of what *can* be done, the strategist begins to converge on a new concept of the business—a new strategic thrust. Our guess is that the experience here—of one or two basic driving ideas—is typical: In the final analysis, change in mind set is stimulated by a small number of key events, probably one critical incident in most cases. Continuous bombardment of facts, opinions, problems, and so on may have had to prepare the mind for the change, but one simple insight likely creates the synthesis—brings all the disparate data together in one sudden "Eureka!"-type flash.

Once the mind is set, assuming it has read the new environment correctly and has not seized prematurely on trends that have not themselves stabilized, then the refreezing stage begins. Here the object is not to read the environment, at least not in a global sense, but in effect to block it out. This is not time for the monitoring precepts of strategic management. It is time to work out the consequences of a new strategic thrust. It has been claimed that obsession is an ingredient in effective organizations (Peters, 1980). For the period of refreezing (not unfreezing or changing), we would agree. This is not the time for questioning but for pursuing the new orientation—the new mind set—with full vigor. When we asked the president how the post-1970 period differed from that of the two previous years, he commented: "Any idea is acceptable so long as it's. . . ." And he motioned with his hands in two parallel lines to indicate: so long as it is strictly within the bounds of the new concept. A management that was open and divergent in its thinking must now become closed and convergent. We wonder how many executives fail in one or the other—remaining convergent when divergence becomes necessary or failing to settle down to a convergent pattern after a period of divergence.

Whereas unfreezing was a time of great discomfort, refreezing must be one of great excitement (at least for those who accept the reorientation). The organization now knows where it is going; the object of the exercise is to use all the skills at its command to get there. This is not to say that all is creative. Refreezing is characterized by an analytic mode of behavior, with heavy emphasis on formal evaluation, perhaps closer to the planning mode. Of course, some members will not accept the reorientation; for them, the discomfort now begins, and this can spill over to the strategist if considerable resistance arises.

To conclude, leadership in the simple structure—what we are calling the entrepreneurial mode—is very much tied up with the creation of vision, essentially with *concept attainment*. Since the vision is personal, the overall form of the strategy may be described as deliberate. But in the absence of specific plans the details are likely to emerge. And the vision can change, too. In other words, the leader is able to adapt en route —he or she can learn. We describe this form of strategy making in Figure 2. The focus is on the leader, the organization is mal-

Figure 2. Leadership Taking the Lead in Simple Structure.

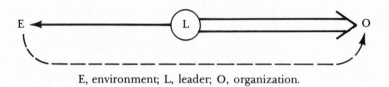

E, environment; L, leader; O, organization.

leable and responsive to the leader's initiatives, and the environment for the most part remains benign, the result of the leader's selecting (or enacting) the correct niche for his or her organization. The environment can, of course, flare up occasionally to challenge the organization, forcing the leader to seek out a new and more appropriate niche.

Organization Taking the Lead: Planning in the Machine Bureaucracy

Volkswagenwerk and Air Canada, after their formative years, and the U.S. government with respect to strategy in Vietnam seem closest to the configuration we call machine bureaucracy. What we mean by this is the classic view of formal organization: clear division of labor and subunit differentiation, extensive hierarchy, a large contingent of staff personnel, rather centralized decision making due to the need for tight coordination, and highly standardized behavior patterns. Like everything else, the process of strategy making is supposed to be formalized, presumably through planning. The planning mode was depicted in the "Three Modes" article as follows: an emphasis on analysis, especially assessment of the costs and benefits of competing proposals; a major role for staff personnel; and above all, an attempt to formally integrate decisions and strategies.

In fact, our best hint of what this might really mean comes from the later years of the Steinberg study, when we felt that Sam Steinberg's entrepreneurship began to be captured by planning. The company needed to plan more extensively and

more formally as it became large and its operations more dis-
persed—in other words, as the need for coordination became
paramount and less likely to be effected successfully in one
mind. One particular event really encouraged the start of the
planning mode: the company's entry into capital markets.
Months before Steinberg floated its first bond issue (nonvoting
stock was to come later), Sam Steinberg boasted to a newspaper
reporter that "not a cent of any money outside the family is invested in the company." And asked about future plans, he replied: "Who knows? There is so much to do right ahead that it
would sound like a wild dream to talk about ten years from
now. . . . We will try to go everywhere there seems to be a need
for us." A few months later he announced a $15 million five-
year expansion program, one new store every sixty days for a
total of thirty stores, the doubling of sales, new stores to aver-
age double the size of existing ones, with parking lots, children's playrooms, and so on. What happened in these few
months was the realization in Sam Steinberg's mind that he
needed to enter the shopping center business and that he could
not do so with the company's traditional methods of short-
term and internal financing. And no company goes to capital
markets without a plan.

But what exactly was that plan? It did not formulate a
strategy. Rather, it justified, elaborated, and articulated the
strategy—in other words, the vision—that Sam Steinberg already had. Planning operationalized the strategy, programmed
it. It gave order to vision, putting form on it to comply with
the needs of the organization and its environment. Thus, planning followed the strategy-making process, which was essentially entrepreneurial. But its effect on that process was not inci-
dental. By specifying and articulating the vision, planning constrained it, rendered it less flexible.

Is there, then, such a thing as a planning mode of strategy
making? We suspect not; at least, we have not found it yet. To
be more explicit, we do not find dramatic new strategies formulated through any kind of formal procedure. (Of course, not
everyone equates planning with formalized procedure; to some
people, planning is simply future thinking—see Mintzberg, 1981.

But as Wildavsky, 1973, notes in the title of a paper, "If planning is everything, maybe it's nothing.") Rather, the planning mode seems to encourage extrapolation or marginal change in given strategies (or visions) or else copying of the strategies of other organizations. Planning, in other words, tends to encourage the use of what we are calling "mainline strategies"—standard, accepted ones in the industry. The formulation of a dramatic new strategy is essentially the attainment of a new concept, a new *Weltanschauung*. It derives from synthesis, whereas planning tends to be oriented to analysis. Thus, planning seems to be a mode for operationalizing strategy, not for creating it—indeed, a mode that may discourage the creative side of strategy making.

This seems to come out most clearly in our study of Air Canada. Once the airline was established, around the middle 1950s, particularly once it had developed its basic route structure and established itself as a distinct organization, a number of factors drove it strongly to the planning mode. Above all was the paramount need for coordination on two levels. On the operational level, the airline had to coordinate its flight schedules with its aircraft, its crews, and its maintenance. And on the capital level, it had to coordinate the purchase of expensive aircraft with the introduction of new routes or the servicing of existing ones. (Imagine someone calling out in a hangar: "Hey, Fred, this guy says he has two 747s for us. Do you know who ordered them?") Safety is another factor: The intense need for it in the air breeds a mentality of being very careful about what the organization does on the ground, too. Other factors include the lead times inherent in key decisions such as ordering new airplanes or introducing new routes, the sheer cost of the capital equipment, the size of the organization, the airline's status as a government-owned corporation, and the airline's strong influence in its home markets. In any event, what we find in Air Canada—which we believe is largely a result of the planning orientation—is the absence of major reorientation of strategy for a good part of the study, especially the last two decades of it (to 1976). Aircraft certainly changed—they became larger and faster—but routes did not, nor did markets. Air Canada gave only marginal attention, for example, to cargo, charter, and shuttle operations.

How, then, does the planning-oriented machine bureaucracy change its strategy when it has to? Our best indication comes from the study of an organization that had to—Volkswagenwerk (Mintzberg, 1978). We interpret the history of Volkswagenwerk from 1934 to 1974 as one long strategy life cycle. The original concept of the "people's car" was conceived by Porsche; the factory to produce it was built just before the war but never went into civilian automobile production; a man named Nordhoff was given control of the organization in 1948, and he developed the other necessary components of the strategy, notably those related to service, internal expansion, and so on; the company enjoyed dramatic success through the 1950s; when problems began to appear, it grafted new pieces onto its existing strategy (the Variant models) without changing its essential concept; then, when the problems became serious, it reacted almost frantically, introducing, under a new leader from outside the industry, all kinds of new models with very little sense of its own direction; finally, under another leader (named Leiding) who developed within the industry, it consolidated a new strategy around one of its new models.

What does all this suggest? First, we see the effect of bureaucratic momentum. Even if we leave aside the influence of planning, the effort of setting up assembly lines and creating sales and service networks for a given automobile locked the company into a certain posture. But bureaucratic momentum here was psychological no less than material. Nordhoff, who had been the driving force behind the development and success of the organization, became a chief impediment to change when the environment demanded it. Leadership had been co-opted by bureaucratic momentum. (The capture of leadership by bureaucratic momentum was even more dramatically illustrated in our study of U.S. strategy in Vietnam, notably in 1965 when the forces for escalation overwhelmed Lyndon Johnson.) Moreover, in Volkswagenwerk, the uniqueness and

tight integration of the strategy—we called it a "gestalt strategy"—impeded strategic change. Change an element of a tightly
integrated Gestalt, and it *dis*integrates. Thus success can breed
failure.

To return to the strategic change in this configuration is also impeded by
the very nature of the structure. In machine bureaucracy the
leadership is removed from the operations by an extensive hierarchy. This means that there is a sharp dichotomy between the
formulation of strategy and its implementation. The leadership
has to impose its strategies through the hierarchy, which it
does first by specifying detailed plans and then by monitoring
performance through impersonal controls to ensure that these
plans are carried out. But that puts leadership out of touch with
the details of the operations—in other words, the development
of real knowledge of the business is impeded—and that, together
with the specificity of the plans, discourages the kind of adaptation found in simple structure, where the formulator *is* the
implementer.

To return to our original question, how, then, does the
strategy change? Using Miller and Friesen's (1980) term, we believe by "revolution": A new, strong leader comes in with a new
vision (perhaps because he or she has been closer to the operations, as with Leiding, who turned Volkswagen around), suspends established procedures, ignores staff planners, and consolidates power around himself or herself personally—and then
does what is necessary. In other words, the machine bureaucracy reverts to simple structure temporarily, the planning mode
to an entrepreneurial mode, in order to realize necessary change.
But the large, established organization typically cannot tolerate such personalized control for long and is as likely as not to
spit out its entrepreneur once he or she has rendered the necessary changes (which is exactly what Volkswagen did in 1974).
Thus, the process of strategic change can be described in quan-
tum terms (Miller and Friesen, 1980)—long periods of stability
of strategy interrupted occasionally by short periods of revolutionary change.

To conclude, as shown in Figure 3, in machine bureaucracy it is the organization that takes the lead, with its systems

Figure 3. Organization Taking the Lead in Machine Bureaucracy.

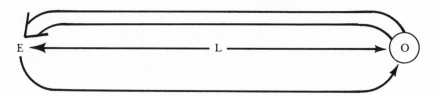

and procedures, its methods of planning, and its own bureau-cratic momentum. Of course, an organization cannot undertake on a piecemeal basis massive commitments of resources, such as producing a new-model automobile or flying wide-body jets, testing before plunging. Detailed plans and a carefully struc-tured organization are required before anything can be done. But the price of these is high. The environment may demand change, especially after the strategy has had some years of suc-cess, but the organization inevitably resists. Indeed, particular-ly when it is large and powerful, as many machine bureaucracies are, it is the organization that seeks to impose itself on the envi-ronment—for example, by trying to stabilize markets so that they will accept its products. Pfeffer and Salancik (1978) de-scribe all kinds of methods that organizations use to do so—ver-tical integration to control suppliers and customers, the estab-lishment of cartels, the development of arrangements with governments, and so on. Leadership in the machine bureaucracy may try to mediate, encouraging the organization to respond to environmental change while seeking to buffer it from the forces of the environment in recognition of its need to maintain stabil-ity. But time encourages momentum, and often the leadership gets captured by the organization, too, so that reversion to sim-ple structure and the entrepreneurial mode (under a new leader) becomes necessary for change.

    If the strategist of the simple structure is a concept attainer, then that of the machine bureaucracy is a planner, or perhaps a pigeonholer who slots generic strategies into well-defined conditions and then hangs onto them for dear life.

Environment Taking the Lead:
Adaptation in the Adhocracy

The National Film Board of Canada, a government-owned
company that makes mostly short and many highly innovative
films, and Arcop, a small architectural firm well known in Canada
for its innovative work, closely fit the characteristics of what we
are calling adhocracy. By *adhocracy* we mean essentially project
structure, more specifically structure in which various experts
combine their talents on teams or task forces to innovate. In the
National Film Board, the teams create novel films; in Arcop,
they design unique buildings. Such organizations tend to decen-
tralize rather extensively but selectively (that is, decision by decision according to expertise) and to rely heavily on devices to
encourage mutual adjustment (such as integrating managers and
matrix structure) but to discourage the more conventional
parameters of structure (common in machine bureaucracy) in
order to avoid standardization and formalization. The mode of
strategy making labeled "adaptive," characterized by the writings of Lindblom (1959, 1968; Braybrooke and Lindblom,
1963) and Cyert and March (1963), would appear to fit best in
adhocracy. The adaptive mode was described as appropriate for
the organization that has no clear goals but instead divides its
power among members of a complex coalition; organizations
using this mode were characterized as reacting to existing problems rather than searching for new opportunities and were characterized by decisions that are disjointed and made in serial,
incremental steps.

Our study of the two adhocracies would appear to confirm the flavor of this description, although not some of its specific details. Because the adhocracy must respond continuously
to a complex environment that it cannot predict, it is unable to
rely on deliberate strategies. In other words, it cannot predeter-
mine patterns in its streams of activities. Rather, its decisions or
actions must be made one at a time, largely according to the
needs of the moment. And these must be under the control of
whoever has the expertise to deal with the issue in question.
The result is that power over strategy making in adhocracy is dif-

fused in ways unheard of in simple structures or machine bureaucracies, where it tends to be focused at the top of the hierarchy.

But does continuous response to the environment necessarily imply the reaction to problems rather than the proactive
search for opportunities? On one hand, adhocracies appear to
be very reactive, continuously trying to read the environment to
know which way to go next. On the other hand, they do so to
innovate, to create new outputs to serve that environment. So
perhaps strategy making in adhocracy is best described as op-
portunistic reaction.

That decisions are serial and incremental seems to be true
in the sense that adhocracies are reluctant to make grand decisions that commit resources for long periods of time. In the
words of Lindblom, they prefer "continual nibbling" to "a
good bite" (1968, p. 25). But that such decisions are disjointed
—distinct from one another—is one assumption that proved
overly simple. What happened in our studies was most interesting. At times decisions and actions showed a curious propensity
to converge—that is, to exhibit patterning. In other words, we
do find strategies in adhocracies, even though these are typically
emergent.

Most surprising in our study of the National Film Board
were the ways in which the content of films tended to converge
on certain themes periodically and then to diverge, despite an
almost complete absence of direction on film content from the
central management. We classified almost 3,000 films made at
the National Film Board from 1939 to 1976 into thirty-nine
categories of content (for example, experimental, mental
health, defense, native people). We then distinguished what we
called "focused strategies"—situations in which a content category received some sustained attention (essentially five or more
films per year for more than two years)—from "trickles"
(streams with fewer than five films per year) and "blips" (five
or more films but for only one or two years). Figure 4 is a plot
of the percentage of films categorized in focused strategies (and
the inverse, trickles plus blips) by year. Here we can see the tendency to converge and diverge periodically, or as we put it in the

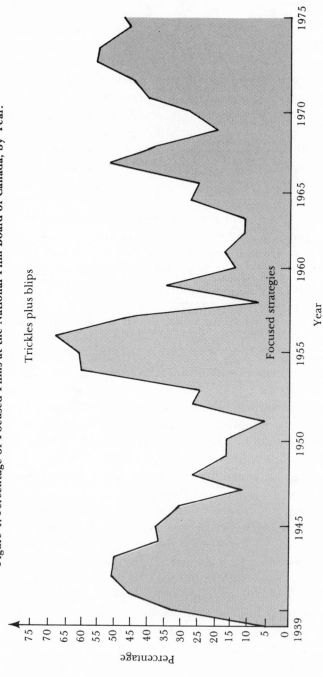

Figure 4. Percentage of Focused Films at the National Film Board of Canada, by Year.

report (if we can be forgiven for this reference to a film company), the cycling into and out of focus. The first convergence was largely around defense and related films to support the war effort. Then until the early 1950s there was a great deal of diversity with little focus. The advent of television in Canada captured the Film Board for a few years in the 1950s as no theme ever did before or since. But that focus ended just as quickly as it began and was followed by another period of divergence. Then, in the middle 1960s, there was a brief period of convergence around the themes of experimentation and social commentary, which was interrupted briefly and then renewed in somewhat modified form in the late 1960s and 1970s around social issues.

What role does leadership play in the adhocracy? Implied in the description above is a possible role for *informal* leadership. One filmmaker can make a new type of film, which can serve as a model for other filmmakers and so lead to a focused strategy. That, in fact, is how the television focus of the 1950s came about—one filmmaker took the plunge, and many of the others quickly followed suit, converging on the theme. Figure 5, a plot of all the films that we categorized as experimental, shows another example, except that this convergence was far less sudden or pervasive. What is of interest here is that every film on this chart until 1960, with one exception, was made by Norman McLaren, the Board's most celebrated filmmaker. What we have, in effect, from the organization's point of view, is a trickle, although from the individual's point of view it can be labeled the personal strategy of Norman McLaren. Then in the 1960s others finally followed McLaren's lead and began to experiment too, so that the personal strategy became an organizational one (although not dominant).

Where does all this leave the formal leadership, the people who do not make films but sit in executive offices? Clearly, to use the formal language of organization theory, they must spend a good deal of time managing the boundary conditions. The managerial roles of liaison, monitor (external), spokesman, and negotiator assume great importance in organizations that face unpredictable environments. And the general managers

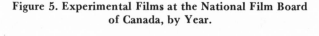

Figure 5. Experimental Films at the National Film Board
of Canada, by Year.

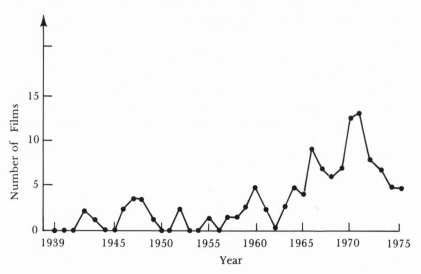

must also spend a fair amount of time resolving conflict, given
the flexibility of the internal structure (Mintzberg, 1979, pp.
447–449). But what about their role in strategy making? Must
the general managers defer totally to the experts? In two ways
we find that they need not. First, the general managers can try
to manage the process of strategy making, if not the content of
strategy. In other words, they can set up the structures to encourage certain kinds of behavior patterns and hire the people
who themselves will create those patterns. Had there been no
Norman McLaren, for example, there might not have been an
experimental film strategy in the 1960s. And second, they can
provide general guidelines for strategy, seeking to define certain
boundaries outside which the experts should not take action.
We call this an *umbrella* strategy and found it most clearly in
Arcop. The leadership always imposed one basic umbrella: Arcop devoted its effort to "public celebration" buildings—unique,
visible ones that would have an impact on the community and
celebrate its spirit. Within that umbrella, anything went—cultural

centers, hotels, office buildings, churches, and so on. Periodically, there was in fact convergence, as there was in the National Film Board. At one point, for example, the firm was repeatedly contracted to design performing arts centers. But that convergence was largely emergent—the architects were open to a wide variety of work and happened to be successful in one particular sphere. In other words, in some sense the environment imposed the strategy (that is, the pattern). Only the umbrella—the broad set of guidelines—was clearly deliberate.

To conclude, as shown in Figure 6, in adhocracy it is the

Figure 6. Environment Taking the Lead in Adhocracy.

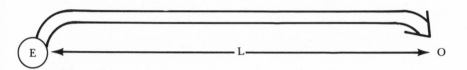

environment that takes the lead. It drives the organization, which responds continuously and eclectically, nevertheless periodically achieving convergence for a time. (We have wondered what *organizational intuition* might mean; perhaps the convergence in strategic theme as a result of spontaneous mutual adjustments is one place to apply the term appropriately.) The formal leadership seeks somehow to influence both sides in this relationship, negotiating with the environment for support and trying to impose some broad general guidelines (an umbrella) on the organization. If the strategist of the simple structure is a concept attainer and that of the machine bureaucracy is a planner, then the strategist of the adhocracy is a *pattern recognizer,* seeking to detect emerging patterns (inside and outside the umbrella). That way the appropriate ones can be encouraged through more conscious attention and concentration of resources (narrowing the umbrella or moving it over), while others deemed inappropriate can be discouraged. In the former case we may find the paradoxical situation of a leadership changing its

intentions to fit the realizations of its organization. But that can
be a key to successful learning in the adhocracy.

The Strategists' Mind

Who is the strategist, and how does his, her, its, or their
mind work? As suggested at the outset, we do not pretend to
know much about anyone's mind. But at least we can try to
identify whose mind is in question in strategy making.

Our three situations reveal quite different answers. The
mind of the strategist is easiest to identify in the simple structure. There is one leader, and that person invents or conceives
strategy. He or she is best described as a concept attainer, which
is just a way of saying that the black box of the strategist's
mind is indeed black instead of green or fuchsia.

Machine bureaucracy appears to be more complex but
may in fact prove simpler. That is because, in a sense, there is
no strategist in machine bureaucracy, at least no active one. At
best there may have been one in the organization's past—the
person who conceived the original vision—or there may be one
in another organization whose ideas are copied. And there may,
of course, be dormant ones in the organization itself, people
with vision waiting for the chance to impose their intentions or
people who already had their chance and have since run dry. In
any event, those who call themselves strategists in machine bureaucracy tend to be planners of sorts, protecting, extrapolating, and marginally modifying—in effect, programming or implementing—the strategies the organization already pursues.

It is really in adhocracy that the complexity appears.
"Every man a strategist" would not be an unfair characterization of strategy making in adhocracy, except to its women. Yet
the fact that convergence does periodically occur raises an interesting point—namely, that there can be an "organizational
mind." We can talk of the strategists' mind (as opposed to the
strategist's mind or the strategists' minds) and even begin to talk
of "organizational intuition." Again, we can say little about
how the mind functions except that pattern recognition seems
to be one of its important capabilities. In other words, this box

is not black but multicolored, and marbled. And because this mind comprises behaviors more than neurons (at least at our level of analysis), we may be able to learn a good deal about it. Perhaps organization theorists who study collective minds may ultimately make greater headway in understanding the functioning of the executive mind than psychologists who study single ones!

4

Cultivating
Timely Executive Action

William R. Torbert

The Americans are,
to use their favorite expression,
a highly executive people.
—James B. Bryce, *The American Commonwealth*, 1888

The word *executive* descends from the Latin *ex*, "out," and *sequire*, "to follow," and thus means "to follow out," or in one contemporary definition "to carry out . . . a purpose" and in another "apt, skillful" (*Oxford English Dictionary*). Hence, the very notion of "Executive Mind" carries within it the no-

The author wishes to thank the faculty members of the Boston College School of Management who participated in the initial "Work in Progress" seminar, which contributed to his thinking about the themes of this paper, and would like to offer special thanks to Jean Bartunek, Stavros Cademenos, Mark Krieger, Jack Neuhauser, Richard Nielsen, and Paul Shiman, who offered critical comments on an early draft of the paper.

tion of functioning—indeed, the notion of purposeful and effective functioning.

"Executive Mind" bespeaks an immense discipline relating the very sources of human aspiration to the ultimate ends of human action—an immense discipline which few persons imagine as a possibility, let alone discover as a practical direction, which still fewer persons actually undertake, which fewer yet master, and which virtually no institutions actively cultivate.

This essay begins with repeated efforts to characterize and to illustrate the concerns and the disciplines relevant to "Executive Mind." The point is not to "prove" from the outside that such a quality as Executive Mind exists, not to "prove" that each historical character mentioned consciously exercised Executive Mind, but, rather, to evoke an appreciation from the inside that, rare as it is in historical and personal experience, such a quality is worth seeking for oneself and for the situations in life to which one wishes to be responsible.

In a sense, then, the initial strategy of this paper corresponds to Abraham Maslow's early efforts to seek out examples of "self-actualizing" persons. He wished to elaborate a category of motivation that, though statistically rare, could be argued to be an evolutionary aim for many or all, as well as a more effectual, less restricted and conflicted source of motivation for those who experience it.

Toward the end of his life, Maslow recognized that human beings harbor an even deeper and more dignifying need than that for self-actualization: a need to achieve meaningful participation in human projects that last beyond ourselves, that span the generations. He was, in effect, seeking to explicate an aspiration to act in ways that are at the same time personally expressive and culturally reverberative. And this means, in turn, to act in ways dictated neither by inner impulses nor by external demands, to act freely and artfully rather than compulsively and conformingly, to sculpt action so responsive to both inner and outer worlds that it is timely, not timebound. I will argue that the cultivation and exercise of Executive Mind is the discipline that leads to timely action, to action meaningful beyond oneself, through the generations.

After the initial efforts to characterize and illustrate

Executive Mind, the final section of this chapter attempts to sketch the outlines of the kind of research that serves to cultivate Executive Mind and timely action.

Four Complementary Disciplines: Observing Mind, Theorizing Mind, Passionate Mind, Executive Mind

Actually the notion of Executive Mind points to more than one rare mental discipline. Influenced by the typologies of Jung (1923) and Mitroff and Kilmann (1978), we can speak of "Observing Mind," "Theorizing Mind," and "Passionate Mind" as complements to Executive Mind (see Figure 1). In contrast to the typologies of Jung and of Mitroff and Kilmann, however, the present typology of four types of mind does not describe the universe of human mental processes. It does not refer to what Freud called primary- and secondary-process thinking (dreamlike and logical thinking). Instead, the present typology refers to "tertiary"-process thinking (Torbert, 1973), to four rare mental disciplines, each of which involves a special, paradoxical action of the attention different from ordinary logical, discursive, or imaginative thought. For example, Observing Mind is virtually the reverse of our ordinary inner chatter about our condition; instead, it involves a continuous clarifying action whereby preconceptions are "swept aside" each moment and one's vigilance and receptivity to whatever is happening inside and outside increase.

Moreover, unlike the Jungian types, which can be highly unbalanced and for which attaining balance and integration is a difficult, voluntary, adult activity, the four types of mind presented here "incline" toward one another. Indeed, they represent the balancing and integrating activities of mature adulthood and thus *require* one another. In particular, Executive Mind can do no good work without the material provided by Observing Mind, the form provided by Theorizing Mind, and the motivation provided by Passionate Mind.

As a brief introduction to these four mental disciplines, we can ask where they are cultivated in today's universities and

Figure 1. Four Qualities of Mind.

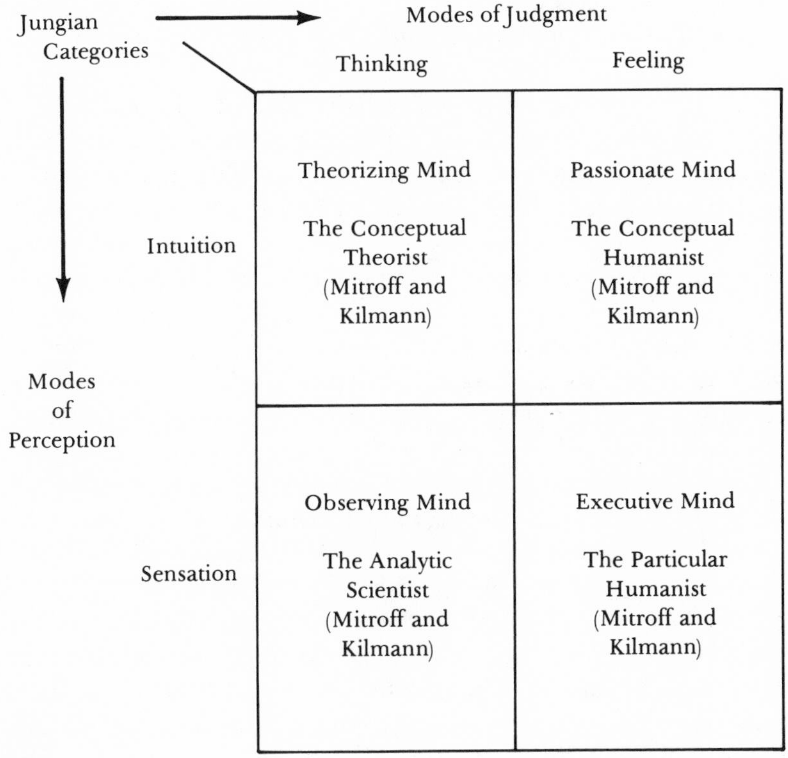

Jungian Categories → Modes of Judgment	Thinking	Feeling
Intuition	Theorizing Mind The Conceptual Theorist (Mitroff and Kilmann)	Passionate Mind The Conceptual Humanist (Mitroff and Kilmann)
Sensation	Observing Mind The Analytic Scientist (Mitroff and Kilmann)	Executive Mind The Particular Humanist (Mitroff and Kilmann)

Modes of Perception ↓

what historical figure can serve as an archetypal representative of each.

The notions of Observing Mind and Theorizing Mind are most familiar to the social scientist, although even within the modern university the appreciative stillness of Observing Mind is today cultivated only by the clinically-oriented methodologies, being epitomized by nineteenth-century natural scientists such as Darwin and Lyell. (Audubon's illustrations of birds represent a quintessence of the interplay of observation and execution.) Fully cultivated, Observing Mind includes within its purview not

only the outside world but also the subject's own thoughts, feelings, and actions (Torbert, 1973).
   The Buddha as archetypal embodiment of Observing Mind.

   If Observing Mind is rarely cultivated, the eternal dynamic tension of cosmogonic construction characteristic of Theorizing Mind is glimpsed almost solely through personal contact with truly philosophical teachers. The literary forms to which we have become habituated virtually preclude the exhibition and cultivation of Theorizing Mind. I can count only four twentieth-century literary works that fully accept the discipline of instantiating Theorizing Mind: Joyce's *Finnegans Wake,* Heidegger's *What Is Called Thinking?,* Wittgenstein's *Philosophical Investigations,* and Gurdjieff's *All and Everything: Beelzebub's Tales to His Grandson.*
   Socrates as voice for Theorizing Mind;
   Periclean Athens as chorus.

   As for the disciplines of Passionate Mind and Executive Mind, these are relegated at the modern university almost entirely to peripheral activities such as drama and sports. The pedagogy of group dynamics self-study is only very occasionally understood as cultivating the disciplines of naming, containing, appreciating, refining, reverencing, recognizing, and appropriately expressing the lifetime pulse of passion. Generally, the passions are reduced to mere emotions, proclaimed irrational, and excluded from the academic curriculum. Religion, in the ultimate inversion of traditional teachings, is treated as a private matter.
   Jesus, epiphany of Passionate Mind.

   Executive Mind depends on these three other rare disciplines both for discriminating valid data about the outside and inside worlds where the executive works and for vivifying the purposiveness of the overall enterprise that the executive serves.
   Executive Mind is for the mental muscle that can operate at the fulcrum between a person's inner life and the outer world; the mental muscle that can embody thought, transform-

ing habitual, predetermined behavior into inspired, creative, timely action; the mental muscle that can manage the play of attention at the interface of time and space. Just as bodily musculature provides a person leverage in space, so Executive Mind provides leverage in time (appropriate financial leveraging for a family, an enterprise, or a nation representing one subordinate manifestation of this capacity). Just as the ultimate development of bodily leverage gives the greatest athletes (such as Nadia Comaneci at the 1976 Olympics) the appearance of almost effortless ease, grace, and spaciousness in the midst of the most complex movements, so the highest development of mental leverage gives the greatest executives the appearance of leisureliness amid the most complex schedule, the most dire emergency, the most momentous decisions.

Executive Mind shapes space-time by acting so appropriately that the actions become mythical foundations reframing subsequent culture. In the Communist Chinese collectivist hagiography, the miraculous Long March, whereby Mao, Chou, and the Red Army escaped encirclement by Chiang Kai-shek in the south and marched 6,000 miles north in virtually continuous battle over the course of an entire year to refound the Communist state in Shensi, is regarded as the ultimate demonstration of virility and virtue—as the actualization of an "impossible" dream.

The surest sign of the continuing, balanced development of Executive Mind in the young adult (circa ages twenty to forty) is the preeminent application of his or her current executive capacities to cultivating the disciplines opening toward Observing Mind, Theorizing Mind, and Passionate Mind. Executive Mind is unlikely to manifest itself in a constructive, culturally transforming manner before the second half of life. Before that, the passion for recognition tempts one to seek excellence, power, glory, or truth in terms defined by others. Who achieves early in life the self-recognition from which, alone, temperate and just actions proceed?

Within the academy, the pedagogical methods of case study, simulation, oral competitions, and clinical internships, pioneered primarily at schools of management and other professional schools, all seek to cultivate executive qualities.

Gandhi as inquirer seeking integration of Observing Mind, Theoretical Mind, and Passionate Mind through Executive Mind, redefining manhood and nationhood for India in so doing (and Huxley's Grey Eminence, *a searing portrait of another spiritual/political figure whose initially parallel search deviated diabolically).*

Barnard's View of the Executive

Although the foregoing introductory comments may seem at some remove from the practice of executive leadership in today's world, a few brief references to Chester Barnard's classic work *The Functions of the Executive* (1938) should suggest otherwise.

Observing Mind. The role of Observing Mind in executive leadership is intimated by the following passages:

> The fine art of executive decision consists in not deciding questions that are not now pertinent, in not deciding prematurely, in not making decisions that cannot be made effective, and in not making decisions that others should make [p. 135].

> There is no principle of executive conduct better established in good organizations than that orders will not be issued that cannot or will not be obeyed. . . . To do so destroys authority, discipline, and morale [p. 167]

> The decision as to whether an order has authority or not lies with the persons to whom it is addressed [p. 163].

All three of these remarks emphasize how crucial it is for the executive to be attuned to those about him or her—to their ways of construing the world, the organization, and the executive—to temporal rhythms in human affairs, and to fostering a dynamic balance of initiatives between self and others.

The three quotations communicate an aura of modesty or humility about what the executive can and should do; or, still more simply, they imply an executive capable of observing without distortion what genuinely requires doing. One of the constant dangers that executives court by virtue of their explicit mandate to make decisions is ego inflation—the usually implicit belief that they should make any and all decisions of interest, or as many as possible, the more and the quicker the better. Such ego inflation leads into a vicious cycle of fear and ineffectiveness: Addiction to decision-making work reduces the leisureliness characteristic of all four of the higher mental disciplines, gradually distancing the executive from a vivid commitment to an order appealing to those about him or her; then, as the executive meets with increasing resistance to decisions, he or she becomes less willing to entrust decisions to others, further increasing the burden of decision making; and so on.

Of all Alexander's generals and relatives, only Ptolemy observed the limits of his own range of command, preserving Egypt in peace, building Alexandria, and dying with the satisfaction of completed work and a continuing line, while the others all struggled for the whole of Alexander's heritage, dying young and enjoying none of it.

The capacity to listen to temporary rhythms—whether within a morning, within a year, or within a lifetime—and to await the moment when action can be effective has been most dramatically illustrated in this century by Charles de Gaulle's retirement of more than a decade after World War II, during which time his moral authority increased while that of the Fourth Republic dissipated, until he was called in 1958 to end the Algerian War and to found the Fifth Republic—to redress France in a nobler image of which he, by virtue as much of his observant retirement after World War II as of his military role during the war, was the very embodiment. A more recent and more complex choreography of retirement and return to action is being enacted by Konosuke Matsushita of Matsushita Electric Company (Pascale and Athos, 1981). (The capacity for voluntary retirement is, of course, only one of many possible manifestations of Observing Mind.)

Theorizing Mind. The role of Theorizing Mind in executive leadership is suggested by the following quotations from Barnard:

> A formal and orderly conception of the whole is rarely present, perhaps even rarely possible, except to a few men of executive genius. . . . Even the notion which is here in question seems rarely to be stressed either in practical or scientific studies [p. 239].
>
> The distinguishing mark of the executive responsibility is that it requires not merely conformance to a complex code of morals, but also the creation of moral codes for others. . . . Organizations endure . . . in proportion to the breadth of the morality by which they are governed. This is only to say that foresight, long purposes, high ideals, are the basis for the persistence of cooperation [pp. 281–282].

The executive, as Mintzberg's (1973a) careful empirical studies have shown, is constantly besieged by a multitude of apparently competing demands. Ideally, the executive has a normative, synthetic theoretical perspective that reveals hidden complementarities among issues, establishes priorities, provides a meaningful frame for activities (that is, a coherent, encouraging, dignifying frame), and endows the executive with the vigilance and the balance to foresee and to respond in a measured fashion to the otherwise unexpected. In the absence of such a theoretical perspective, the executive's own activity becomes fragmented, and that of the organization as a whole descends toward "loosely coupled" "organized anarchy" (Cohen and March, 1974; Weick, 1979). In world affairs during the past generation, perhaps the most striking demonstration of the executive leverage provided by a synthetic theory that redefines the entire "stage" is Gamal Abdel Nasser's creation of "the Third World." This conception, so immediately persuasive to so many that we have already virtually forgotten who originated it, facilitated the transformation of the frozen bipolarity of the postwar world into the dynamic dialectical interplay we know today. It encouraged and dignified all "Third World" countries, which had until then worn the sobriquet "underdeveloped" with appropriate dispiritedness—none more so than Egypt itself, which, alone among Arab countries, has been able to struggle toward a new, more positive relationship to Israel in recent years, just as a person who forms a strong, positive self-concept thereby becomes enabled to explore relationships to persons very different from himself or herself.

Passionate Mind. The role of Passionate Mind in executive leadership can be elaborated from the following comments in Barnard's *Functions of the Executive*:

> Purpose is essential to give any meaning to the rest of the environment. The environment must be looked at from some point of view to be intelligible [p. 195].

> The inculcation of belief in the real existence of a common purpose is an essential executive function [p. 87].

> Purpose is defined more nearly by the aggregate of action taken than by any formulation in words [p. 231].

An executive's sense of purpose is, obviously, closely related to his or her world view, to an implicit or explicit theory about the nature of individuals, of organizations and societies, and of the cosmos. But, equally obviously, a sense of purpose is no mere logical deduction from theoretical premises. A sense of purpose is a passionate, motivating quality that, as Barnard suggests above, is a precondition for intelligibility (a precondition for theorizing) and a more profound shaper of action than theory is.

Isaiah Berlin (1980) attributes just such a capacity to Winston Churchill during the Battle of Britain and does so in words that highlight the dialectical tension between the qualities of Observing Mind and those of Passionate Mind:

> Churchill is not a sensitive lens which absorbs and concentrates and reflects and amplifies the sentiments of others; unlike the European dictators, he does not play on public opinion like an instrument. In 1940 he assumed an indomitable stoutness, an unsurrendering quality on the part of his people, and carried on. . . . He idealized them

with such intensity that in the end they approached his ideal and began to see themselves as he saw them: "the buoyant and imperturbable temper of Britain which I had the honour to express"—it was indeed, but he had a lion's share in creating it. So hypnotic was the force of his words, so strong his faith, that by the sheer intensity of his eloquence he bound his spell upon them until it seemed to them that he was indeed speaking what was in their hearts and minds. Doubtless it was there; but largely dormant until he had awoken it within them.

After he had spoken to them in the summer of 1940 as no one has ever before or since, they conceived a new idea of themselves which their own prowess and the admiration of the world [have] since established as a heroic image in the history of mankind, like Thermopylae or the defeat of the Spanish Armada. They went forward into battle transformed by his words. The spirit which they found within them he had created within himself from his inner resources, and poured it into his nation, and took their vivid reaction for an original impulse on their part, which he merely had the honour to clothe in suitable words. He created a heroic mood and turned the fortunes of the Battle of Britain not by catching the mood of his surroundings but by being stubbornly impervious to it, as he has been to so many of the passing shades and tones of which the life around him has been composed.

The peculiar quality of heroic pride and a sense of the sublimity of the occasion arises in him ... from a capacity for sustained introspective brooding, great depth and constancy of feeling—in particular, feeling for and fidelity to the great tradition for which he assumes a personal responsibility, a tradition which he bears upon his shoulders and must deliver, not only sound and undamaged but strengthened and embellished, to successors worthy of accepting the sacred burden [pp. 14–15].

Churchill's impact on England in its darkest hour illustrates a fundamental tension between the academic mind and Executive Mind. Where the "objective" academic mind might see only darkness and might regard any other construction of events as a form of dishonesty, Executive Mind is fired by a passion to accomplish an improbable purpose and is, consequently, fundamentally optimistic even at the darkest moment of despair. This optimism is in no sense a fatalistic "just wait, everything will be all right" attitude but, rather, the ability to draw energy from a supreme challenge or demand.

Executive Mind. The role of Executive Mind in executive leadership is to balance observation, strategy, and passion in artistic, timely, responsible, effective action. Or, in words more directly connected to the very definition of *executive* with which we began, Executive Mind so coordinates action that it effectively transforms (past, empirical) physical and social realities in the direction of (future, normative) purposes. In Barnard's words, to develop "the nonlogical, the intuitional, even the inspirational processes . . . means developing the artistic principle in the use of the mind, attaining proportion between speed and caution, between broad outlines and fineness of detail, between solidity and flexibility. As in other arts, . . . constant practice is required" (1938, p. 322).

To penetrate beyond the surface of these initial statements about Executive Mind, it is necessary first to destroy the sense of antagonism between science and art with which many of us are bred, as well as the accompanying sense that science is objective and precise whereas art is subjective and imprecise. In particular, we are all familiar with essays and discussions about whether management has now become a science, clear and certain, or still remains an art, mysterious and uncertain. But anyone familiar with traditional arts—whether we think of the pyramids, of ju jitsu, of sitar ragas, of the commedia dell' arte, of Shakespearean sonnets, or of a Balanchine ballet—recognizes that mathematical precision and predictable, definite (objective) effects on participants and observers are of the essence in the arts. Conversely, anyone familiar with the frontiers of science today recognizes that the foundations of mathematics, of matter, of time, and of intelligence are all shrouded in mystery. The distinction between science and art is not between two kinds of knowing but between knowing and doing. At their best, management sciences and management arts will complement each other; and management will certainly remain an art so long as there is anything to manage and anyone who has mastered the relevant, artistic disciplines.

The Transforming Power of Executive Mind

Not every executive whose desk is clear, whose office is quiet, and who creates a personal relationship with a visitor before doing business has mastered the disciplines of Executive Mind: The executive may merely have succeeded in outwardly imitating (perhaps inadvertently parodying) an impressive mentor. Nevertheless, a clear desk would seem to symbolize control over one's own time—over one's worlds of concern—whether as an accomplished fact, as a distant aspiration, or as a subterfuge. (In fact, empirical studies show that executives frequently experience themselves as losing the battle for sufficient control over their time to address the issues they regard as most significant [Cohen and March, 1974; Perkins, 1967].)

In an executive role, the experience of control over one's own time, the experience of clear mind amid multiple demands, can come only from passionate familiarity with three interpenetrating "scales" of time—with one's own lifetime calling, with the temporal rhythms of one's enterprise, and with world historical currents. With this knowledge—or, better, with the continuous thirst for this knowledge, since it is never complete, static, or fully explicit—comes the ability to meet each new demand calmly and actively, to seek how each new demand can be woven into the tapestry of one's life work. In this way, Executive Mind exercises a transforming influence within its sphere of activity. As suggested earlier by the mention of Churchill, de Gaulle, Gandhi, and Nasser, the exercise of Executive Mind can transform the very definition of a local situation, of a nation, or of the international balance of power.

Thus, Executive Mind operates beyond the frontier of conventional judgment (but without losing sight of the dumb power, the unconscious wisdom, and the sheer necessity of conventional judgment). Conventional praise and blame play a role in defining the context within which continuing action occurs, but they do not directly affect Executive Mind. Indeed, certain Sufi masters choose "the path of blame," whereby they intentionally counterbalance the attractive power of their charisma by sculpting actions that attract blame as well. In this way they seek to cultivate a passionately and precisely ambiguous arena within which aspirants can struggle to discover what is up to them. Similarly, some psychotherapists and organizational consultants (for example, Perls, Argyris) cultivate negative transference among their clients with the intention of minimizing any tendency in the clients to become passively dependent on the interventionist as a heroic savior. To choose "the path of blame," or, more generally, to operate in a balanced fashion beyond the frontier of conventional judgment, requires egoic detachment from the outcomes of action—"works wrought uninvolved," in the words of the *Bhagavad Gita.* The Buddhist phase for this state of mind is "No praise, no blame," and we are all familiar with Henry Ford's vulgar version: "Never complain, never explain."

Excerpts from Oriana Fallaci's interview with Lech Walesa (Fallaci, 1981) can serve as summary illustration of the complementarity among the four qualities of higher mind and of the capacity these qualities bequeath to change the very definition of a situation:

1. Observing Mind

Q. Don't you ever feel scared . . . inadequate . . . by the responsibility you took in front of your country and of history?

A. Nie, nie, nie, because I am a man of faith and because I know that this moment needs a guy like me. A guy who can make decisions with good sense and solve problems in a cautious, moderate way. I am not a fool. I do understand that too many injustices got accumulated during these thirty-six years, so things cannot change from morning to night. It takes patience, it takes wisdom. I mean, the rage that people would like to burst like a bomb must be controlled. And I know how to control it, because I know how to reason, though I am not a learned—*I simply know that I smell things, I feel situations, and when the crowd is silent, I understand what it silently says. And I say it with a voice, with the proper words.*

Q.   Let's talk about the day you jumped beyond the fences [of the Lenin shipyards in Gdansk].

A.   Well, long before it happened we had considered the possibility of some big strike in Gdansk. We had considered it in our meetings, when we taught the workers the history of Poland and the union laws. In fact, I had made myself ready to avoid an excessive situation and I had told the workers if there is an uproar, I want to be informed at once. And when I was informed, I immediately realized that the uproar had burst early because the situation was ripe, thus I had to get into the shipyards. The trouble was that four gentlemen, I mean four policemen, watched me day and night. I got them lost—I won't tell you how because I might need that trick again in the future—and I got to the shipyards and I jumped inside. I got there at a crucial moment. In fact, there was a meeting of 2,000 workers and the big boss was asking them to leave, making his promises. And nobody cared to oppose him. As a matter of fact, they were already leaving.

2. Theorizing Mind

Q.   Has communism failed?

A.   Ha! It depends on the way you measure the concept of good, bad, better, worse. Because if you choose the example of what we Polish have in our pockets and in our shops, then I answer that communism has done very little for us. If you choose the example of what is in our souls instead, I answer that communism has done very much for us. In fact, our souls contain exactly the contrary of what they wanted. They wanted us not to believe in God, and our churches are full. They wanted us to be materialistic and incapable of sacrifices; we are antimaterialistic, capable of sacrifice. They wanted us to be afraid of the tanks, of the guns, and instead we don't fear them at all. . . .

Q. Lech, where did you learn to talk like that, from whom?
A. I don't know. I told you that I never read a book, anything. I never had teachers either, nor examples to imitate. I always solved problems alone. Even the technical ones, like to fix a TV set or a sink, I think them over and I fix them in my way. Politics is the same. I think it over and I find the solution, or at least a solution. As for the moderate line I gave to Solidarity, however, I can tell you that I set it after the defeats of 1968 and 1970. It was then that I realized the necessity of working without impatience; otherwise, we would break our heads. I said to myself: Lech, a wall cannot be demolished with butts. We must move slowly, step by step, otherwise the wall remains untouched and we break our heads. You know, I have been arrested 100 times, more or less, usually forty-eight-hour arrests, and one thinks very well in jail, because in jail there aren't noises and one is alone. It was in jail that I also found the way of sowing doubt into the minds of my jailers, to make them release me and to make them understand how wrong they were toward the country and themselves. Finally, it was in jail that I discovered the system of informing people about my arrests. Because it is useless to be arrested if people don't know.
Q. What was this system, Lech?
A. Well, when they released me and I went home, I placed myself in front of a bus stop and even if I had money to buy my ticket, I pretended to be penniless. So I asked the people to buy my ticket, explaining that I had been arrested and why. People got interested and bought my ticket. Then I took the bus and during the trip I continued to explain; I held sort of a rally for them to warm up feelings.

3. Passionate Mind

Q. This is great politics, Lech.
A. Nie, nie, nie. I am no politician. I have never been. Maybe one day I'll be one. I have just started to look around and understand their tricks, their calculations, but today I am no politician. The proof is that, if I were a politician, I

would like doing what I do now. I would never have enough
of it. Instead, I'm fed up, and I tell you at once what I am:
I am a man full of anger, an anger I have kept in my stomach since I was a boy, a youngster. And when a man accumulates the anger I have accumulated for so many years,
he learns to manage it all right. Which explains why I control so well the crowds and the strikes. Ha! One has to be
very angry in order to know how to control the anger of
the people. One has to have learned to live with it. Listen,
my rage has been stored up for so long that I could keep it
in at least five more years.

4. Executive Mind

[Continuing from the moment at the Lenin shipyard in
Gdansk, when the workers were leaving] I felt my blood
boil. I elbowed my way through the crowd, I set myself in
front of him and—do you know boxing? I landed him a
straight left and I put him down so quickly that he almost
fell out of the ring. I mean, I shouted at him that the workers wouldn't go anywhere if they weren't sure they had obtained what they wanted. So they felt strong, and I became
their leader, and I still am.

Q. Lech, what does it mean to be a leader?
A. It means to have determination, it means to be resolute inside and outside, with ourselves and with the others. . . .
      I know how to say things with the proper words,
like I did with the peasants at the strike in Jelenia Gora,
for instance, when I yelled at them: "You've started the
wrong strike, you idiots, you champions of stupidity, I'm
against you." And 300 people remained speechless. Well,
speaking to the crowds isn't always the art of going with
the crowds. Sometimes it's the art of going against the
crowds. . . .
      Demands must be put at the right time, without im-
patience. Look at the monument we erected for our dead,
our workers killed by the police in 1970. Had we built it at
once or two years later, now it would be simply the branch
of a tree, easy to cut. Instead, today it's a tree and its roots

are so deep that nobody can extirpate them, and if it will be cut, it will blossom again.

Illustrations of Executive Mind

The most felicitous recent artistic rendering of Executive Mind is Kurosawa's film *Kagemusha* (*The Shadow Warrior*). Depicting the jousting for supremacy among three warlords, just before the establishment of the shogunate in Japan, Kurosawa focuses on the warlord known as the Shadow Warrior. During his lifetime the Shadow Warrior gains his name from the practice of having one of his brothers impersonate him at times on the battlefield so that the enemy never knows whether he is actually present. After his death (which occurs early in the film), the Shadow Warrior's name gains an additional dimension of meaning, for his final will to his circle of brothers and generals is to keep his death a secret for three years and to continue to impersonate him for that time (using a common thief who looks like him and who has been trained to enact his role) in order to keep their enemies off balance. Here is an ultimate exercise of Executive Mind: arranging to continue to act effectively even after death.

I mentioned earlier that Executive Mind cultivates such an intimacy with the rhythms of time—of social history, of institutional development, and of the personal evolution of one's immediate circle—that it conveys a dynamic quality of stillness, of situatedness. This quality permeates the traditional Japanese disciplines of balanced movement and attentive sitting, visible throughout Kurosawa's film (and almost unendurably deliberate to the overexcited Western observer). This quality of situatedness is also vividly illustrated by the strategic disposition of the forces of the Shadow Warrior in battle. There are four "divisions" of troops, named Forest, Wind, Fire, and Mountain. Forest is the infantry, which attacks first, Wind is one wing of cavalry, Fire is the other wing, which enters at a decisive moment with short swords, and Mountain is the force that surrounds the Shadow Warrior himself. The Shadow Warrior (or his substitute) sits immobile atop a mountain behind the battle, observing. Should the enemy break through to his position, the warriors of the Mountain division create a human shield around their leader, who maintains his posture throughout. The legend is that the clan cannot be defeated so long as its leader remains still.

The executive, Barnard tells us, must balance solidity with flexibility. Kagemusha blends mountain and shadow, solid, enduring immobility with the simultaneous evanescent flexibility to be in two places at once, moving invisibly at will. As "mountain," Kagemusha empowers his own forces; as "shadow," he confuses the enemy.

The Dilemma of Entering the Executive Role. A second central character in *The Shadow Warrior* is the common thief (read "sinner," in Christian terms) who is first pressed into the role of impersonating the Shadow Warrior at the latter's death and only gradually learns to "take" the role. Even though the thief is an accomplished actor in the external sense, the executive role makes a spiritual demand on him—to maintain a continuous performance throughout his waking life—for which he is utterly unprepared and by which he is utterly humbled.

In the most deeply affecting scene of this powerful film, the thief is introduced by the Shadow Warrior's generals to his household retainers, who are to be the only others to share in the secret of his true identity. With these men the thief can relax temporarily and be himself, to his immense relief. They can also offer him further advice about the Shadow Warrior's intimate habits of movement, expression, and speech. In the course of the joking that follows, it is clear the retainers do not believe that the friendly, anxious, unprepossessing thief could ever play the Shadow Warrior convincingly. On horseback and in battle regalia he may deceive the troops, but close up he simply lacks the tangible but undefinable situatedness of the Shadow Warrior, his calm, immobile, ceaselessly vigilant presence. How will the thief possibly succeed in deceiving the Shadow Warrior's own grandson, let alone his concubines? It is inconceivable that the act will work for three days, let alone three years.

In the midst of the slightly derisive jocularity, the thief asks lightly, "How's this?" Instantaneously he becomes the

Shadow Warrior, so undeniably bringing his rhythm and his aura of authority back to life that tears spring to the eyes of his retainers and of the audience. The act is no longer merely an act: The thief has demonstrated the authority of Executive Mind, the authority to transform the very definition and atmosphere of a situation. He has, in fact, visibly become, by a supreme act of attunement, imagination, and will and by his undeniable effect on others, what he earlier merely pretended to be. At the very moment when his opportunity to "play" the executive was vanishing in anxious hilarity, he "saw" in a new way what the challenge was and "rose to the occasion."

Each of us is called to exercise Executive Mind in our adult life, at the very least in regard to our own life as a whole and in regard to our children, if not also in the organizations, professions, and polities of which we are members. And each of us enters the executive role as unprepared as the common thief, no matter what our previous training. Ordinary analytic and calculative thought is incommensurable with—the merest shadow of—Executive Mind. We can gain access to Executive Mind only through the continuous humility of accepting the inadequacy of our ordinary thoughts, emotions, and movements to our calling. Only such humility can motivate a listening for other voices beyond our ordinary thought, a listening which quiets our ordinary, lumbering, grandiose, anxious Walter Mitty daydreams, which gradually attunes us to the awesome complex of personal, social, and cosmic rhythm, and which thereby grants us the authority to enact a role voluntarily.

In order to help the Tibetan Dalai Lama achieve the proper state of quiet, receptivity, and transmission—the proper state of in-formation—for his role in the highest rituals, the Song of Heaven is played for him. The Song of Heaven consists of a seemingly unbearable din, cymbals clashing and mountain horns bleating atonally and irregularly. Such is our dilemma in everyday life: to become in-formed amid the inner and outer noise. Genuinely effective organizing—the gift of Executive Mind—generates order from chaos. Unlike even the most efficient machine conceivable, which generates greater order locally at the expense of a general increase in entropy universally, effective organizing is ("magically") universally uplifting. So far are we from effective organizing; so much does humility become us.

Like the common thief and like the actor in a stage play, we will inevitably feel imprisoned within our role on occasion. We will not be listening to our lifetime calling, or the call will conflict with various momentary whims. We will want to retire temporarily from the publicity of the stage. We will want to cease being artful and just be ourselves. And it is, of course, necessary and desirable to meditate in solitude and to relax in the spontaneity of friendship. Indeed, as stated before, leisureliness is of the essence to all the higher states of mind: All are achieved through a purely voluntary, playful process (Torbert, 1972). But, paradoxically, to be oneself, to be spontaneous, to be leisurely, to be friendly are the highest disciplines, the consummate arts. These possibilities are not natural in the ordinary sense; they belong primarily neither to our biological nature, "first nature," nor to social convention, "second nature," but rather to yet a "third nature," for which the biological and the sociological are material to be transformed and to which only a lifetime commitment to artful inquiry and performance can gain us access.

Thus, Executive Mind treats life as a whole as an artform —a form of theater with stages and wings, with rehearsals and performances, with active collaborators, antagonists, "straight men," and audiences, requiring the interplay of strategy and spontaneity, but also requiring a great deal of "undramatic," craftlike work in setting one scene or another (Mangham and Overington, 1983).

Executive Mind accepts and works with the distances between inner self and one's performance at any given time, as well as the distance between one's performance and others' perceptions. Likewise, Executive Mind accepts and works with the distances between the inner circle of colleagues who share one's vision and who take acting roles and the wider audience, which may very well not share one's vision or appreciate the distinction between acting and reacting—although its action inclines toward bridging rather than maintaining those distances. And, finally, Executive Mind accepts and works with the distances between contemporary political, economic, esthetic, religious, and scientistic ideologies and the praxis of voluntarily creating nonelitist high cultures through the exercise of Executive Mind.

In this sense, Executive Mind is profoundly antiutopian. The vision of collapsing all distances and tensions into effortless, "classless" harmony strikes the active imagination as mere passive lunacy. Quite the contrary, it is the very distance and tension between the thief's nature and the executive role he assumes that, accepted at the critical moment when he is most tempted to relax in the bosom of his household—in the classless harmony of camaraderie—raise him and the whole "play" from the farce it could so easily have become to tragic stature.

The Dilemma of Executive Succession. A third character in *The Shadow Warrior* not yet mentioned here is Kagemusha's son. If the thief can lead us beyond grandiose symbols to the humility appropriate to entering an executive role (see Jentz, 1981, for a systematic treatment of the dilemmas of entering an executive role), the son can lead us to the humility appropriate to leaving an executive role.

The dilemma of leaving an executive role is, of course, the dilemma of succession. The Shadow Warrior does not, in fact, resolve the dilemma of succession by having the thief take his role. He only prolongs the dilemma. But to prolong the dilemma of succession may have been the principal aim underlying the entire magnificent charade. For Kagemusha's son is a querulous sort who seems at once insecure, jealous of and alienated from his father, not yet prepared to take the executive role. The three-year interregnum may be the father's effort to allow the son further seasoning after the father is no longer present to overshadow him.

In any event, the interregnum does not achieve this purpose. The son undoes the father's lifetime work as soon as he gains the father's seat. Order descends into violence and chaos.

The highest art of Executive Mind is confounded by the dilemma of succession, the dilemma of parentage, the dilemma of the generations. Anyone who believes himself or herself the consummate executive need only refer to his or her family life for evidence to the contrary. (Which is simply to say that our own family is close enough to us to make it difficult for us to blind ourselves to the fact that it is beyond our control. Whether our family flourishes or disintegrates, we properly pray for guidance rather than crediting ourselves.) The dilemma of succession faces the executive with his or her limits, his or her mortality. The greatest leaders face their limits throughout their lifetime, continually seeking worthy colleagues and successors to complement and to confront them. Lesser leaders turn away from their own limits and collude with their followers' desire for irresponsible security by cultivating rather than disowning legends of omniscience, omnipotence, and infallibility.

Creating Executive Teams. These considerations lead us to the greatest single concern of Executive Mind between entry to and exit from the executive role: the cultivation of a genuine executive team—that is, a team in which every member takes the executive role, takes responsibility for the welfare of the entire enterprise (Mills, 1965). One major reason for this concern is the one just described—namely, the desire to provide continuity for the enterprise beyond the lifetime of the individual chief executive. A second major reason for this concern has also been implied—namely, the need for different channels of access to, different perspectives on, and confrontation among assumptions about top-level decisions if they are to remain apt over the long term. These different channels and perspectives can be provided only by human beings (an all-embracing MIS cannot do the trick) because the relevant information is frequently not yet codable in conventional terms. It is still subtle and implicit rather than categorical and explicit (recall Walesa's comment "I smell things. I feel situations, and when the crowd is silent, I understand what it silently says"). Moreover, the assumptions to be confronted in making, implementing, and evaluating top-level decisions are often held in a fiercely subjective manner that yields more readily to continuing courageous confrontation or artful indirection by trusted and respected colleagues than to "objective" information, which can be interpreted away until it is too late to benefit from it.

An interesting example of executive succession and of the development of an executive team is found at Delta Airlines, the world's most profitable airline over the past thirty years. Part of the interest of the example is that the founding chief executive of Delta, C. E. Woolman, does not appear to be primarily responsible for the development of the executive team that succeeded him. Rather, as Woolman approached his seventies and after he had suffered a heart attack, his cadre of top officers began, first imperceptibly and then more openly, to shift the management to themselves, learning how to manage by consensus. When Woolman died, in 1966, the senior management team continued right on without the difficulties of succession experienced by other major airlines. Today at Delta the office of the chairman in effect includes not only the CEO and the vice-chairman but also the seven senior vice-presidents. This senior management team meets every Monday morning, and although each member has a clearly defined area of responsibility (for example, marketing, finance, flight operations), all operate interchangeably, important decisions taken quickly by whoever is in the office ("Delta . . . ," 1981).

As the Delta example suggests, Executive Mind (indeed, each of the higher mental capacities) derives not solely from individual genius and discipline but, rather, from a collaborative exercise in which the playful vigilance and the proper subordination of each member uplift the team as a whole (Vail, 1978).

Nevertheless, insofar as a single executive exercises Executive Mind, one important sign of executive greatness is the capacity to generate more than one great team during the executive's career. By this standard, one might nominate Red Auerbach, general manager of the Boston Celtics and organizer of three championship basketball "dynasties" during his career, as the greatest contemporary American executive. The elusive but unmistakable common theme of these three teams is the running and passing and rebounding (the discipline and the self-subordination) of their greatest stars and the regular capacity of the team as a whole for playing "above their heads" in emergencies rather than falling apart. The Celtics at play represent the best physical metaphor for Executive Mind of which I am aware (so long as we recall that their play occurs within a formal, well-defined game, with the result that the greatest strategy chal-

lenges to Executive Mind—the continual reconceptualization
and transformation of the very rules of the game—are not being
exercised). It hardly seems coincidental that the coaching ranks
of the NBA have been disproportionately populated by former
Celtics during the past generation. At the same time, the Celtics'
disastrous finale during the 1983 season, losing four straight
playoff games despite one of their most talented teams ever, can
serve as a final reminder that Executive Mind is neither a matter
of talent nor a quality that can be achieved once and for all.

5

Problem Management: Learning from Experience

David A. Kolb

For many scholars who study organizations and management, the central characteristic of organizations is that they are problem-solving systems whose success is measured by how efficiently they solve the routine problems associated with accomplishing their primary mission and how effectively they respond to the emergent problems and opportunities associated with survival and growth in a changing world. The vitality and success of organizations are determined, in this view, by "doing the right thing" (problem finding) and by "doing things right" (problem solving). Kilmann's approach (1979, pp. 214–215) is representative of this perspective: "One might even define the essence of management as problem defining and problem solving, whether

The problem-management model described here was developed in collaboration with Richard Baker and Juliann Spoth.

the problems are well structured, ill structured, technical, human, or even environmental. Managers of organizations would then be viewed as *problem managers,* regardless of the types of products and services they help their organizations provide. It should be noted that managers have often been considered as generic decision makers rather than as problem solvers or problem managers. Perhaps decision making is more akin to solving well-structured problems where the nature of the problem is so obvious that one can already begin the process of deciding among clear-cut alternatives. However, decisions cannot be made effectively if the problem is not yet defined and if it is not at all clear what the alternatives are, can, or should be." In this view, the core task of the executive is problem management. Although experience, personality, and specific technical expertise are important, the primary skill of the successful executive is the ability to manage the problem-solving process in such a way that important problems are identified and solutions of high quality are found and carried out with the full commitment of organization members.

A problem-management perspective on executive behavior has much promise. It is a rational, proactive view of management, one that is useful for describing, as well as prescribing, executive action. In addition, the framework of problem management has phenomenological validity; it fits well with executives' subjective experiences of their role in managing their organization's problem-finding and problem-solving activities. Yet important criticisms have been made of previous attempts to fit managerial behavior into existing problem-solving models —criticisms that need to be addressed before a problem-management perspective can be taken seriously.

The first of these criticisms was alluded to in the quotation from Kilmann. Previous attempts to describe executive behavior in problem-*solving* or decision-making frameworks are too narrow, excluding a most important strategic executive function—finding and defining the right problems to work on.

A second criticism is that problem-solving models of management are too rational and too linear. Many executive activities appear to be guided more by nonrational, "intuitive" ways of knowing than by the kind of logical step-by-step analysis suggested in problem-solving models (Mintzberg, 1973a, 1976). As Weick puts it in his contribution to this volume, "Decisions are not made at specific points in time, they accrete. . . . Linear models and step models have only modest relevance to everyday thinking. Even if people tried to implement them, they would find them foreign to what they are trying to do."

Third, theorists who view organizational action as strongly determined by environmental forces see problem-solving models of management as misleading because they are too proactive, failing to recognize the ways in which executive action is reactive, determined by demands from the organization's environment.

Finally, problem-solving models have emphasized individual cognitive aspects of executive behavior at the expense of the socioemotional dimensions of management. Problem management is not just an activity of the individual executive mind; it is fundamentally a social process. Solutions to problems are inevitably combinations, new applications, or modifications of old solutions. From other people we get new dreams, new ideas, information, and help in getting things done. Language, communication, and conflicting views are central in problem management. Particularly in organizations it is difficult to conceive of a problem that does not in some way involve other people either in choosing the problem, in supplying information about it, in helping to solve it, or in implementing the solution.

This chapter is an attempt to realize the promise of the problem-management perspective on executive action by creating a problem-management model that takes account of the forgoing criticisms. This model, based on the theory of experiential learning (Kolb, 1983), conceives of problem management in a way that includes the following:

- Problem finding as well as problem solving.
- A nonlinear description of the process of problem management that is dialectic and emergent.
- Both rational and intuitive modes of knowing.
- Both the active and reflective aspects of the executive role.

• Both the cognitive and social/emotional aspects of problem management.

Model of Problem Management Based on
the Theory of Experiential Learning

In previous writings (Kolb, Rubin, and McIntyre, 1979; Kolb, 1983) I have argued that an understanding of problem solving and so-called academic learning can be enhanced by viewing both processes as specialized modifications of a single, more holistic, adaptive process of learning from experience. The experiential learning process consists of four phases: concrete experience, reflective observation, abstract conceptualization, and active experimentation. Common-sense notions of problem solving tend to focus on the phases of concrete experience and active experimentation—on the specific difficulties experienced in immediate situations and the actions taken to overcome them. Traditional educational ideas about learning, however, tend to focus on the phases of reflective observation and abstract conceptualization—emphasizing the gathering of information and development of general concepts. Just as it has been proposed that the process of traditional education is improved when the concrete and active emphasis of problem solving is added (Keeton and Tate, 1978; Chickering, 1977), it can correspondingly be suggested that the effectiveness of problem solving is enhanced by the addition of the academic learning perspectives of reflection and conceptualization. In both cases what results is a more holistic and integrated adaptive process.

The model of problem management derived from the theory of experiential learning is, like that theory, holistic and normative. It describes an idealized problem-management process that is characteristic of the fully functioning executive in optimal circumstances. Ineffective problem management is seen as the result of deviations from that normative process because of personal habits and skill limitations or because of situational constraints such as time pressure or limits on access to information that can result from one's position in the organization or from mistrusting relationships with subordinates. The model consists of four analytic stages, which correspond to the four stages of the experiential learning cycle. Stage one, situation analysis, corresponds to concrete experience; stage two, problem analysis, to reflective observation; stage three, solution analysis, to abstract conceptualization; and stage four, implementation analysis, to active experimentation. These four stages form a nested sequence of analytic activities such that each stage requires the solution of a particular analytic task to properly frame the succeeding stage.

The task of *situation analysis* is to examine the immediate situational context in order to determine the right problem to work on. Although problem-solving activity is often initiated by urgent symptomatic pressures, urgency alone is not a sufficient criterion for choosing which problem to work on. As every manager knows, the press of urgent problems can easily divert attention from more important but less pressing long-term problems and opportunities. Every concrete situation contains a range of problems and opportunities that vary in urgency and importance. Some of these are obvious, while others are hidden or disguised. Situation analysis requires exploration to identify the full range of problems and opportunities in the situation and priority setting to choose the right problem to work on— that is, the problem that takes precedence by criteria of both urgency and importance.

Given the appropriate choice of a problem, the task of *problem analysis* is to properly define the problem in terms of the essential variables or factors that influence it. Here the task is to gather information about the nature of the problem and to evaluate it by constructing a model of the factors that are influencing the problem. This model serves to sort relevant from irrelevant information and guides the search for further information to test its validity. The result of problem analysis is to define the problem so that criteria to be met in solving it are identified.

Given a problem as defined in problem analysis, the third stage, *solution analysis,* seeks to generate possible solutions and to test their feasibility for solving the problem against the criteria defined in stage two. This is the most intensively studied stage of problem solving, best known through Osborn's (1953) early work on brainstorming.

The solution chosen in solution analysis is next implemented in the fourth stage of problem solving: *implementation analysis.* Tasks essential for implementing the solution must be identified and organized into a coherent plan with appropriate time deadlines and follow-up evaluations. Responsibility for implementing the plan is developed through participation of those individuals and groups not already involved in the problem-solving activity who will be directly affected by the solution. Implementation activities from stage four are carried out in the situation identified in stage one and thus modify that situation, creating new opportunities, problems, and priorities. Effective problem management is thus a continuing iterative cycle paralleling the experiential learning cycle. For example, when the participation of affected individuals is elicited in implementation analysis, new problems and opportunities may come to light as priorities for continuing problem-solving efforts.

Carlsson, Keane, and Martin (1976), using the experiential learning framework, have documented this iterative four-stage problem-solving process in their historical study of R&D projects. Through analysis of monthly project reports and team-member interviews, they studied the histories of R&D projects in a major consumer products R&D laboratory. In one project they found that key steps in the progress of the project could be interpreted as representing a clockwise sequence through the learning model (see Figure 1 and Table 1). Critical examination of this analysis by other project managers and their higher-level R&D managers confirmed that the model represented the realities of the project. In subsequent analysis of other projects they found "instances of stages being skipped, of project teams 'stuck' in a stage, and even instances of reverse movement through the stages. The managers involved generally agreed that the pictures were accurate and that the deviations indicated problems deserving of management attention" (p. 6).

Figure 1 shows the details of the iterative problem-solving process in one of the projects that Carlsson, Keane, and Martin studied. Numbers on the spiral refer to activity descriptions listed in Table 1. As indicated by the "Type of Analysis" column in Table 1, the sequence of activities in the project followed successive iterations of the four-stage problem-solving model.

Dialectics of Problem Management. The protocol of the R&D project activities described above contains another pattern widely recognized by students of creativity and problem solving. The process of problem solving does not proceed in a logical, linear fashion from beginning to end but, rather, is characterized by wavelike expansions and contractions alternately moving outward to gather and consider alternatives, information, and ideas and inward to focus, evaluate, and decide. These expansions and contractions have been variously labeled "green light/red light" in brainstorming (Osborn, 1953), "ideation/evaluation" (Basadur, 1979), and "divergence/convergence" (Guilford and Hoepfner, 1971). The existence of such a pulsation process strongly suggests that problem solving is not the result of a single mental function such as logical thinking but, rather, that effective problem solving involves the integration of dialectically opposed mental orientations. The experiential learning theory of adult cognitive development (Kolb, 1983, chap. 6) offers some insight into the specific dynamics of these dialectical processes as they occur in each of the four analytical stages of problem management. This theory describes the process whereby individual orientations toward the four learning modes become more sophisticated and integrated with one another. A brief overview of the theory will draw out its relevance for problem management. The experiential learning cycle is driven by two sets of dialectically opposed processes, one set of opposing ways to grasp reality and one set of opposing ways to transform reality. In the first set, reality can be grasped by apprehension of concrete experiences or by comprehension of symbolic representations. In the second set, these "prehensions" of reality can be transformed by extension, outwardly oriented active experimentation, or by intention, inwardly oriented reflective observation.

That there are two distinct and dialectically opposed modes of knowing the world or grasping reality has long been recognized by philosophers, most notably the pragmatists. John

Figure 1. Effective Problem Solving as a Process of Experiential
Learning: An R&D Project History.

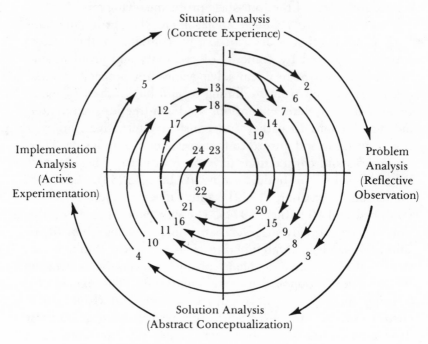

Source: Adapted from Carlsson, Keane, and Martin (1976).

Table 1. R&D Project Activities.

	Type of Analysis	Expansion/ Contraction
1. Planning activity initiated by a management question: "What businesses should this division be in?"	Situation	E
2. Generation of nine alternatives.	Situation	E
3. Establishment of criteria for selection made jointly with marketing.	Problem	C
4. Evaluation of the nine alternatives against the criteria, resulting in the selection of three projects to pursue.	Solution	C
5. Assignments of staff to activate three projects, one of which is the subject of this study.	Implementation	E

Table 1. R&D Project Activities, Cont'd.

	Type of Analysis	*Expansion/ Contraction*
6. Identifying the options for position-ing the product in the market.	Situation	E
7. Identifying the potential process routes to making the product.	Situation	E
8. Establishing the criteria for decid-ing the competitive targets.	Problem	C
9. Examining standing criteria in the division for choice of processes and weighing flexibility higher than normal for this project.	Problem	C
10. Deciding on the specific objective for this product.	Solution	C
11. Choosing the process route to be developed.	Solution	C
12. Making the product and placing a consumer test.	Implementation	C
13. Obtaining consumer test results that confirmed that the product targets had been met.	Implementation	E/C
14. Generation of alternatives for ob-taining a more favorable economic position in the marketplace.	Situation	E
15. Analyzing the alternatives from the standpoint of the user.	Problem	E
16. Selection of the specific target and the attribute to be optimized.	Solution	C
17. Making the product and placing a consumer test. (The path from 16 to 17 is shown as a broken line be-cause the work was incomplete; that is, the consumer test was placed without having the opti-mum product.)	Implementation	C
18. Obtaining and analyzing consumer test results, which were worse than predicted.	Situation	E/C
19. Generation of alternatives for the project in view of the outcome of the consumer test.	Situation	E
20. Reexamination of criteria.	Problem	E
21. Optimizing product/process vari-ables.	Problem	C

(continued on next page)

Table 1. R&D Project Activities, Cont'd.

	Type of Analysis	Expansion/ Contraction
22. Specifying the process details for the test market production and trimming costs to fit within the appropriation.	Solution	C
23. Meeting specific requirements for the test market plant.	Implementation	C
24. Making product and placing next consumer test.	Implementation	C

Adapted from Carlsson, Keane, and Martin (1976). "Type of Analysis" and "Expansion/Contraction" columns added by the author.

Dewey, for example, states: "Our intellectual process consists ... of a rhythm of direct understanding technically called *ap*prehension—with indirect mediated understanding technically called *com*prehension" (1910, p. 120). In addition, there is considerable physiological evidence that the hemispheres of the human brain are typically specialized around these functions—the left hemisphere on comprehension and the right hemisphere on apprehension (Edwards, 1979; Kolb, 1983). Comprehension is logical, is digital, and operates in linear time, with a past, present, and future. Apprehension is based on sensations and feelings, is holistic, and is synchronous, existing only in the present. Knowing by comprehension is typically accomplished by critical analysis of symbols, while knowing by apprehension is typically accomplished by the appreciative synthesis of the elements of concrete situations.

Intention and *extension* are terms that are likewise familiar to philosophers. In logic, *extension* refers to the denotation of a concept, the set of objects in the external world to which the concept applies; *intention* refers to the connotation, or meaning, of the concept—that is, the attributes that make it up (Cohen and Nagel, 1934). The most significant work on these processes, however, is that of Carl Jung, who distinguished between the introverted (intention) and extroverted (extension) ways of knowing. In the extroverted, or extensional, way of dealing with the world, one emphasizes objects in the world over the subject who perceives them, whereas the introverted (intentional) way of dealing with the world emphasizes subjective meanings over the objects that stimulate them. Jung (1923, p. 13) emphasizes the dialectic relationship between these two processes: "These opposite attitudes are merely opposite mechanisms—a diastolic going out and seizing of the object and a systolic concentration and release of energy from the object seized. Every human being possesses both mechanisms as an expression of his natural life-rhythm." There is some evidence to support a physiological base for these two processes in the differential arousal of the sympathetic and parasympathetic nervous systems (Broverman and others, 1968; Diekman, 1971), suggesting that when the sympathetic nervous system is dominant, the basic adaptive orientation is outward toward action and mastery of the environment, and when the parasympathetic system dominates, the orientation is receptive, more toward perception and reflection than action.*

Each of the four learning processes just described is dominant in one of the four problem-solving stages. It is through the process of apprehension that we directly experience situations. Through the process of intentional transformation we determine the meaning of our experiences and define problems. The process of comprehension shapes the generation of solutions— that is, future-oriented conceptualizations of how the problem might be changed—and the process of extensional transformation dominates in the active implementation of solutions (see Figure 2). The developmental theory of experiential learning suggests that the way each of these processes is developed and refined is through service as the focal point for resolution of the dialectic processes of the opposing dimension. Specifically, apprehension of concrete situations is refined and elaborated by the transformation dialectics of intention and extension—that

*It is not the assumed physiological/anatomical locations of intention/extension and apprehension/comprehension processes that is primary here, for this is currently highly speculative. Rather, what is important is the description and identification of these as pivotal psychological functions in learning.

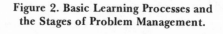

Figure 2. Basic Learning Processes and
the Stages of Problem Management.

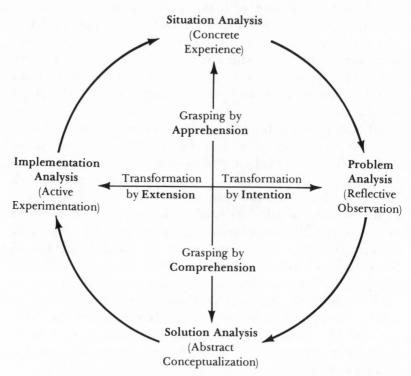

is, by orienting oneself in concrete situations by action (extension) and relating what happens to values (intention). Problems are defined through intention by the integration of the grasping dialectics of apprehension and comprehension—that is, gathering information about the problem and its concrete manifestations (apprehension) and organizing this information into a model or theory about what is causing the problem (comprehension). Comprehension of solutions is developed by the transformation dialectics of intention and extension—that is, developing ideas about how to change critical attributes of the problem (intention) and evaluating the feasibility of these ideas in reality (extension). The process of implementation through extension is refined by the grasping dialectics of apprehension and comprehension—that is, plans are developed (comprehension) and concretely carried out with the involvement of others in the situation (apprehension). The experiential learning model thus suggests specific analytic activities based on dialectic conflict resolution for each stage of problem management. This refined model is diagramed in Figure 3 and is described below.

Situation Analysis—Valuing and Priority Setting. Most problem-solving activity begins with a problem as given—some circumstance, task, or assignment that demands attention. The task of situation analysis is to transform this problem as given into a problem that is consciously chosen to meet the dual criteria of urgency and importance. To understand the dialectics of situation analysis, it is first necessary to understand the nature of problems. A problem is a discrepancy between some desired state or goal and current circumstances in reality. In the simplest sense, problems have three structural components: the current state, or reality (R), the goal (G), and the process whereby reality can be transformed to match the goal state— that is, the solution ($\rightarrow$). Depending on which of these three factors are known, we have different types of problems. When all three are known (R $\rightarrow$ G), there is no problem, simply a task to be accomplished. When current circumstances and the desired state are known, but the means for transformation are unknown (R $\overset{?}{\rightarrow}$ G), we have a structured problem, perhaps the most common form of a problem as given. When both the current state and the means of transformation are unknown ($\overset{?}{R} \overset{?}{\rightarrow}$ G), the problem is unstructured and needs to be defined before solutions can be developed. Next comes that particular subclass of problems known as opportunities. These are cases in which the goal is not yet known or articulated. R $\rightarrow \overset{?}{G}$ defines a structured opportunity such that a current state and means for transforming it exist but no goal has been articulated. Two common examples are a plant with unutilized capacity and a potentially marketable production waste by-product. Finally, there are opportunities that are unstructured in varying degrees: $\overset{?}{R} \overset{?}{\rightarrow} \overset{?}{G}$, a known situation without clear goals or ways of achieving them;

Figure 3. Problem Management as a Dialectic Process.

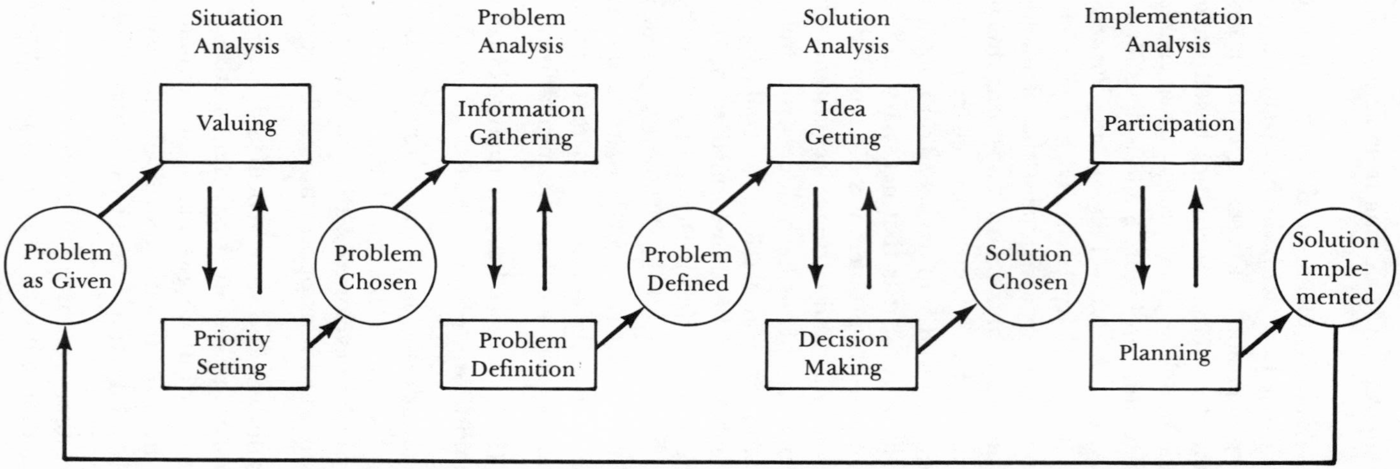

$\overset{?}{R} \rightarrow \overset{?}{G}$, a known solution in search of a worthwhile problem to solve; and $\overset{?}{R} \overset{?}{\rightarrow} \overset{?}{G}$, a totally undefined opportunity.

Without conscious situation analysis, problems tend to be chosen in roughly the order presented here. First, we do tasks; then we tackle defined problems. Unstructured problems are less likely to be chosen for attention, and structured and unstructured opportunities often are never recognized. This "natural" approach to choosing problems in situations is biased toward short-term survival in the immediate situation, since urgent problems, almost by definition, have clear realities and states to be desired or avoided. This approach is most appropriate for lower-level jobs in organizations where the time span of discretion is short and tasks are well defined (Jaques, 1979). At higher management levels, as the time span of discretion increases and tasks become less structured, the natural approach becomes less effective. Successful long-term adaptation in organizations, particularly in environments that are turbulent and rapidly changing, requires a process of careful strategic choice of the right problem to work on that resists "knee jerk" reactions to symptomatic environmental pressures. Urgent structured problems in organizations are often the result of failure to address unstructured problems that lie behind them; for example, the continued urgent need to replace bank tellers may result from failure to address more unstructured problems of worker morale or career opportunities. In addition, for many organizations in rapidly changing environments, aggressive opportunity seeking is essential to maintain stability and growth. Careful situation analysis is therefore most critical when long-term adaptation to a changing environment takes precedence over expedient action.

The dialectics of situation analysis involve the successive articulation of possible goal states (G) and the exploration of current realities (R) in order to create a menu of problems and opportunities in the situation, from which one can be chosen that satisfies the criteria of urgency and importance. The process of articulating desired goal states is the process of valuing.

Valuing is an intentional process focused on the affective meaning of goal statements. The affective component of goals and objectives is their "energy core," that part of a goal that stimulates, focuses, and channels human energy. Surrounding this core is usually a conceptual or symbolic component of goals that relates them to the current situational realities. An automotive assembly unit, for example, may have a goal of reducing quality control rejects from the paint room from 5 percent to 2 percent. This statement reflects only the symbolic component of the goal. The affective component is unexpressed. Possibly it is pride in one's work, fear of losing one's job because of foreign competition, reluctant obedience to an order from above, or some combination of these emotional values. Although the affective core of goals and objectives is typically latent, it is the summative impact of these emotional values that determines the actual importance of a goal.

The task of the valuing phase of situation analysis is to identify and articulate these often-latent emotional values, for it is these values that are stimulating and channeling human energy in the situation. To be successful, the valuing process must overcome barriers that exist in most organizational settings to open sharing of values. Foremost among these barriers is the organizational press to be realistic. George Prince, one of the developers of synectics, describes the following dialogue with one of his friends about wishing (a technique for valuing):

I asked a business friend to explain to me why he found wishing difficult and distasteful. "I have spent my adult life doing my best to be realistic and deal with situations the way they really are, not the way I wish they were," he said.

"If you don't wish about a situation, how do you know how it ought to be?" I asked.

"You have a point, but I do not call that wishing. I call that having a goal or objective—it is not a wish, it is something it is possible to achieve. Wishing, by my definition, is hoping for something to happen that you *know* can't happen," he replied.

It is understandable that practical people have trouble tolerating wishfulness. However, I see wishing as an additional form of exploratory thinking, of goal setting. Because it is not concerned

> with reality, it has the capacity for opening one's
> eyes to new possibilities. If one is constantly real-
> istic and precise in wanting (goal setting), one
> automatically rules out exploring many lines of
> thought that might be profitable [Prince, 1975, p.
> 171].

Wishing, wanting, and valuing must be explored independent of reality in order to develop fully. In dialectic terms, the thesis of value must first be fully articulated before facing the antithesis of reality from which the synthesis of a chosen problem can be developed.

Two other barriers to the valuing process are the fear of conflict and the threat of isolation. Charles Lindblom (1959) noted some time ago that it is easier to find agreement on a course of action than to get agreement on the goals for the action. Discussion of values accentuates human individuality and emotional commitment, with a resulting increase in conflict among viewpoints. In the dialectic view, such conflict is essential for the discovery of truth, although most executives shy away from conflict because it is unpleasant and because they do not know how to use disagreement constructively. A related barrier to valuing is the threat of isolation that comes from holding values different from the majority's. It is this barrier that gives rise to conformity and groupthink (Janis, 1971) in problem finding. A worker, for example, may suppress his or her genuine values for achievement and excellence in order not to violate group norms of mediocrity. For this reason an effective valuing process requires an environment that gives security and support for individuality.

The contrasting pole to valuing in the situation-analysis dialectic is priority setting. Priority setting is an extensional process concerned with actively shaping concrete reality by choosing areas to be changed and improved. As with any dialectic, valuing and priority setting enhance each other—valuing gives direction and energy to priority setting, and priority setting gives substance and reality to valuing. Priority setting has three specific tasks: (1) to explore the current situation for features that facilitate or hinder goal achievement, (2) to test the feasibility of changing those features, and (3) to articulate reality-based goal statements that give substance to values and allow them to be realized. Priority setting is not a rational, analytic process of reflective planning. It is an active, intuitive process of trial-and-error exploration of what is going on in the situation. It involves "knocking on doors," listening to people, trying things out, and taking risks.

Overall, the central issue in situation analysis is leadership, and the basic social role of the problem manager is that of a leader whose responsibility is to guide the problem-solving attention of the organization to those problems and opportunities whose solution will be of maximum benefit to the long-run effectiveness of the organization. Someone once said that the key to successful leadership is to find out which way people are going and then run out in front of them. There is an element of truth in this, for the successful leader in situation analysis identifies the values and goals of those in the situation and then holds up those that are most important as priorities for action.

Problem Analysis—Information Gathering and Problem Definition. Problem analysis begins with the problem chosen in situation analysis and seeks to understand and define the problem in such a way that solutions can be developed. Problem analysis is an intentional process that focuses on determining the meaning of a problem by determining the critical attributes that make it up. This determination of meaning is achieved through resolution of the grasping dialectics of apprehension and comprehension.

In the apprehension mode, information about the concrete problem situation is gathered. Knowledge of the specific problem situation is critical to problem solving because, as Dunckner notes, "we find that a solution always consists in a variation of some critical element of the situation. . . . Thus every solution takes place so to speak on the concrete specific substratum of its problem situation. . . . This is as important as it seems to be banal. For it follows from this that in seeking a solution, one must bring the given problem situation as clearly as possible into focus" (1945, p. 20).

The information-gathering phase of problem analysis is a

receptive, open-minded phase in which all information associated with the problem is sought and accepted. This receptive stance has both a cognitive and an interpersonal component. Cognitively, it is important in the information-gathering phase to avoid biases and preconceptions about the nature of the problem and its causes in favor of letting the data about the problem speak for themselves. Interpersonally, information gathering requires skills in the development of trusting relationships so that others do not hold back or modify information to say "what the boss wants to hear" or to avoid reprisals. In many organizations the cognitive and interpersonal components of information gathering interact negatively with each other to produce a climate where gathering accurate information is very difficult. Mistrust and threat cause workers to withhold information, and management must therefore rely on its own prejudgments about the nature of problems. By acting on these prejudgments, managers reinforce worker mistrust and perpetuate a cycle that restricts accurate information exchange.

In the comprehension mode, problem definition, the task is to define the problem on the basis of the information gathered. Problem definition is basically a process of building a model portraying how the problem works—factors that cause the problem, factors that influence its manifestation, and factors mediating the application of solutions. Two skills are critical in building a model that defines a problem—causal analysis and imagery. Causal analysis uses the inductive logic of experimental inquiry to evaluate data in order to identify the invariant causal relationships that define the problem, thus sorting relevant from irrelevant information. Its principles, articulated long ago by J. S. Mill, are useful, though not definitive, heuristics for evaluating information in problem definition:

1. The method of agreement—nothing can be the cause of a problem that is not a common circumstance in all occurrences of the problem.
2. The method of differences—nothing can be the cause of a problem if the problem does not occur when the supposed cause does.

3. The method of concomitant variation—a supposed cause of a problem is not causally related to the problem if the two do not vary together.
4. The method of residues—take away from a problem those parts known to be the effects of other causes, and the remainder is the effect of the remaining causes.

Use of these principles serves as an evaluation filter to eliminate irrelevant information and to suggest hypotheses about the causes of the problem. For many problems, however, this evaluation alone is not sufficient to understand the complex dynamics involved. Imaging is a way to further refine the problem definition by imagining its dynamics and subjecting them to "thought experiments." Stated simply, imaging is the process of creating in one's mind, on paper, or by computer a model or scenario of how the problem occurs and then subjecting that model to various transformations to understand how the model operates and how the problem might be solved. Prince (1975, p. 168) describes this process nicely: "Imaging is our most important thinking skill because it accompanies and facilitates all other thinking operations. I find it useful to think of my imaging as my display system or readout of my thinking processes."

With practice, imaging can create richly detailed problem scenarios and can portray large amounts of information in complex interrelationships. Most important, these images can be manipulated and transformed at will. Dunckner (1945, pp. 20–21) describes the details of such transformational thinking:

> We can therefore say that insistent analysis of the situation, especially the endeavor to vary appropriate elements meaningfully *sub-specie* of the goal, must belong to the essential nature of a solution through thinking. We may call such relatively general procedures heuristic methods of thinking.
> The inquiry after elements which should be varied in a suitable fashion is identical with the question "Just why doesn't it work?" or "What is the ground of the trouble (the conflict)?" . . . To each solution corresponds a ground of conflict

present in the situation analysis of the situation,
therefore primarily an analysis of conflict . . . that
seeks to penetrate more deeply into the nature,
into the grounds of the conflict. . . . Besides elements which in the solution undergo elimination
or alteration (so-called conflict elements), these
are also areas which are actually used by the solution (material elements) . . . which answer the
question "What can I use?" Analysis of the problem situation appears therefore in two forms: as
analysis of conflict and as analysis of material.

Information gathered through apprehension of a concrete
problem, when juxtaposed against a conceptual model of the
problem, serves to evaluate that model, while the model created
serves to guide the search for new relevant information. In a
sense the problem manager in problem analysis is in the role of
detective—gathering clues and information about how the
"crime" was committed, organizing these clues into a scenario
of "who done it," and using that scenario to gather more information to prove or disprove the original hunch. The dialectic
between information gathering and the problem definition has
a synergetic power over information or model alone, since in
their combination one can learn from what does not occur or
has not happened as well as from what has. As in Sherlock
Holmes' famous case "The Dog Who Didn't Bark," a model suggests events that should occur if the model is true, and their
nonoccurrence in reality can therefore invalidate the model.
The output of the problem-analysis phase is a model of the
problem validated through the interplay of information gathering and problem definition—a problem as defined. The problem
as defined describes the problem in terms of those essential variables that need to be managed in order to solve it.

Solution Analysis—Idea Getting and Decision Making.
Solution analysis is a symbolic, conceptual activity based on the
process of comprehension. Comprehension of solutions to the
problem as defined is achieved through the interplay between
intention—the development of ideas about how the problem can
be solved—and extension—decision making about the feasibility
of ideas generated. This two-stage process has been highly devel-

oped in brainstorming (Osborn, 1953). The first step of solution analysis focuses on creative imagination. This is the green-light stage of brainstorming, whose aim is to generate as wide a range of potential solutions as possible in an atmosphere free from evaluation and supportive of all ideas. The second substage, the red-light stage of brainstorming, focuses on evaluation—sorting through the ideas generated in the first substage and evaluating them systematically against the criteria that need to be met in order for a potential solution to most effectively solve the problem. In the solution phase, the problem solver is in the role of inventor, creatively searching for ideas and then carefully evaluating them against feasibility criteria.

Implementation Analysis—Participation and Planning. Implementation analysis is an extensional process aimed at carrying out abstract solutions in concrete reality. It is accomplished through the interplay of comprehension in the planning process and apprehension in the process of carrying out plans. Because implementation of solutions in organizational settings is most often done by or with other people, the critical apprehension task is participation, enlisting the appropriate involvement of those actors in the situation who are essential to carrying out the problem solution. Three subtasks are involved here:

1. Anticipation of the consequences that will result from implementing the solution and involvement of those who will experience these consequences in the development of ways to deal with them.
2. Identification of those key persons who, by virtue of expertise and/or motivation, are best qualified to carry out the various tasks in implementation.
3. Involvement of key persons in another cycle through the problem-solving process to reevaluate whether the most important problem has been chosen, whether the problem is properly defined, and whether the best solution has been identified. This step sometimes becomes necessary in the process of accomplishing (1) and (2) above.

In the participation phase of implementation, the essential attitude to adopt is inclusion of others, receptivity, and openness to their concerns and ideas.

The planning phase of implementation analysis is an analytic process involving the definition of tasks to be accomplished in implementing the solution, the assignment of responsibility to qualified persons, setting of deadlines, and planning for follow-up monitoring and evaluation of the implementation process. If the problem and its solution are very complex, planning may be quite complicated, using network planning methods such as PERT or critical path analysis. Often, however, a simple chart listing key tasks, responsible persons, and time deadlines is sufficient for planning and monitoring implementation.

Implementation analysis involves two dialectically related processes. The first is to develop plans for implementation and the concrete apprehension of the potential consequences of implementing these plans. An iterative process is often useful here —scout out potential issues that may arise in implementation, develop a rough plan, share it with those involved in the situation to get reactions, and then modify the plan. The other dialectic can be termed the "Whos and the Whats." Executives appear to have distinct stylistic preferences about how they deal with this issue. Some prefer to define the "Whats" first—the plan and tasks to be accomplished—and then assign these tasks to persons to carry them out. Others begin with the "Whos," first identifying qualified and interested persons and then developing plans with them. The best approach to take probably varies with the situation and task, but beginning with the "Whos" has the advantages of giving priority to often-scarce human resources and maximizing participation and delegation. In synthesizing these dialectics, the problem solver in implementation analysis adopts the role of coordinator working to accomplish tasks with other people.

Mind Sets and the Mental Discipline
of Problem Management

Some systems for practical problem solving (such as that of Kepner and Trego, 1965) present a logical and somewhat mechanical step-by-step procedure for solving problems. Other approaches emphasize the mystery and emergent quality of the process. Bruner (1962a), for example, sees the creative process as emerging from dialectically opposed orientations—detachment and commitment, passion and decorum, deferral and immediacy, and freedom to be dominated by the object and by one's inquiry. In the problem-management model presented here, it is not appropriate to view the steps as a rigid, invariant sequence, for three reasons. First, it is not practical for a manager to subject every problem that comes up to a thorough examination in the four analysis stages. Second, depending on one's role responsibilities and the nature of the particular problem one faces, different facets of the problem-solving process will be more critical than others. Sometimes, for example, the problem has already been solved when it reaches your desk; your task is to implement the solution, not to solve it again, redefine it, or choose another problem in the situation. Thus, the critical analytic stage for this problem is implementation analysis. Attention is given to the stages of situation analysis, problem analysis, and solution analysis only for review and evaluation purposes. Similarly, in some problems the critical, evaluative component is most important—for example, the instrument checkout before a flight—while in others the creative, imaginative component is central. Third, as anyone who has observed problem solving in action can attest, there *is* a nonrational, intuitive, mysterious component in human problem-solving behavior. New ideas pop up in the evaluation stage, important facts get remembered after the problem is defined, and so on. Too rigid adherence to a mechanical step-by-step process denies the benefits of these flashes of inspiration. However, to simply stand in awe of the mysteries of intuition and creativity is of little practical value.

The approach taken here seeks a middle ground between these two extremes by introducing the concept of mind sets into the problem-solving process. Mind sets are higher-level mental heuristics or thinking styles that guide the direction and focus of the problem-management process. Through conscious choice of the appropriate mind set and management of the transitions and interrelationships among mind sets in the stages of problem management, it is possible to increase problem-solving effectiveness. The mental discipline of problem solving involves learning how, first of all, to be aware of the mind set we and others are using in working on a problem and, then, how to consciously adopt the appropriate mind set for the particular issue at hand. Thus, problem solving is the process of using our minds to control the world around us. It is literally the way we achieve the power of mind over matter.

There are two physiologically based mind sets, called "red mode" and "green mode" in deference to their similarity to the red-light and green-light phases of brainstorming, and four role-based mind sets that correspond to the four analytic stages of problem solving (see Figure 4).

The red- and green-mode mind sets correspond to the two predominant orientations of consciousness identified by Hilgard (1979) in his review of psychological research on human consciousness. Diekman (1971, p. 481) describes the physiological and psychological characteristics of these two orientations:

> The action mode [red mode] is a state organized to manipulate the environment. The striate muscle system and the sympathetic nervous system are the dominant physiological agencies. The EEG shows beta waves and baseline muscle tension is increased. The principal psychological manifestations of this state are focal attention, object-based logic, heightened boundary perception, and the dominance of formal characteristics over the sensory; shapes and meanings have a preference over colors and textures. The action mode is a state of striving, oriented toward achieving personal goals that range from nutrition to defense to obtaining social rewards, plus a variety of symbolic and sensual pleasures, as well as the avoidance of a comparable variety of pain.
>
> The attributes of the action mode develop as the human organism interacts with its environment. For example, very early in life focusing attention is associated not only with the use of the intrinsic muscles of the eyes but also becomes associated with muscle movements of the neck, head, and body, whereby visual interest is directed toward

Figure 4. Managerial Mind Sets and Roles in Problem Management.

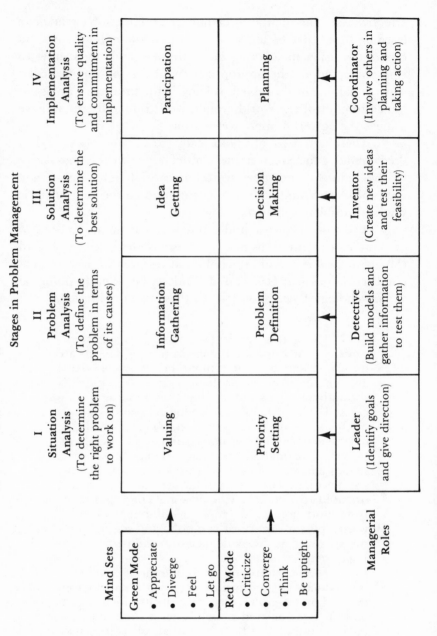

Mind Sets	I Situation Analysis (To determine the right problem to work on)	II Problem Analysis (To define the problem in terms of its causes)	III Solution Analysis (To determine the best solution)	IV Implementation Analysis (To ensure quality and commitment in implementation)
Green Mode • Appreciate • Diverge • Feel • Let go	Valuing	Information Gathering	Idea Getting	Participation
Red Mode • Criticize • Converge • Think • Be uptight	Priority Setting	Problem Definition	Decision Making	Planning
Managerial Roles	Leader (Identify goals and give direction)	Detective (Build models and gather information to test them)	Inventor (Create new ideas and test their feasibility)	Coordinator (Involve others in planning and taking action)

Stages in Problem Management

objects. Likewise, thinking develops in conjunction with the perception and manipulation of objects and, because of this, object-oriented thought becomes intimately associated with the striate muscle effort of voluntary activity, particularly eye muscle activity. Specific qualities of perception, such as sharp boundaries, become key features of the mode because sharp boundaries are important for the perception and manipulation of objects and for acquiring knowledge of the mechanical properties of objects. Sharp perceptual boundaries are matched by sharp conceptual boundaries, for success in acting on the world requires a clear sense of self-object difference. Thus, a variety of physiological and psychological processes develop together to form an organismic mode, a multidimensional unity adapted to the requirements of manipulating the environment. . . .

In contrast, the receptive mode [green mode] is a state organized around intake of the environment rather than manipulation. The sensory-perceptual system is the dominant agency rather than the muscle system, and parasympathetic functions tend to be most prominent. The EEG tends toward alpha waves and baseline muscle tension is decreased. Other attributes of the receptive mode are diffuse attending, paralogical thought processes, decreased boundary perception, and the dominance of the sensory over the formal.

These mind sets are not analytically independent processes, as were the learning processes identified earlier, but are pragmatic, holistic orientations that people adopt to cope with their environment. The red-mode mind set facilitates analysis, criticism, logical thinking, and active coping with the external environment. The green-mode mind set facilitates creative imagination, sensitivity to the immediate situation, and empathy with other people. The red-mode mind set is therefore most appropriate for the contraction phases of problem management —priority setting in situation analysis, problem definition in problem analysis, decision making in solution analysis, and planning in implementation analysis. The green-mode mind set, in contrast, facilitates the expansion phases of problem management—valuing, information gathering, idea getting, and participation. Effectiveness in problem solving is enhanced by approaching the expansion/contraction phases of each problem-management stage in the appropriate mind set. For problem solvers to accomplish this matching of mind set and problem-solving task, they must first become aware of when they are in the red or green mode of consciousness and then learn to shift from one mode to another. With some practice this can be accomplished quite easily, and usually practice in identifying and separating the two mind sets has the effect of increasing the intensity of both. This purity of conscious mind set increases problem-management effectiveness by enhancing the dialectics of each analytical stage. Similarly, managing the problem-solving process with groups of people requires the creation of a climate that stimulates and reinforces the appropriate mind set in participants.

The problem-management process is further guided by four managerial role sets that focus the dialectic interplay of red and green mind sets on the relevant stage of the problem-management process. In situation analysis this role set is that of a leader focused on identifying goals and values in the situation in the green mode and setting priorities in the red mode. In problem analysis the role set is that of a detective focused on gathering information in the green mode and building and evaluating models in the red mode. In solution analysis the role set is inventor: generating ideas in the green mode and testing their feasibility in the red mode. In implementation analysis the role set is coordinator: developing participation in the green mode and planning in the red mode. Conscious attention to these role sets serves to focus attention on the priorities of each analytic stage, and shifting role set signals the transition from one stage to another.

Problem Solving as a Social Process

How does the mind of the executive differ from the minds of other adults? What most distinguishes the way executives think and solve problems is the particular social system they live and work in. Executives' minds are shaped by their organizations and their positions in them—by the values, norms, and climate created there and the mind sets that are rewarded. Managers with whom we have shared the problem-management model described above are quick to realize that their organizations have a strong influence on their personal problem-management process. Typical comments are "I often know I'm working on the wrong problem, but my boss has defined the situation for me and won't listen to my views" and "I realize I operate too much in the critical red mode, but that's the way my organization is."

Organizational Structure and the Managerial Role. Organizations as a whole are problem-solving systems, and the structure of the organization is a problem-solving heuristic—it provides a way of defining and sorting problems and matching them with predetermined solutions. This can perhaps best be illustrated by comparing the typical organizational structure with the "family tree," or branching structure, of an individual problem-solving process. It was the German psychologist Karl Dunckner, in his seminal monograph "On Problem Solving" (1945), who first noted that individual problem-solving protocols could be ordered in a series of successively more concrete statements that reformulate the problem in such a way that each statement "in retrospect possesses the character of a solution and in prospect that of a problem" (p. 9). Figure 5 shows this successive ordering of problem-solving statements for his classic problem—how to treat an internal stomach tumor by x ray without destroying the healthy tissue surrounding it. This particular protocol shows the attempt to define three alternative approaches at the first problem-definition level—avoiding contact between the rays and healthy tissue, desensitizing the healthy tissue, and lowering the intensity of the rays on their way through the healthy tissue. These statements then branch into one or two levels of more specific solutions. The most feasible solution in this problem—use of a lens to focus the rays most intensely on the tumor—comes by way of the third branch of initial problem definition. Thus, attempts to solve this problem that begin with the third branch reach the solution more quickly than those choosing the first two branches. Pursuit of

Figure 5. Branching Structure of an Individual Problem-Solving Protocol.

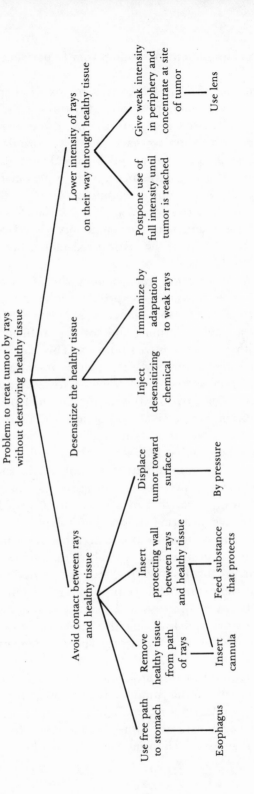

the first two lines of thought, in fact, takes the problem solver further from the solution.

The visual analogy between the branching protocol and an organization chart is obvious, and in function the branching process is the same: Problems are stated most generally and abstractly in a mission statement at the top of the organization and are subdivided into specialized divisions, departments, and sections that concretize the mission statement in different ways —finance, marketing, production, and so on. At each successive level of the organization, the task is to assign a given problem to that branch below it that represents the best solution path—for example, to treat a particular case as a production problem or a marketing problem. The organizational structure thus serves to predefine problems for managers who occupy roles at these different levels—a process which can be efficient but whose effectiveness depends on properly defining and sorting problems at higher organizational levels, a task that is quite difficult in uncertain and rapidly changing environments. This constriction of the range of a manager's problem-definition process serves to reinforce a native human tendency to define problems too concretely. As Dunckner states: "In very many cases the mediating phases (of problem definition) are not mentioned because the [subject] simply does not realize that he has already modified the original demand of the problem. The thing seems to him so self-evident that he does not have at all the feeling of having already taken a step forward. This can go so far that [he] deprives himself of freedom of movement to a dangerous degree. By substituting a much narrower problem for the original, he will therefore remain in the framework of this narrower problem just because he confuses it with the original" (1945, p. 11).

The tendency for executives to define problems narrowly in terms of their organizational role is illustrated dramatically in Dearborn and Simon's (1958) study of how executives from different organizational functions defined the most important problems facing the Castengo Steel Company. In analyzing this complex, detailed case describing the company's situation, sales managers described sales as the most important problem facing the company significantly more often than managers from other functions. Production executives, in contrast, saw organization problems as more important, and managers from other functions also tended to see the company's problems in the light of their organizational roles.

Because executive problem management takes place in an organizational structure, problem solving involves not only cognitive analysis but interpersonal communication and influence. Effective situation analysis, for example, often involves a process of upward influence with one's superiors, challenging and exploring the choice of problem on the basis of what is often a more detailed and intricate knowledge of the problem situation at lower levels of the organization. Similarly, effective problem definition can require integrated communication and negotiation with peers in other functional specialties to determine which specialized resources should be allocated to deal with the problem.

The Red-Mode Climate of Organizations. A second social factor that conditions executive problem management is the tendency for most organizations to emphasize and reward the red-mode mind set over the green-mode mind set. Organizations have a tendency to become arthritic and constricted in their problem-solving processes because of forces that combine to emphasize criticism, evaluation, and avoidance of risk at the cost of positive appreciation, creativity, and exploration. Chief among these factors is the tendency to manage by exception, to attend to issues only when something goes wrong. This approach tends to emphasize problems at the expense of recognizing opportunities and reinforces a climate where managers avoid mistakes at all costs because the way to get ahead is to look good and avoid being the focus of executive scrutiny. Critical and analytical remarks dominate in this climate, since the emphasis is on spotting mistakes and deviations from normal procedure. In addition, it is easier and safer to be critical than to be creative.

George Prince (1972, p. 47) describes the impact of what he calls the judgmental (red mode) managerial style and then describes how the introduction of a climate that emphasizes the green-mode mind set can improve problem-solving productivity:

If you could watch and listen to video and sound tapes of business meetings, you would note the pervasiveness of the judgmental managerial style in corporate life. In watching and listening to hundreds of these tapes over many years, I have been impressed again and again by these observations.

- Even mild rejection has a significant negative effect on people.
- Pointing out flaws in the ideas and actions of others occupies much of the time.
- Approval has a positive effect on people and creates a climate for resolution of the problem. . . .

The beginning of improvement in conditions comes when the manager recognizes that for productivity's sake, at least, he must avoid transactions between individuals that arouse defensive or revengeful reactions. Instead he must establish a climate in which it is appropriate to voice imperfect thoughts and ideas. In this climate all ideas are explored and used by the group. Flaws are dealt with, but as drawbacks to be overcome by everyone.

In my experience, when this climate is present, rejections, unfriendly queries, and pointing-out-a-flaw behavior are practically eliminated. Idea production rises dramatically. Every idea is noted and explored to some extent. According to the participants, they often come out of these meetings feeling exhilarated, pleased with having made worthwhile contributions, and sometimes even personally enriched.

Conflict Management: Dialectics and Dialogue. In the dialectic problem-management model proposed here, conflict is essential; it is the spark that ignites problem solving and the energy source that stimulates the generation and refinement of ideas. Typical organizational attitudes toward conflict are quite different, however. Table 2 describes some of the differences between typical organizational attitudes about conflict and problem solving and the stance toward conflict that is inherent in dialectic problem solving.

Table 2. Differences Between Typical Organizational Attitudes
Toward Conflict and the Dialectic Attitude.

Feature of Conflict	Typical Organizational Attitude	Dialectic Attitude
Centrality of conflict in problem solving	An undesirable side effect of problem solving	Essential to the process of problem solving
Source of conflict	Conflict is between persons; pride is at stake	Conflict is in the problem situation; actors are observers and representatives
Assumptions about outcomes	I am right and you are wrong; the outcome is likely to be win/lose	We are both probably right and wrong; an integrated win/win solution can result
How to handle conflict	Decrease intensity by avoidance, forcing, smoothing, or compromise	Keep at moderate intensity—"hot" enough to flush out assumptions and critical elements but "cool" enough to maintain an analytic stance

Effective dialectical problem management requires a new set of attitudes and organizational norms about conflict management. Executives need to learn to use conflict constructively and avoid the ego-involved and personalized stances toward conflict that cause great personal stress and thereby result in strategies to avoid or suppress disagreement. Paulo Freire, whose revolutionary approach to experiential learning is based on dialectic problem solving, recommends dialogue as the appropriate social process for problem management:

> Dialogue is the encounter between men mediated by the world in order to name the world. ... And since dialogue is the encounter in which the united reflection and action of the dialoguers are addressed to the world which is to be transformed and humanized, this dialogue cannot be reduced to the act of one person's depositing of ideas in an-

other, nor can it become a simple exchange of ideas to be consumed by the discussants. Nor yet is it a hostile, polemical argument between men who are committed neither to the naming of the world, nor to the search for truth, but rather to the imposition of their own truth. . . . Founding itself upon love, humility, and faith, dialogue becomes a horizontal relationship of which mutual trust between dialoguers is the logical consequence. . . . Nor yet can dialogue exist without hope. . . . Finally, true dialogue cannot exist unless the dialoguers engage in critical thinking—thinking which discerns an indivisible solidarity between the world and men and admits of no dichotomy between them—thinking which perceives reality as process, as transformation, rather than as a static entity— thinking which does not separate itself from action, but constantly immerses itself in temporality without fear of the risks involved [1974, pp. 76–81].

Summary

This chapter has described a dialectical model of problem management based on the theory of experiential learning. The model identifies four analytic stages in problem management— situation analysis, problem analysis, solution analysis, and implementation analysis. Within each stage, analysis is based on dialectically opposed phases—valuing and priority setting in situation analysis, information gathering and problem definition in problem analysis, idea getting and decision making in solution analysis, and participation and planning in implementation analysis. Problem management involves adopting the appropriate cognitive mind set for each stage and phase. Problem solving is both a cognitive and a social process. Social factors that can facilitate or hinder effective problem-solving management are the organization's structure and an executive's role in it, the extent to which the organization emphasizes the red-mode or green-mode mind set, and the way conflict is used in problem management.

6

Stakeholders of Executive Decision Making

Ian I. Mitroff
Richard O. Mason

> In the beginning, consciousness rises
> up like an island with whatever contents
> it has, but soon sinks back again into
> the unconscious.
> —Erich Neumann

One of the highest, and thereby most fundamental, of aims of any science is unification. Unification is so powerful a drive in science because the rewards it promises to bestow are so great. It promises to bring under one framework, one idea, the seemingly most disparate of phenomena. It says that all the more that things differ from one another, underneath it all, there is a common thread.

The phenomena with which we are concerned in this paper are as diverse as any we know. In keeping with an earlier tradition in science, we can pose our concern in the form of a question: "What do social system analysis, organization behavior, small-group behavior, and individual behavior have in common?" If that is not enough, then we can ask it in the following form: "What do strategic plans and policies, myths, fairy tales, and individual psychological scripts and stories have in common; what, if anything, could unite such seemingly diverse phenomena?"

We trust that the significance of our concern will not be lost because of the directness with which we have stated it. In a word, we are asking, "Is there a relation between very different levels of social life—that is, from the single individual to the institutional—and if so, what could it possibly be?" We are thereby seeking no less than an integrated view of human beings.

Because of the magnitude and difficulty of the task—not to mention the extreme challenge to which our attempt is subject—it is fitting to present our ideas, as much as possible, in the order in which they were discovered. In the main, scientific writing is intentionally designed to hide the genesis of "its" ideas. The ease with which the small word *its* occurs in the preceding sentence is testimony to what we mean. The alleged impersonality of science is both one of its greatest strengths and one of its greatest weaknesses (Mitroff and Kilmann, 1978). When the controversy of the ideas expressed is so obviously apparent, we do not believe that such impersonality is warranted. Given the magnitude of the attempt, we believe it is vital that we spell out something of the history—or, at the very least, the chronology—of our attempt so that the reader can better judge the rationale of our effort.

As we proceed, we shall be ever mindful of Philip Slater's biting, but not undeserved, remark: "To demand an exclusive interpretation [of myth] is equivalent to insisting that a Spanish peasant, a tropical flower, the Hudson River, an oyster, and the fountains of the Villa d'Este are identical because they contain H_2O. It is a point in common, yet it hardly exhausts their significance" (Slater, 1968, p. xii). To say the least, we hope that our effort rises above this plane.

Jungian Psychology—The Types

Anyone who encounters the history of philosophy in a
deep and reflective way and does not eschew all psychological
considerations as inherently demeaning or irrelevant to philosophical concerns cannot fail to be continually impressed by the
fact that one is dealing with an area in which very different tem-
peraments, to put it mildly, are operating. It was our good fortune both philosophically and psychologically—that is, it suited
our temperament—to study with two men whose view of philosophy was neither in competition with nor in opposition to psychology. As a result, our readings of the basic texts in Western
philosophy, from the pre-Socratics to Dewey, was accompanied
by a simultaneous reading of Carl Jung's *Psychological Types*
(1923). The purpose of this simultaneous reading was not in the
least to reduce serious philosophical problems and questions to
a mere matter of psychological preference or style. If it had, it
would have justified the philosopher's worst fear: Philosophy
was being summarily reduced to psychology so that "it was all a
matter of psychology, nothing more." We shall not pause here
to refute in detail both philosophically and psychologically the
claim of psychological reductionism. We need merely note that
the claim of *psychological* reductionism is itself a highly dubious and contentious *philosophical* doctrine. The important
thing is that it is a *philosophical* assertion and thus, if only in
part, runs counter in spirit to the gist of the original assertion.

Our purpose in reading Jung was instead to understand
better the different patterns of reasoning, the structure of
thought, with which different minds approached the subject
matter of philosophy. Why is it that what is so self-evident, so
taken for granted, so beyond needed proof for one thinker is so
dubious, if not outright false, for another? More important still,
could the different answers and systems that different philosophers have concocted to the great questions be fitted into
some pattern, some broader system? If the purpose of reading
Jung was not to assert arrogantly that he provided an answer
where all others before had failed, did he nonetheless provide a
valuable insight, a glimpse, however fragile and contentious,
into a possible pattern?

To our way of thinking, Jung's *Psychological Types* (1923) is a landmark in the history of humanity's attempt to understand itself. Two things distinguish Jung's effort, either of which would be enough to establish a person's reputation for all time. The first is an encyclopedic command and survey of previous attempts in Western culture to construct systems of different types of personality. The second is an attempt to construct his own system based on a critical appraisal of previous systems and his own enormous clinical experience. The result is still the most comprehensive and fruitful description and system of personality types that we know of (Mitroff and Kilmann, 1978).

This early study of Jung, which occurred while we were still in graduate school, was followed over the next thirteen years by efforts to extend Jungian personality theory and to apply it to such areas as the design of management information systems (Mason and Mitroff, 1981), organizational problem solving (Mitroff and Kilmann, 1975, 1976; Mitroff and Mitroff, 1980), strategic planning (Mason and Mitroff, 1981), and even social science methodology itself (Mitroff and Kilmann, 1978). The effort in the area of social science methodology culminated in a book by Mitroff and Kilmann, *Methodological Approaches to Social Science: Integrating Divergent Concepts and Theories* (1978). In that book it was shown that social science methodology itself could be viewed, and presumably better understood, as the projection of at least four very different psychologies onto the world. Each practices and embodies a very different concept of science.

Thus, for instance, the "analytic scientist" is the scientific equivalent of Jung's sensing-thinking type. As such, the analytic scientist embraces the methods of the natural scientist. Primary, if not sole, emphasis is placed on knowledge and on methods for acquiring it, which are exact, precise, specific, and impersonal. The key ideas are "control" and "elimination of ambiguity"—that is, removal of as many factors as possible that interfere with or contaminate our knowledge of precisely what can be said to cause what. It should come as no surprise to find that the analytic scientist's prime, if not exclusive, mode of gaining knowledge and of certifying it is the rigorously controlled experiment.

In sharp contrast is the "conceptual theorist," the social scientific equivalent of Jung's intuitive thinker. This kind of scientist values new and, particularly, radical ideas, those that shake the scientific enterprise to its very foundation, at times almost for their own sake. This scientist's method for gaining knowledge is much more difficult to describe briefly. Suffice it to say that, in the social realm, it is dialectical. We will say a bit more about this in a moment when we discuss the application of Jungian psychology to organizational problem solving and strategic planning.

The latter two types of social scientist are the hardest to describe, no matter how many pages we are given. The reason is that they are the styles or qualities of mind that are most at variance with the historical and still largely prevailing conception of science. And yet it is precisely for this reason that they may be the most important. Both types are founded on Jung's concept of feeling. Whereas thinking abstracts, classifies, distances, and generally removes itself from all direct human contact or experience with its subject matter (better yet, "objects"), feeling forms a bond between itself and what is studied. The aim is not impersonal but personal knowledge of the highest form—that is, knowledge that is as esthetic and ethical as it is scientific. When feeling takes the form of a social scientific attitude, it is not concerned with pure knowledge for its own sake but, rather, with that kind of knowledge and with the means for obtaining it that serve the "farthest reaches of human nature," our esthetic, ethical, and spiritual nature. There are critical differences between the forms that feeling takes in science—the "conceptual humanist," or Jung's intuitive-feeling type, and the "particular humanist," or Jung's sensing-feeling type, but we shall not bother to pursue these differences here.

Along the way, the authors also discovered how Jung's ideas about personality could be put to practical use in helping groups, individuals, and organizations deal with their problems. A simple method was discovered for helping people "see" their personality and its effects on others (Mitroff and Kilmann, 1975, 1976; Mitroff and Mitroff, 1980). A short personality test based on Jung's ideas is administered individually to a group of almost any size (Myers and Briggs, 1962). Smaller, homogeneous groups are then formed from the larger, heterogeneous group by placing all persons with the same personality profile into one group. That is, all those persons who have a sensing-thinking orientation are placed in one group, all those who have an intuitive-thinking orientation into another, and so on. Each smaller group is then given a standardized Tinkertoy set, a common set of pictures cut out of a magazine, or similar materials and is asked to build a construction out of the Tinkertoy parts or to construct a story out of the magazine pictures. Each group's construction is intended to be its "best expression" of some common issue or problem that the larger group or organization as a whole is experiencing. If there is no such common problem at the surface, groups may be asked to build constructions that best express their perception of "society's most important problem" or their "ideal organization."

Since there are no absolute right or wrong answers to such exercises and, further, since there are few "experts" in Tinkertoy construction, especially among adults, the exercises allow us to see and to compare systematically one of the most difficult of all phenomena to witness, personality. Needless to say, over the years that we have conducted this exercise, we have rarely ceased to find strong and systematic differences between the products of the various groups. The constructions typically differ in their use of color and symmetry. The subjects of the constructions differ even more. In general, they range from the efficient use of technology, in the case of thinking, to how to get more human caring in the world, in the case of feeling; from the tried and true, the concrete and specific, in the case of sensing, to the holistic, the systemic, the untried, the new, novel, and radical, in the case of intuition. More important, because the differences are "there" for all to see and from which to learn, personality itself can be seen. In effect, this feature of the process is phenomenological in the truest sense of the term. It allows the participants to witness the phenomenon of personality and to see its effects on problem solving. This, in our understanding, is the basic meaning of phenomenology—that is, of making the phenomenon visible. It is especially true to the intended meaning in that it makes a phenomenon visible to those who are responsible for producing it.

As we shall discuss later, more important still and, as a result, vastly more difficult to achieve is the integration of these differences in ways of perceiving the world into a "whole." For now, however, the thing we want to emphasize is that, building on the work of others, we were able to transform a system that is primarily intellectual into a tool for practical problem solving.

Dialectical Planning as Social System Analysis—Stakeholders

Throughout the aforementioned period, a parallel development was also occurring. As we were learning how to extend the Jungian personality framework so that it could be used as a tool for organizational and interpersonal learning, we were also discovering how to operationalize the philosophical concept of dialectics so that it could be used for organizational learning and strategic planning as well (Mitroff and Mason, 1981b). Of the two, dialectics was the much more difficult to discover how to transform into a practical device. A previous paper (Mitroff and Mason, 1981a) recounts this part of our journey, so we will not repeat it here.

The philosophical concept of dialectics has great relevance to the management of large-scale institutions. As the problems of large institutions become bigger, more complex, more critical, and more dynamic, it behooves the management of such institutions to have a more appropriate method of treating such problems. Most of our traditional problem-solving methods were largely developed for, and hence are appropriate for simple problems, not complex, systemic ones.

The problems of the world are not like the problems found at the end of most texts. Problems in the world do not come neatly labeled and packaged as such, let alone neatly compartmentalized from other problems. Universities may, because of their extreme disciplinary specialization and general narrowness, segregate technical problems from personal and social ones, but most problems in most organizations do not respect these arbitrary lines. By definition, most important problems involve the whole of an organization.

At the same time, most organizational problems are so complex and malleable that, like the Tinkertoy exercise, they constitute an enormous projective device; that is, persons of different training and psychological type will see and hence define "the problem" in different ways. As a result, complex problems can be molded and shaped into those that the individual instinctively fears, likes, prefers, or knows how to handle. Now, if organizational problems, unlike most textbook exercises, no longer constitute a natural or a fixed "given"—that is, they are not inherently the same for all interested parties—then management needs to assure itself that it is working on the "right" definition or version of the "right" problem, as much as or perhaps more than that it is finding the right solutions to agreed-on problems. In a word, as the world becomes more complex and volatile, problem *defining,* problem *finding,* problem *formulating,* and problem *selecting* become more important than problem solving.

It is here that an appropriate concept of dialectics is needed. What dialectics, appropriately constituted, allows one to do is to compare systematically various competing definitions of important organizational problems and their attendant solutions or policies. One of the most basic reasons, perhaps *the* most basic, that people differ in their perceptions and definitions of important problems is that they differ fundamentally in the basic assumptions they hold about the world. What we and others were able to discover is a simple yet effective method of getting at such assumptions in a relatively nonthreatening way. The full details of accomplishing this are reported in a recent book, *Challenging Strategic Planning Assumptions* (Mason and Mitroff, 1981).

Briefly, the procedure involves working backward from any proposed definition of a problem, or tentative strategy for resolving it, to the assumptions that undergird it. Since few persons are able to deal at the abstract level of assumptions, we had to find a more direct and practical way of getting at them. Stakeholder analysis proved to be the key here.

Stakeholder analysis regards any social system as composed of a possibly indeterminate number of teleological—that is, purposeful—entities (Ackoff and Emery, 1974). Stakeholders are all those individuals, groups, institutions—past, present, and future—that both affect and are affected by any proposed policy or strategy in dealing with a problem. In effect, stakeholders are the relatively concrete, interested parties on whose cooperation any plan depends and, in turn, those who may be affected, intentionally or not, by any proposed plan.

Assumptions are the properties that must be posited of stakeholders in order for a plan to succeed. For example, in the 1960s and 1970s, the Detroit auto companies made a number of critical assumptions about their competitors and their buying public in order to justify the correctness of their policies—that is, the decision to produce certain kinds of bulky, inefficient, out-of-style automobiles and to discount the seriousness of the foreign-car invasion. The gravity of this example shows just how critical the assumptions one entertains about the social world are. It also shows that one's assumptions deserve constant challenging and monitoring. To cite an additional example, one can only wonder, first, whether our support for the Shah of Iran would have been as firm or taken the direction it did if we had been more aware of the assumptions on which it was based and, second, how fragile those assumptions were.

Elsewhere (Mason and Mitroff, 1981) we have given the details of the methods for surfacing stakeholders and assumptions. For the most part, stakeholders comprise familiar social system roles—competitors, suppliers, allies, government, employees, unions, and so on. Also for the most part, assumptions cover such things as stakeholders' will, motivations, purposes, beliefs, values, power, authority, responsibility, resources, and legal requirements.

One feature of the method in particular has proved invaluable as a problem-solving and strategy-setting device. This is the feature that allows the proponents of different policies to compare their visions of the world, much as the Tinkertoy exercise does. This is accomplished by having the proponents of a particular policy plot their assumptions on two simple axes, the perceived importance of an assumption and its perceived certainty. Typically, the assumptions made about some stakeholders are more important or critical to the perceived success of a policy than others. If some assumptions are false, a policy is hurt more than if others are. Similarly, we typically feel more confident about the truth or certainty of some assumptions than others. Plotting assumptions on these two axes allows us to identify two important sets of assumptions: (1) those regarded as important and certain and (2) those regarded as important and uncertain. This technique also allows us to compare precisely how the proponents view the world and, as a result, to have a more productive debate about the nature of reality.

The importance of the preceding cannot be overemphasized. Assumptions are like the weather: Everybody talks about their extreme importance, but beyond that, nobody does anything about them. Our claim is not to have found *the* definitive method for getting at them but, rather, to have taken them seriously enough to work on a methodology, crude as it is, for dealing with them. If, as we shall argue later, assumptions constitute one of the deepest grounds of human reality, then it is of the utmost importance to have a method for getting at their profound influence.

Jungian Psychology—The Archetypes

As anyone who has studied Jungian psychology knows, the personality types of Jung are only the tip of the iceberg, the smallest part of the system. This does not diminish their tremendous importance. It only puts them in proper perspective. In Maria von Franz's chillingly accurate phrase, the ego—that is, that part of the psyche that is accessible to consciousness—is only the tiniest and barest of patches on the incredibly larger sphere of the total human psyche.

Long before the methods of social problem solving described in the previous two sections reached their present form and stage of application and development, the first author embarked on a study of Jung's archetypal psychology. The purpose for such a study can perhaps best be explained by recounting an experience the first author had many years after he began study of this aspect of Jung's psychology. If, as we believe, life, and certainly its understanding, is not linear, then it is understandable that often one has to come to a later part of one's journey to understand why one began it in the first place.

The first author had long been vaguely aware of transactional analysis (Berne, 1964) but had never really taken it seriously. As almost everyone knows, Berne founded his system to make Freud more accessible to a wider audience. As part of this effort, he replaced Freud's technical machinery and vocabulary with concepts and words that were more readily understandable. Thus, for example, Freud's superego, ego, and id were replaced by Berne's Parent, Adult, and Child. Although Berne's system is actually much more complicated and sophisticated than that (Klein, 1980), it is enough for our purposes to point this out.

A moment of taking Berne seriously occurred one day when the first author suddenly realized how Berne could be used to enrich Jung's types. One of the most offensive things about any typology is that it "types" people. Jung was painfully aware of this consideration and went to great lengths to avoid it. Throughout his various descriptions of the types, he repeatedly cautions against putting people into "neat little boxes." That is not the purpose of his typology. Its fundamental purpose is to give people a framework and a series of concepts, a vocabulary, for, first of all, recognizing their differences and, second, working through them (Jung, 1968). The typology is not meant to imply rigid classification or permanent fixity for all of one's life. For instance, sensing-thinking types are not alike in all their characteristics.

The thought that occurred was that *one* of the reasons that sensing-thinking (ST) differs from person to person is that a person's conscious psychological function takes on a very different expression and operation depending on which of Berne's three characters, Parent, Adult, or Child, it manifests itself through. That is, if one is an ST in the conscious mode but is guided by underlying forces of the Parent mode, then one's attitude, often observed, will be that only the ST version of reality

—for example, the analytic scientist's approach—is valid. All other attitudes are wrong. If, however, one's ST is under the influence of the Child, then—depending on which of Berne's Child characters is operating—one will feel either inferior, small, and helpless or so wildly creative and uninhibited that others might have extreme difficulty in understanding one's thoughts. If, finally, one's ST is guided by the Adult character, or aspect of the personality, then one's attitude will be entirely different. The Adult is the character whose ego is presumably developed enough to deal realistically with the world. Notice that we did not say "developed enough to deal realistically with reality," for each type's conscious function is, for all practical purposes, "reality" for that type. Hence, there is little breaking out of the circle except through the recognition that reality consists in the bringing together of the "realities" of the other types. But this is precisely the attitude of the Adult character, which in effect says, "I have my way of viewing the world, and to me it often seems so natural that there could be no other way; but others are just as convinced of their way. If it is not an either/or, if others do not represent a threat to me as they do to the Parent or Child, then the questions I must ask myself are: What can I learn from and give to others? How can we combine our different visions of the world to achieve a more powerful one?"

In essence, the thought that occurred was that the Parent, Adult, and Child characters could be overlaid on the Jungian personality dimensions to achieve a richer framework both for explaining and for understanding human behavior. Lest the significance of this idea be lost or undermined, let us state it somewhat differently. One of the great strengths of the Tinkertoy exercise and the stakeholder approach to social system analysis and/or design is that they allow people of different education, intellectual ability, temperament, and training to literally see one of the most difficult of all phenomena to witness—personality, that is, inner differences. Tinkertoy constructions and stakeholder parties are concrete entities. So are Berne's three characters, Parent, Adult, and Child. As social scientists, we believe we have a deep responsibility to help others observe, in their own terms and words, the phenomena of which they are

fundamentally a part and which they hence constitute. To repeat once again, this to us is the central meaning of the term
phenomenology. As such, there is nothing mysterious or esoteric about it all. It simply means "making visible the psychological phenomena which are inside all of us and which run and
give meaning to our lives."

Actually, the overlay of the two systems is much more
complicated than we have suggested here (Mitroff, 1981). But
this is not for our purposes the essential point. The essential
point is that, no matter what brand of depth psychology one
turns to, one finds a number of common features. The first is
that the deepest layers of the human psyche are **revealed** (that
is, *known*) in terms of the broadest and most diverse cast of
personalized characters. Second, these personalized characters
assume the wildest variety of shapes and forms. For instance,
some of the characters are real in that they stand for our actual
parents, siblings, relatives, clan, and so on, while others are
archetypal and symbolic, for example, the ideas of woman and
man in general. These, in turn, are divided into the most bewildering and fascinating variety and array of forms—for instance, young man, young woman, the wise old woman, the
wise old man, sorcerer, temptress, seductress, witch, priest,
Adam, king, queen, hunter. They even assume animal and physical form—fire, water, and so on. The family of shapes is so
broad that we know of no taxonomy or effort to classify the
characters that different systems of depth psychology treat!
We are ourselves engaged in a basic research effort to accomplish precisely this. It is truly amazing that we have a periodic
table of the basic elements—the constituents of inorganic matter—but not of the constituents of the human psyche.

Third, not merely is the structure of the psyche revealed
in terms of these characters, but it appears that its structure *is*
the assemblage of the characters that constitute it. That is, the
ontology of the mind, its basic structure, and its epistemology,
the knowledge of it, exist in a very tight couple. The *relationship among the characters themselves* that constitute the mind
may be somewhat loosely coupled, but the relationship between
what the kind "is" and how we know what " 'it' is" is very

tightly coupled. Fourth, the functioning, meaning, and properties of the characters are made known (revealed) through a variety of storytelling mechanisms: dreams, fairy tales, myths, and
scripts. Although there are critical differences among these
forms (Bettelheim, 1977), for our purposes they all point to the
same thing, our fifth point.

The various storytelling mechanisms serve a number of
important mechanisms. At one level they help the individual to
cope, to vent his or her conflicts in such a fashion that they can
be dealt with in an acceptable—that is, healthy—way. At another, they help individuals to share their stories with one
another and, by so doing, recognize the universality of their
condition. In the latter sense, one of the most fascinating aspects of fairy tales and myths is that they recount the developmental phases that the psyche goes through from birth to
death (Neumann, 1954). Fairy tales and myths, in other words,
represent humankind's attempts to cope and to develop psychologically writ largest, that is, on the grandest scale imaginable.

Sixth, the nature of the characters is such that they are
subject to the most profound splitting of attributes. The ability
to tolerate good and bad, strength and weakness, love and hate
as attributes of a single character is, psychologically speaking, so
difficult that it poses one of the greatest challenges in life. In
general, it comes only to the most mature and healthiest of
egos. As a result, good and evil tend to be split, the good being
projected onto one character and the evil onto another.

Because of the obvious importance of these points, and
particularly for the implications to follow, we have chosen to
quote from three of the giants in this area, Carl Jung, Erich
Neumann, and Bruno Bettelheim. There are many more from
whom we could have chosen, but the writings of these three
testify repeatedly to our six points. One would be hard put to
find three who have written more powerfully on the nature of
symbols and their relation to the structure, if not the very con-
stitution, of the psyche. We quote:

> Although the alchemists came very close to
> realizing that the ego was the mysteriously elusive

arcane substance and the longed-for lapis, they
were not aware that with their sun symbol they
were establishing an intimate connection between
God and the ego . . . projection is not an involun-
tary act; it is a natural phenomenon beyond the
interference of the conscious mind and peculiar to
the nature of the human psyche. If, therefore, it is
this nature that produced the sun symbol, nature
herself is expressing an identity of God and ego. In
that case, only unconscious nature can be accused
of blasphemy, but not the man who is its victim. . . .
    The alchemists rightly regarded "mental
union in the overcoming of the body" as only the
first stage of conjunction or individuation, in the
same way that Khunrath understood Christ as the
"Saviour of the Microcosm" but not of the Macro-
cosm, whose saviour was the lapis. In general, the
alchemists strove for a *total* union of opposites in
symbolic form, and this they regarded as the indis-
pensable condition for the healing of all ills. Hence
they sought to find ways and means to produce
that substance in which all opposites were united.
It has to be material as well as spiritual, living as
well as inert, masculine as well as feminine, old as
well as young, and—presumably—neutral. It had to
be created by man, and at the same time, since it
was "increatum" by God himself, the *Deus terres-
tris* [Jung, 1963, pp. 109, 475].

Jung is saying here that what the alchemists were doing, largely unbeknownst to their conscious awareness, was projective
psychology. They were projecting the structure of their minds
onto the search for the magical substance. Hence, the proper
reading of the alchemical texts is that of depth psychology, not
science, not chemistry. Through Jung we are granted a rare and
fascinating glimpse into the structure of the medieval mind.
    Neumann speaks to what the figures of myths contribute
to our understanding of the origin and development of human
consciousness:

    The dangers of the unconscious, its render-
ing, destroying, devouring, and castrating charac-

ter, confront the hero as monsters, prodigies, beasts, giants, and so forth, which he has to conquer. An analysis of these figures shows that they are bisexual like the uroboros, possessing masculine and feminine symbolic qualities. . . .

The tests of masculinity and the proofs of ego stability, will, power, bravery, knowledge of "heaven," and so forth, which are demanded of the hero, have their historical equivalents in the rites of puberty. Just as the problem of the First Parents is resolved in [the story or myth of] the dragon fight, and in turn succeeded by the hero's encounter with woman as his partner and his soul, so, through the initiation ceremony, the neophyte is detached from the parental sphere, and becomes a marriageable young man capable of founding a family. But what happens in myth and in history also happens in the individual and on the basis of archetypal determinism. The central feature of puberty psychology is [revealed in] the syndrome of the dragon fight. . . . The personal aspects of this situation, a small part of which has been formulated psychoanalytically as the personalistic Oedipus complex, are merely surface aspects of the conflict with the First Parents, that is, with the parental archetypes. And in this process, [the person] has to "kill the parents" [or slay the dragon to achieve selfhood or autonomy] [1954, pp. 170, 205].

What Jung and Neumann are discussing in the most abstract of terms, Bettelheim makes perfectly concrete in his inspiring discussion of fairy tales:

Contrary to what takes place in many modern children's stories, in fairy tales evil is as omnipresent as virtue. In practically every fairy tale, good and evil are given body in the form of some figures and their actions, as good and evil are omnipresent in life and the propensities for both are present in every man. It is this duality which poses the moral problem and requires the struggle to solve it.

Evil is not without its attractions—symbolized by the mighty giant or dragon, the power of

the witch, the cunning queen in "Snow White"—
and often it is temporarily in the ascendancy. . . .
It is not the fact that virtue wins out at the end
which promotes reality, but the hero is most attractive to the child who identified with the hero
in all his struggles. . . .

The figures in fairy tales are not ambivalent
—not good and bad at the same time, as we all are
in reality. But since polarization dominates the
child's mind, it also dominates fairy tales. A person
is either good or bad, nothing in between. One
brother is stupid, the other is clever. . . . One parent is all good, the other evil. . . . Presenting the polarities of character permits the child to comprehend easily the difference between the two, which
he could not do as readily were the figures drawn
more true to life, with all the complexities that
characterize real people. Ambiguities must wait until a relatively firm personality has been established
on the basis of positive identifications. . . .

A child's choices are based, not so much on
right versus wrong, as on who arouses his sympathy
and who is antipathy. The more simple and straight-
forward a good character, the easier it is for a child
to identify with it and to reject the other. . . . The
child decides this on the basis of projecting himself
wholeheartedly onto one character. . . .

The witch—more than the other creations of
our imagination in which we have invested magic
powers, the fairy and the sorcerer—in her opposite
aspects is a reincarnation of the all-good mother of
infancy and the all-bad mother of the oedipal crisis. But she is no longer seen halfway realistically,
as a mother who is lovingly all-giving and an opposite stepmother who is rejectingly demanding, but
entirely unrealistically, as either superhumanly rewarding or inhumanly destructive [1977, pp. 8-10,
94].

And finally:

"Cinderella" sets forth the steps in personality development required to reach self-fulfillment,
and presents them in fairy-tale fashion so that every
person can understand what is required of him to be-

come a full human being. This is hardly surprising, since the fairy tale, as I have tried to show throughout this book, represents extremely well the workings of our psyche: what our psychological problems are, and how these can best be mastered. Erikson, in his model of [the] human life cycle, suggests that the ideal human being develops through what he calls "phase-specific psychosocial crises" if he achieves the ideal goals of each phase in succession. These crises in their sequence are: First, basic trust —represented by Cinderella's experience with the original good mother, and what this firmly implanted in her personality. Second, autonomy—as Cinderella accepts her unique role and makes the best of it. Third, initiative—Cinderella develops this as she plants the twig and makes it grow with the expression of her personal feelings, tears, and prayers. Fourth, industry—represented by Cinderella's hard labors, such as sorting out the lentils. Fifth, identity—Cinderella escapes from the ball, hides in the dovecote and tree, and insists that the prince see and accept her in her negative identity as "Cinderella" before she assumes her positive identity as his bride because any true identity has its negative as well as its positive aspects. According to Erikson's scheme, having ideally solved these psychosocial crises by having achieved the personality attributes just enumerated, one becomes ready for true intimacy with the other [Bettelheim, 1977, p. 275].

The Group and the Organization— Types and Archetypes

All the aforementioned processes that operate in the individual also operate in small groups and in organizations (Berne, 1964). As we advance up the scale of human phenomena from the single individual to the organization, there is a difference in degree, but not in kind, in the explanation of human behavior. Characters, both real and imagined, actual and symbolic, develop in small groups. Groups develop myths and stories no less than individuals do to give meaning to their existence and to structure their relationships. As individuals develop their character structure—and, as we have emphasized, the structure of their characters—through such mechanisms as identification, introjection, and projection, groups utilize these very same mechanisms as well. Groups, like individuals, develop split characters to handle the split feelings of goodness and badness with which they must deal. We quote from a volume on groups that summarizes, as best we know, the state of our knowledge:

> The group situation recreates the basic nuclear-family conditions that spawn the Oedipus complex. The leader is regarded as father, and some female member or the female subgroup or the group as a whole is regarded as the mother (assuming the leader is male). . . . One additional view of the small group has provocative, but largely unexplored, developmental implications—the notion that the group is unconsciously experienced as a maternal entity. Bion, Durkin, Gibbard and Hartman, Jaques, Ruiz, and Scheidlinger see the group as a pre-oedipal mother. Slater, too, adopts this point of view as it relates to boundary evolution. . . .
>
> In small groups there is an effort to split good and bad and to put the good into the group and the bad into the leader or disorganizing subgroup. This effort culminates in the revolt against the leader. There is an attempt to force him in the group fully on the group's terms (make him good) or to exclude him fully by destroying him. The revolt is preceded by the expression of several components of distress. Whatever the antecedents, there is an effort to get back into the group anyone or anything (symbols, ideas) experienced as good. This situation occurs because members may at the same time have projected onto the leader good, "ideal" qualities which are then recaptured and introjected during the revolt. Although the leader is ostensibly excluded in the revolt, he is simultaneously included by the mechanism of introjection. . . .
>
> Groups are replete with mythological and mythlike assumptions about themselves. Members and leaders make use of conscious fantasy productions, involve their fellows in issues of political faith and ideology, have rituals and ritualistic activ-

ity, and invent religiouslike beliefs as well [Gibbard, Hartman, and Mann, 1973, pp. 8, 173, 274].

On Quirks and Quarks

With poetic insight and imagination, modern physicists, borrowing a term from James Joyce, have named the basic building blocks of the universe "quarks." They have shown that these entities are complex and interesting almost beyond belief. The basic building blocks of the mind, of social life in general, are no less complex and certainly no less interesting. Whereas the basic building blocks of the physicist are abstract, impersonal, mathematical entities, ours are all-too-human entities. The phenomena with which the physicist deals are completely impersonal; the elements with which we as social scientists deal are intensely personal. As we have argued, the very elements that constitute the mind and social life take a distinctly human form: They are characters. Following Joyce's lead, we prefer to term these elements "quirks." Quirks are the basic building blocks of human experience. Stories, myths, fairy tales, and assumptions are the unifying force, the social glue, that binds the characters into a united whole or theme.

To say that human experience is basically constituted in terms of a host of characters is not to say that the range and type of characters in individual, small-group, organizational, and social system behavior are the same. They are not. More important, however, a full analysis would show both considerable distinctness and overlap between the clusters or populations of characters that those fields of human behavior treat. Thus, each field constitutes a distinct galaxy of characters, which pertains specifically to that field. At the same time there are both an influence and an overlap between galaxies. In psychological terms, there are mutual infection, influence, integration, and contamination between the characters that inhabit and constitute the supposedly separate ranges of human experience. But this conclusion helps to resolve one of the great controversies of social science—namely, "Is the social system a reflection of individual personality, or is it the other way around?" In terms of the image we have been exploring, our response is that the two equally "cause" as well as "influence" each other simultaneously. If there is considerable overlap between the characters that shape and constitute human behavior at all levels, then it is a serious mistake to view the arrow of influence as one-way.

The view of social system integration we have outlined here is very different from previous attempts and thus has serious consequences for social knowledge. However, our effort is in no way intended to belittle previous efforts. We are indebted to them. We do believe, however, that previous attempts have been founded on an implicit mechanical view of nature. Little wonder, then, that integration was sought in terms of the structural, mechanical, or mathematical features of human systems. Our attempt, in contrast, is frankly teleological and, as such, is founded on a teleological theory of human systems (Ackoff and Emery, 1974; Churchman, 1971). Above all, we believe it has the distinct advantage of revealing the phenomenological nature of human systems to the very persons who constitute such systems themselves. Mechanical attempts at unification are valuable only to the extent that they identify the relevant properties of important characters or stakeholders.

We believe that such an approach has other advantages as well. For instance, as we move from level to level, there is a distinct difference in the range of psychological language in terms of which the characters supposedly speak. For example, supposedly the characters—which we have termed stakeholders—that make up a policy system are "real"; that is, they function at the level of ego reality. However, anyone who has ever worked with "real" managers knows that the characters onto whom they project their policies are anything but completely ego-governed. There is a great deal of superego and id projection as well. We always have a great tendency to make our enemies or competitors seem worse than they actually are and, conversely, to make our allies seem better or more benign than they actually are. If we can begin to be the least bit honest with ourselves, then we have to acknowledge that our conscious plans are more infected—certainly affected—by our unconscious than we have dared acknowledge. Our best analysts of the mind have appreciated this better than our best policy analysts. We quote from Bettelheim:

> The myth of Hercules deals with the choice between following the pleasure principle or the reality principle in life. So, likewise, does the fairy story of "The Three Little Pigs."
>
> Stories like "The Three Little Pigs" are much favored by children over all "realistic" tales, particularly if they are presented with feeling by the storyteller. Children are enraptured when the huffing and puffing of the wolf at the pig's door is acted out for them. "The Three Little Pigs" teaches the nursery-age child in a most enjoyable and dramatic form that we must not be lazy and take things easy, for if we do, we may perish. Intelligent planning and foresight combined with hard labor will make us victorious over even our most ferocious enemy—the wolf! The story also shows the advantages of growing up, since the third and wisest pig is usually depicted as the biggest and oldest.
>
> The houses the three pigs build are symbolic of man's progress in history: from a lean-to shack to a wooden house, finally to a house of solid brick. Internally, the pigs' actions show progress from the id-dominated personality to the superego-influenced but essentially ego-controlled personality.
>
> The littlest pig builds his house with the least care out of straw; the second uses sticks; both throw their shelters together as quickly and effortlessly as they can so they can play for the rest of the day. Living in accordance with the pleasure principle, the younger pigs seek immediate gratification, without a thought for the future and the dangers of reality, although the middle pig shows some growth in trying to build a somewhat more substantial house than the youngest.
>
> Only the third and oldest pig has learned to behave in accordance with the reality principle; he is able to postpone his desire to play, and instead acts in line with his ability to foresee what may happen in the future. He is even able to predict correctly the behavior of the wolf—the enemy, or

stranger within, which tries to seduce and trap us; and therefore the third pig is able to defeat powers both stronger and more ferocious than he is. The wild and destructive wolf stands for all asocial, unconscious, devouring powers against which one must learn to protect oneself, and which one can defeat through the strength of one's ego [1977, pp. 41-42].

If Bettelheim is not talking about strategic planning as much as he is about fairy tales, then perhaps we are missing the point. We do not think we are.

This is not to say that the lessons to be taught are one-sided. The field of strategic planning has as much to teach archetypal or depth psychology as the latter presumably has to teach the former. If depth psychology has much to teach planning about the underlying meaning of the characters and symbols it discusses, then planning also has a great deal to teach depth psychology about how to organize its material into a more coherent format. For instance, as we illustrated earlier, the influence of stakeholders can be assessed on two dimensions, importance and certainty. In a similar fashion, the broader stakeholders that govern individual, group, and organizational behavior can be assessed on two primary dimensions, the "potency" of their influence and the "degree of awareness" an individual or group has of the operation or effect of a particular stakeholder on behavior. From another perspective, planning can offer depth psychology a focusing concern—that is, a field of application. In other words, if depth psychology has been interested mainly in the interpretation and meaning of symbols for their own sake or for individual growth, then planning asks, "What does all this mean for collective behavior? What does it mean for such 'real' problems as hunger, transportation, crime, and governance?" In short, planning and depth psychology need each other more than ever, more than they realize.

To see just how much the two fields need each other, consider the act of synthesis or integration, the very subject motivating this chapter. The integration of opposing or competing plans is one of the most important, yet least understood, aspects of strategic planning. Depth psychology shows precisely why this is so difficult. If synthesis means the putting back together of qualities that have been split apart and projected onto the separate characters, then synthesis literally entails finding a single stakeholder that is capable of containing contradictory qualities. Little wonder that synthesis should be both so difficult and so mysterious a process! As Jung himself has put it: "What the union of opposites really 'means' transcends human imagination. Therefore, the worldly-wise can dismiss such a 'fantasy' without further ado.... But that doesn't help us much, for we are dealing with an eternal image, an archetype, from which man can turn away his mind for a time, but never permanently. Whenever this image is obscured, his life loses its proper meaning and consequently its balance" (1963, p. 200).

If the view outlined here makes any sense at all, then it means that the social sciences' search for their Newton has been seriously—dangerously—misguided. Newton is an appropriate character for unification in the mechanical sense only. In the teleological sense of unification, the figure of Adam may be a more fitting character, for Adam comes closest to being the symbol of unification. "We can ... understand why Isaac Luria attributed every psychic quality to Adam: he is the psyche *par excellence*. ... Adam stands not only for the psyche, but for its totality; he is a symbol of the self, and hence a visualization of the 'irrepresentable' Godhead.... [We recognize] that the archetypal structure of the unconscious will produce, over and over again and irrespective of tradition, those figures which reappear in the history of all epochs and all peoples, and will endow them with the same significance and numinosity that have been theirs from the beginning" (Jung, 1963, p. 390). If this is so, then we await the coming of our Adam or Adams of social science. The ushering in of a new era in social science is thus equivalent to the creation of a new guiding character. To play on a saying of Freud's, where once Newton was, Adam shall be. May we learn how to develop the kind of science that knows how to nourish and to cherish our Adams wherever they may be!

Finally, one of the greatest strengths of such a view may be that, paradoxically enough, it pinpoints *exactly* the *incom-*

pleteness of human knowledge. No one can pretend to say for sure that he or she knows the full extent of the characters influencing human behavior. For this reason there will always be a certain incompleteness to human knowledge. How people cope with the anxiety this produces takes us back full circle to where we began. Anxiety produces character, and character produces anxiety.

7

Union of Rationality and Intuition in Management Action

Louis R. Pondy

According to a recent story in the *Wall Street Journal,* Sam Ayoub, senior vice-president in charge of foreign currency operations for the Coca-Cola Company, claims to make decisions about foreign currency trading by relying more on his intuition than on elaborate technical reports (Long, 1982). "I rely on my gut feelings," says Ayoub. However, Ayoub's intuitive judgments are not based on ignorance of the facts. Instead, he has created a system of acquiring timely information that informs his intuition: Managers in the field provide him with hourly updates of the prices of major currencies, including a regular Monday morning 4:00 A.M. report of how European markets opened; and he travels extensively for informal conversations with local bottlers about each country's economic and political developments so that he will not have to rely on incomplete and outdated newspaper accounts. By relying, apparently, on informed intuition rather than on a detailed, rational analysis of systematically collected data, Ayoub has been able to capitalize financially for Coke on exchange-rate fluctuations.

This brief vignette of the role of intuition in one executive's decision-making style highlights a long-standing dilemma in theories of managerial action: Is effective managerial action better served by employing the techniques of rational analysis or by trusting to the unarticulated processes of creative intuition? The field of organizational behavior has provided no clear resolution of this dilemma.

In this chapter I shall argue that dilemmas frequently result from asking the wrong question or from asking a question in the wrong way. By posing the dilemma as a choice between two opposing styles of decision making, students of organizational behavior have excluded the possibility that those apparent opposites could be combined into a third, more powerful hybrid style that incorporates the best of both. My aim is to ask whether and how "rationality" and "intuition" can be combined at the level of primary human processes and whether and how such a combination can be institutionalized in the context of organizational and managerial practices.

My claim is that a union of rationality and intuition *is* possible, that they are *not* antithetical, and that each of these primary human processes functions most effectively in combination with the other. Furthermore, I shall argue that a recently developed model of strategic change, "logical incrementalism" (Quinn, 1982), embodies many of the features of a rational/ intuitive union in a management context. Thus, the possibility of joining rational and intuitive processes is not merely of academic interest but may also have practical implications for improved managerial action.

According to Quinn (1982, p. 199), logical incrementalism is a loosely connected set of management practices that constitute "an adaptation to the practical psychological and informational problems of getting a constantly changing group of people with diverse talents and interests to move *together* effectively in a continually dynamic environment." Though incremental, these processes are described by Quinn as conscious, proactive, and purposeful on the part of the manager; hence the phrase *"logical* incrementalism." Taken together, the processes serve to create an awareness among members of problems and possibilities, to initiate partial solutions, and to produce a novel strategic synthesis for the organization. The emergence of a new strategic synthesis takes place continuously over many months or even years, with few well-defined marking points. There is no instant when the executive or the organization shifts dramatically from the old to the new synthesis.

This model represents a puzzle because Quinn provides no explanation at the level of primary processes for why his model should work; the model has no theory, so to speak. It is my contention in this chapter that logical incrementalism works, in part, because it provides a way of bringing about the union of rational (or analytic) and intuitive (or synthetic) modes of inquiry by placing them jointly in a stream of action-over-time. Implicit in this contention is my claim that both rationality and intuition are necessary in any creative act, including the act of producing a new strategic synthesis. To foreshadow the argument, rationality requires understanding as a precursor to intelligent action, and intuition requires action as the basis of understanding. How to achieve *both* action-based knowledge and knowledge-based action, when starting with neither, is the puzzle. I shall argue that Quinn's logical incrementalism model points the way toward a solution to the practical management problem, that it provides a mechanism for joining rationality and intuition in organizational settings.

The remainder of the chapter is divided into three sections:

First, I shall review what some others have said about the possibility of joining rational and intuitive modes of inquiry. Although much has been written about the distinctiveness of the two modes, surprisingly little has been written about their union.

Second, I shall describe Quinn's model in somewhat more detail.

Third, I shall examine the extent to which Quinn's model of strategic change, at the level of secondary organizational processes, embodies the primary human-process features of a union of rationality and intuition. In doing so I hope to shed new light on at least one aspect of the executive mind.

Rationality and Intuition: Duality or Union

Basic Differences. Since the research on split-brain functioning, it has been popular to emphasize the differences between two modes of consciousness, one variously described as analytic, rational, sequential, convergent, detailed, logical, scientific, objective, digital, or explicit and a second typically characterized as synthetic, intuitive, simultaneous, divergent, holistic, artistic, pattern-recognizing, subjective, analogue, or tacit. Bogen (1969), for example, has compiled from the literature a list of more than thirty such dualities of mind and has added his own distinction between propositional and appositional modes of thought, the latter term suggesting a capacity for comparing perceptions and schemata. Although Bogen develops the differences between the two modes of thought in some detail and argues forcefully for a better understanding of the appositional mode, he stops short of suggesting that they might be integrated. To accept the duality of rational and intuitive knowing but to fail to consider their union has been the common practice.

There are some exceptions. Jerome Bruner conjectures about the remote possibility of union: "The elegant rationality of science and the metaphoric nonrationality of art operate with deeply different grammars; perhaps they even represent a profound complementarity" (1962b, p. 74). (But note his primary emphasis on their "deeply different grammars.")

Blackburn (1971, p. 1007) argues for the complementarity of intuitive and quantitative knowledge in scientific inquiry but says little about how to achieve it: "To 'see' a complex system as an organic whole requires an act of trained intuition . . . such perceptions . . . follow only after long periods of total immersion in a problem. . . . The intuitive knowledge essential to a full understanding of complex systems can be encouraged and prepared for by (i) training scientists to be aware of sensuous clues about their surroundings; (ii) insisting on sensuous knowledge as part of the intellectual structure of science, not as an afterthought; and (iii) approaching complex systems openly, respecting their organic complexity before choosing an abstract quantification space onto which to project them."

Three points are worth noting about Blackburn's view. First, intuition is *trained*; we learn to see whole patterns as much as we learn to see individual parts. Second, abstract quantification must be held in abeyance to prevent premature closure and to permit the trained intuition to operate. Third, total immersion, exposure to the richness of detail, is necessary for intuition to do its work of apprehending the system confronting the scientist. But in this view rationality is only held *temporarily* at bay, permitting intuition a brief period to do its work of seeing the organic complexity. Blackburn's view of union is at best primitive, with little or no interaction between the two modes of inquiry.

Two-Way Flows. Cyril Smith (1978) carries the process of union a step further in his analysis of the role of esthetics in science by postulating a two-way flow between the objective and the subjective. On the one hand, "Although atomistic details are insufficient for full understanding, they cannot be ignored. All the established 'facts' must be considered before imaginative interpretation can be indulged in" (p. 22). On the other hand, "Nothing is a thing by itself: it takes meaning, indeed existence, only as it interacts with something else" (p. 23).

Thus, imaginative interpretations constitute the details, they punctuate the stream of existence into definable things. But the details themselves, once constituted, give rise to new intuitions or images; interpretations cannot arise out of nothing.

Role of Anomalies. This type of interaction or mutual dependence between the analytic and synthetic would still be a relatively primitive and sterile model of union except for the role that Smith gives to "cumulative nuance": "Socially and culturally, the aggregation of nuances in diverse utilitarian things, daily custom, and ritual gives richness without disruption, for the forces are gentle, not overly specific, and nearly invisible" (1978, p. 47).

Nuances form "local clumps," isolated imperfections. It

is the generation and movement of such misfitted details "with-in a predominantly ordered environment" that produces social change (p. 38). (Cumulative nuance is also the mechanism by which new crystalline structures develop in metals. Smith is a metallurgist who uses metallic plasticity as a metaphor for change in any ordered structure.) Thus, analysis of a given struc-ture followed by logical synthesis cannot reconstruct reality, because it omits the cumulative consequences of local historical accident. In Smith's view, the union of the detail and pattern is an ongoing process that feeds on the propagation of local nuances, details that are anomalous within a given structure. Not all anomalies cumulate into a new pattern, of course, but all new patterns are the result of local misfits cumulating gradu-ally in the midst of an old pattern. And the new pattern or form is typically recognized only retrospectively, after it has come to exist and has displaced the old (Smith, pp. 44–45). This view of structural change suggests a model of union that is (1) interactive but (2) incremental, is (3) set in the historical time line of the sys-tem, and thus (4) is emergent from within the old structure.

   Lived Experience of the Actors. For social systems, the "historical time line" might be rendered as the "lived experi-ence of actors" in the system, for it is *in* the minds and social dialogue of actors and *out of* their experience that new patterns are formed. "Lived experience" is a central concept in Boland and Pondy's (1983) analysis of the union of rational and natural aspects of accounting in its organizational context. At one level an accounting system is a set of rational categories and proce-dures, a quantitative model for an economic system, a set of symbols for ordering and interpreting experience. It creates a rational *context* within which natural processes of organization are acted out. But it is not a disembodied rationality; it is set in the lived experience of organizational actors.

   The accounting system itself emerges out of organiza-tional action as an interpretive rationalization. It is a model *of* the organization in that it describes the organization as it is, but it is also a model *for* the organization in that it prescribes what the organization could become. The natural processes of organi-zation, the qualitative details of organizational life, also provide a *context* within which the rational or quantitative develops. The rational aspect of accounting is a socially constructed response to its natural aspect.

Boland and Pondy's view of the union of rational and natural aspects is thus that they stand in a relationship of *mutual context,* alternating as figure and ground in the lived experience of organization members. An accounting system cannot, therefore, be seen exclusively as a disembodied, free-standing, rational model *for* an organization but must also simultaneously be seen as a naturally evolving model *of* the organization. Boland and Pondy do not give the same prominent role to "local imperfection" that Smith does, but their model of union is otherwise similar to his.

Tacit Norms. What is missing from both Smith's and Boland and Pondy's models of union is the role of tacit norms or understandings in critically judging new creative interpretations. But tacit norms play a key part in Vickers' (1978) model of union. Vickers seeks to understand the role of esthetics in science, and he states his program thusly:

> My thesis is that the human mind has available to it at least two different modes of knowing and that it uses both in appropriate or inappropriate combinations in its endless efforts to understand the world in which it finds itself, including its fellow human beings and itself. One of these modes is more dependent on analysis, logical reasoning, calculation, and explicit description. The other is more dependent on synthesis and the recognition of pattern, context, and the multiple relations of figure and ground. The first involves the recognition or creation of form, irrespective of the elements which compose it. Both are normal aspects of the neocortical development which distinguishes man from his fellow mammals. Both are needed and both are used in most normal mental operations.
>
> They are often referred to as rationality and intuition. . . . The main difference to which I refer is that a rational process is fully describable, whereas an intuitive process is not [1978, p. 145].

Vickers goes on to observe, as I have, that until recently "the possibility that the brain might be capable of *both* processes in *combination*" seems not to have been considered (1978, p. 150; emphasis added).

Like Smith, Vickers draws attention to the role of "misfits" in the gradual evolution and dynamic change of patterns and schemata. Like Boland and Pondy, Vickers conceives of the *alternation* of the two basic processes, a "creative process" that presents new hypothetical forms for judgment and an "appreciative process" that exercises a critical judgment of those forms (Vickers, 1978, p. 158). But Vickers' chief contribution to our developing theory of union is his description of the role of tacit or undescribable norms (or "schemata") in the appreciative process.

In Vickers' view, the schemata may consist in part of explicit describable criteria, but in part they are also *necessarily* tacit, although he does not fully explain this necessity. However, he does suggest that the tacit schemata that screen data can only be inferred from observing their operations, because the schemata are themselves products of the process they mediate. It is as though the schemata were like the type of sunglasses that darken automatically in bright sunlight; we become aware of the lenses only indirectly by the effects they produce, unless we cease using them *as lenses* and focus our attention directly on them *as objects*.

Origin of Schemata. Just as Smith argues that patterns emerge from details, Vickers argues that schemata result from "countless particular examples" (p. 150). Just as words name objects, schemata can name patterns; but like words, schemata exhibit an ambiguity, or open-endedness, that evolves over time with their use. This open-endedness also accounts in part for their tacit nature. However, schemata also influence which details are selected for attention or produced through enactment. Thus, the schemata and the situational details *coevolve,* in an ongoing, never-finished process.

Vickers identifies two types of schemata—"value systems" and "reality systems." Value systems express our "concerns" as human beings; reality systems express our "organized readiness" to recognize patterns or to form expectations. Misfits or mismatches result from a comparison of the two types of schemata, and changes in the schemata are driven by the attempt to resolve the mismatches. Vickers draws on the insight of Christopher Alexander (1967) in arguing that the "fit" between form and context is recognized only in the negative, by the absence of specific misfits. (This is another argument for the tacit nature of schemata.) Even though the form and context cannot be fully described, we can move toward a perfect fit by attending to and working to eliminate the sources of mismatch.

Triggers Versus Templates. Here Vickers seems to differ strongly with Smith's view of misfits or imperfections. Whereas Smith, as we have seen, treats local imperfections as the nuances of a future pattern to be propagated from within the old structure, Vickers seems to want to extinguish the imperfection, with the aim of fitting the form ever closer to its context. This would be an accurate characterization of Vickers' position only if the context were given and fixed, only if the situations in which the schemata operate were not themselves subject to redefinition. However, as we have seen, Vickers does treat schemata and situation as coevolving. Nevertheless, Vickers, more than Smith, sees mismatches or imperfections only as mere *triggers* of change, not as *templates* for change. Vickers does not seem to treat misfits themselves as carriers of new patterns, as new forms writ small awaiting an unfolding process of realization from within existing order. The primary mechanisms of change in tacit schemata are due instead to external changes in the embedding context or to "collision with rival appreciative systems" (Vickers, 1978, pp. 159-160). Nevertheless, Vickers does admit the possibility that "such systems [of tacit norms] also contain within themselves the seeds of their own reversals. Each is a work of art, however unconscious, and, like all works of art, attains form only by a process of selection which excludes possible alternative forms. These in time clamor for realization. They are kept alive in the meantime in those individuals and subcultures that are least satisfied by the accepted systems; and they grow at the expense of the accepted system as soon as the system ceases to command the confidence and authority of its heyday" (p. 159).

Vickers' "seeds of reversal" seem to play the same role of internal structural change as Smith's local nuances, but they do not appear to result from a mismatch between value and reality schemata. The latter yields an adaptation process of a different (lower) order, one that is directed at perfecting a particular form/context fit.

The distinction between imperfection as trigger for change and imperfection as template of change is crucial. Each can play a role in the union of rationality and intuition. In his analysis of tacit schemata, Vickers has drawn our attention to the role of misfits as triggers. But Smith's imperfections as templates also represent tacit, implicit patterns not yet fully realized.

Encounter and Performance. Two final concepts need to be developed in our model of union, those of "encounter" and "performance." The central point here is that rationality and intuition, detailing and patterning, are joined not in the abstract but only in the actors' encounter with the world, only in the midst of performing or giving full expression to a particular interpretation and embodiment of a text. That expression, for maximum effectiveness, must combine both universal and unique aspects. Here I shall rely heavily on Rollo May's (1976) treatment of the creative process and Iredell Jenkins' (1970) analysis of performance.

May's views on creativity are relevant to our inquiry because of the central place he gives to the concept of union—a union of the subjective and objective, a union of Dionysian passion and vitality with Apollonian form and order. The Greeks gave to such union the technical term *ecstasy,* deriving from *ex-stasis,* literally "to stand out from," to transcend the subjective/objective split. Ecstasy "is not to be thought of merely as a Bacchic 'letting go'; it involves the total person, with the subconscious and unconscious acting in unity with the conscious. It is not, thus, *irrational*; it is, rather, suprarational. It brings intellectual, volitional, and emotional functions into play altogether" (May, 1976, p. 49).

May's central point is that ecstasy, or ex-stasis, results from the *encounter* of the subjective pole of the artist's imagination with the objective pole of the external, chaotic world.

Creative acts do not result from the unidirectional subjective projection onto the artistic work. Nor does creativity result from the artist's *passive* receptivity to the objective world. Instead, creative acts flow from intense, active, sometimes anxiety-filled encounters with particular instances, until meaning can be given to and forced on the silence of the world. New images, visions, forms do not spring full-blown from our imagination; we must stage intense encounters with the *limits* of the objective world, and it is from overcoming the dialectical tension between possibilities and limitations that new creative insights emerge.

The offspring of creative encounters are typically symbols and myths. May (p. 153) points out that the root meaning of *symbolic* is "to draw together" (*sym-ballein*), in contrast to *diabolic*, "pulling apart" (*dia-ballein*), thus expressing the importance of symbolism in creating and reflecting the union of rationality and intuition that we seek. The artist's encounter with his or her world heightens "the hopeless discrepancy between conception and realization" (Lord, 1965, p. 24), but symbols draw together the resulting diabolic tensions.

Although May draws primarily from artistic creativity for his theory of encounter, he goes on to argue that the passion for form and creativity are "involved in our every experience as we try to make meaning in our self-world relationship" (p. 161). Thus, May's analysis reinforces the emphasis I have placed on the necessity of "lived experience" as the vehicle or crucible within which a union of rationality and intuition takes place. There can be no union without an encounter of the subjective with the objective.

A persistent theme of my analysis has been that rational and intuitive aspects of a situation can be joined only in the actual expression or enactment of ideas and interpretations. Even though tacit judgments of an esthetic character play a necessary part in the achievement of coherence and meaning, those esthetic values can be fully grasped only through what Jenkins (1970) has termed a "performance." Tacit schemata may not be capable of a literal, rational articulation in the language of, say, mathematics, accounting, or other logical structures, but this does not mean they cannot be publicly expressed—for example, through a tangible presentation using some other grammar of action. Just as the artist (or person) requires an *encounter* with the object of his attention in order to achieve a creative insight, he also requires a *performance* of that insight in order to fully express it (and test it) to himself with others. And that performance involves further interpretation, which grows and changes in the course of performance.

But what is it that is "performed?" Jenkins (p. 204) argues that it is a "text"—a script for the actor/director, a score for the musician/conductor, a body of knowledge for the teacher, a strategic plan for the executive, an architectural design for the builder.

In Jenkins' view, a coherent performance of a text requires two processes, or phases, that gradually merge and cumulate into a "full expression" that is meaningful to an audience: (1) an "apprehension" of the text that results from a faithful study of its universal interpretations, plus the performer's own unique interpretations, and (2) the "embodiment" of those interpretations, using in part elements from the currently accepted "artistic cosmos" and in part the performer's own peculiar techniques of embodiment or presentation.

Apprehension and embodiment each require both universal and unique interpretations. Achieving the right mix of universal and unique is essential to a successful performance. Just as Vickers argues that it is easier to describe a form/context mismatch than a match, Jenkins argues that a successful performance can be recognized but is not as easily describable as the *failures* of performance. We can detect when a textual apprehension is too "wooden" (too faithful to standard interpretations) or too idiosyncratic (too heavily loaded with personalistic interpretations). The same can be said for the techniques of embodiment.

Performance is thus seen as making public and explicit a fusion or union of the convergent and divergent elements of the apprehension and embodiment of the given text. Thus does the text become meaningful not only in the lived experience of the actors but also in the lived experience of an audience.

Through "performance" the subjective is made objective,

just as through "encounter" the objective is made subjective. Performance and encounter are thus conjugate aspects of the same unitary process by which a union of intuition and rationality is achieved. Meaning is wrested from the world and given back to it.

Summary. Let us attempt to summarize our model. The proposed union of rationality and intuition is a process, not an abstract state of mind. It is a process set in the world in the midst of concrete action and carried out by persons with concerns. It is an interactive process in which the rational and the intuitive are equal partners, each providing the context within which the other can operate; neither makes sense alone. It is an incremental process in which action inches along, guided by alternate rational and intuitive steps. It is a process feeding off imperfection and even seeking it, recognizing in local nuances and anomalies the triggers and templates of new forms. It is a process tolerant of tacit criteria of judgment, capable of forming such tacit interpretations and yet able to give them public expression in performance.

The proposed model is my attempt at integrating the best of what some others have said about the possibility of the union of rationality and intuition in human endeavor. Whether it is an effective means of union cannot be completely determined on strictly logical grounds. If we take the model seriously, we will realize that the model itself is an intuition that arose from the processes described by it. It poses a question (How best to join rationality and intuition?) and provides the outlines of a tentative answer. The model tells us to engage in an incremental process of refinement. We need to turn now to the appreciative process—judging the model by explicit and tacit criteria in the world. One way to do this is to look at Quinn's analysis of strategic change.

Quinn's Model of Logical Incrementalism

The purpose of this section is to describe in more detail Quinn's (1982) model of "logical incrementalism," a description of the way strategic decisions are made. The next section will examine the degree of congruence between the level of primary processes wherein rational and intuitive mechanisms are joined and the level of secondary processes, of managerial actions described by Quinn. Quinn makes no attempt to ground his observations of strategic change in theoretical statements about psychological functioning or about systems change in general. Rather, they arise out of a series of case studies of major corporations. Nevertheless, as we shall see, there are striking similarities between the two levels of analysis, which should permit us to enrich our description of both levels by transporting ideas from each level to the other.

Recognizing Anomalies. The key idea in Quinn's model is that strategic change is the result of an "unfolding rationality" (my term, not his). A new strategic vision for the firm emerges incrementally, with its origins "vaguely felt" and perceived as "anomalies" within the firm's current operating assumptions, hardly distinguishable from background noise. These anomalies are not only noticed, they are *talked* about; they are given a linguistic representation—the executive invents words and phrases in an attempt to lift out these weak signals from the background noise, using such ill-defined phrases as *product proliferation* or *organizational overlap*. This process of naming anomalies, however vaguely, makes the anomaly socially discussable and thus permits the executive to create for other members an awareness of potentially important new trends or changes in the firm's environment. Thus named, the anomaly serves as the seed of some new vision or strategy for the firm. It permits the firm to continue to operate within the old strategy while creating symbols of what might become the new strategy. The new exists within the old without discrediting the old.

Such a naming process constitutes an incremental approach to change, but one that, Quinn argues, is conscious and proactive on the part of the executive. By articulating his intuition, by putting it into words, the executive is acting rationally "in the small." By contrast, by rationality "in the large," I mean acting logically within some comprehensive, fully developed model of the world with explicit assumptions, constraints, and objectives. Rationality "in the small" means making partial use of left-brained, analytical mechanisms, such as the act of giving names to features of the environment not heretofore named. The incremental but deliberate process of naming isolated anomalies (note that *anomaly* literally means "not named") is one of several incremental steps that together constitute Quinn's model of "logical incrementalism."

Amplifying Changes Locally. Once the anomaly has been identified and named, it can be "amplified"—that is, clarified, elaborated, and enlarged—toward the ultimate end of becoming a full-blown new pattern, structure, or strategy for the firm. And the amplification process can be set in motion even while the anomaly is still poorly understood: "Even when executives do not have in mind specific solutions to emerging problems, they can still proactively guide actions in intuitively desired directions—by defining what issues staffs should investigate, by selecting principal investigators, and by controlling the reporting process" (Quinn, 1982, pp. 190–191).

Indeed, the amplification process serves to increase understanding and to test whether the anomaly is real and to be taken seriously. By thus acting provisionally, the executive preserves his or her option of backing off, of deciding that the anomaly is not the template of some future strategy. Quinn observes that this amplification process takes place "locally" within a subset of trusted colleagues and with minimum public exposure. The anomaly, if it is to grow at all, grows within its own neighborhood. The new initiative is thus subjected to critical judgment, but a *limited* critical judgment. Characterizing the initiative too precisely too early in the process would bring the full force of comprehensive critical judgment of the entire old strategy to bear and would minimize the chances of change. Thus, it can be seen that vagueness and ambiguity of early articulation are *essential* to short-run survival of the new idea. Ambiguity is not merely an artifact of limited understanding; it is a *necessity* of fundamental change.

To the extent that articulation (that is, rendering vague intuitions in verbal and other explicit representations) can be thought of as a "rational" or "analytical" process, then Quinn's research suggests that the effective way to join rationality and intuition is to use a local rationality rather than a global or comprehensive rationality. This leads us to think of rationality as a direction of movement—*incrementally* more detail, *incrementally* more explicitness, *incrementally* broader exposure and support, *incrementally* more formal justification. Quinn might just as well have termed his model "incremental rationality" rather than "logical incrementalism."

So far I have suggested that a new strategic synthesis emerges from a *single* anomaly. In fact, Quinn observes that "partial solutions" are developed simultaneously for apparently unconnected anomalies. Then, "as events unfurl, solutions to several interrelated problems might well flow together in a not-yet-perceived synthesis" (p. 192). (This insight about multiple partial solutions is consistent with Smith's, 1978, theory of local nuances that gradually cumulate into a new pattern, but more of that later.)

A Partial Summary. Let us recapitulate Quinn's model so far. Problems are vaguely felt and named, and through a variety of mechanisms, partial solutions are locally implanted and amplified. By maintaining ambiguity and by not taking personal ownership of the solutions, the executive prevents premature closure for or against the solutions or even the problem definition. The solution or solutions are seen only as local, tactical responses to problems within the firm's existing strategy. In the process of discussing the proposed solutions, the quality of the analysis is improved, and political support for problem definition and solutions is broadened. The executive thus keeps his or her options open for redefinition and reinterpretation of events until he or she has been able to build a consensus around the partial solutions, thus avoiding the trap of providing a focus for otherwise fragmented opposition to the initiatives.

Solidifying Progress. Once a set of partial solutions has been "amplified," refinements made, and coalitions built around the solutions, then, but only then, is it propitious to begin crystallizing the issue by stating goals in more concrete, less ambiguous terms. Partial solutions have probably been implemented, thus providing feedback data on their functioning in actual practice. From these data, the firm can begin to identify "central themes" that will serve as the basis for subsequent evaluation and control. Thus is progress solidified as the firm moves gradually toward a new strategic synthesis.

Systematic Waiting. In his analysis of strategic change, Quinn stresses the importance of time and timing. The types of fundamental changes he observed took place typically over many months, in some cases many years. By simply waiting for the members of a firm to digest and internalize a new interpretation of events, opposition would frequently dissipate; people would become used to the idea. Typically, chief executives would not attempt to carry a strategic change themselves but would wait for the (often unpredictable) appearance of a "champion" of some particular partial solution. "Systematic waiting" for key events that facilitate some next step in the process is crucial to the timing and pacing of the change. The executive needs to wait patiently and to sense accurately when the next step of solidifying progress is feasible.

Symbolic Acts. I have drawn attention to the importance Quinn has given to verbalizing problems, solutions, goals, and themes. But he also stresses the symbolic value of certain non-verbal acts. By appointing a certain committee or reallocating funds in a certain way, the executive can demonstrate his or her seriousness about a given course of action. For example, at the University of Illinois much talk has ensued over the last year or so about the necessity of budgetary caution, but only with the vice-chancellor's recent announcement of the allocation of 2.5 percent budget cuts has the campus community truly come to take that cautionary talk seriously. The timing of such symbolic acts serves to signal the end of the preliminary phase of strategic change and the beginning of solidification of a new synthesis.

Interaction of Planning and Implementation. Finally, Quinn cautions that "many executives and their companies generally have fallen into the trap of thinking about strategic formulation and implementation as separate, sequential processes" (p. 203). His entire analysis explicitly rejects the notion that a strategic vision is created through some intuitive process and then rationally implemented. Instead, the new strategy emerges

in the midst of and out of the gradual implementation of implicit elements of the strategy. Partial implementation provides
new and better information that shapes and reshapes the strategic interpretation as it emerges.

Quinn's Model as a Rational/Intuitive Union?

Let us ask now how much of our model of the union of
rationality and intuition is reflected in Quinn's description of
logical incrementalism. The interactive and incremental features
of our model of union are certainly present in Quinn's process.
This is so obvious as not to need further comment. Both tacit
and explicit elements are also present. Potential problems are
"vaguely felt," symbolic gestures are used to communicate in-
tent, goals and themes are left implicit early in the process, and
the locus of certain decisions is ambiguous and unspecified. At
the same time, details of partial solutions are worked out explicitly through what Quinn calls "formal analytical techniques,"
and eventually goals, themes, and a new synthesis are given explicit verbal statement (but as the *outcome* of the process, not
as its origin).

Emergent Patterns. Smith's notion of "cumulative nuance"
fits almost perfectly with Quinn's idea of "partial solutions."
Just as some (but not all) of Smith's local nuances or imperfections serve as templates for newly emerging patterns, some (but
not all) of Quinn's partial solutions are the seeds of new strategic syntheses that emerge from within the old strategy. There is
a slight, but tantalizing, difference in their treatments. Smith
seems to suggest that a new pattern emerges from the unfolding
of a single anomaly, whereas Quinn introduces the idea of *multiple* partial solutions, each of which may be amplified but
which together form the key elements of a synthesis through
some type of integration.

Performance, Encounter, and Lived Experience. Jenkins'
notion that a "text" is given full expression through a "performance" that embodies both universal and idiosyncratic elements does not seem to match well with Quinn's description. In
Quinn's view, there is no text to begin with; the text develops

over time, unless one is willing to stretch a point and argue that the firm's environment is the "text" that is interpreted and performed. Nevertheless, the concept of "performance" carries over inasmuch as Quinn argues that strategies are acted out, that plans and their interpretation come to be joined only in the process of implementation. In Quinn's view, one prepares for performance in the midst of performing. Rehearsal (or dress rehearsal) or improvisational theater might be a better metaphor for logical incrementalism.

May's concept of "encounter" fits Quinn a bit better. The executive's and the organization's subjective encounter with the objective environment does seem to Quinn to be the source of new strategies for the firm; new strategies do *not* spring forth as a projection of the effective executive's mind, decoupled from his or her world, onto the world. (This may seem an obvious point, but consider the executive Roy Ash's abortive attempt to impose his own personal vision on the Addressograph-Multigraph Corporation. Would he have been more successful if he had steeped himself more deeply in the history of that company and industry before taking action?) However, Quinn does not incorporate in his model the kind of heightened anxiety and awareness that May says accompanies ecstasy in the creative process. Indeed, emotion of any kind, even mere excitement or enthusiasm or ambivalence or nervousness, is absent from Quinn's treatment of strategic change. One reason may be the gradualist, low-profile approach Quinn takes toward conflict resolution or avoidance. At least for humor, and perhaps for other emotional situations as well, a strong emotional response results from a surprising and rapid change of conflicting frames. But Quinn's incrementalist approach is designed precisely to minimize surprise, so it is not unexpected that emotion should be absent from his analysis.

The important role that May gives to symbolism is reflected in Quinn's model, but Quinn sees symbols as primarily signaling devices, whereas May sees them as means by which divergent views can be integrated or drawn together.

The concept of "lived experience" from our model of union is also present in Quinn's treatment, to a limited extent.

He argues that "the real integration of all the components in an enterprise's total strategy eventually takes place only in the minds of high-level executives" (p. 200). Why only "high-level executives"? We would have thought that the painstaking process of gradually building an experience-based consensus around the new strategy had as its aim precisely making it part of the "lived experience" of the organization's members. Indeed, Quinn does say that "much of the impelling force behind logical incrementalism comes from a desire to tap the talents and psychological drives of the whole organization, to create cohesion, and to generate identity with the emerging strategy" (p. 199). Whatever the relationship of "high-level executives" to the rank and file, logical incrementalism as a change process does attempt to ground strategy in firsthand experience.

Major Differences. One key element of our model of union that may be missing from Quinn's model of strategy change is Vickers' notion of concern, depending on how one defines *concern.* Concern, recall from Vickers, is expressed through a person's or organization's value system. Mismatches between that value system and the reality system drive the process of adaptation. Perhaps I am interpreting "concerns" and "values" to be too closely related to basic human values and moral judgments of "good" and "right." If so, then Quinn pays little or no attention to such values. But he does give instrumental "goals" a central place in his description. Furthermore, Quinn's examples of anomalies or mismatches, such as "excessive concentration on one market or one product" suggest that there is, for example, some ideal or valued level of market or product concentration that constitutes part of a value schema. To the extent that these instrumental ideals can be interpreted as "concern," then logical incrementalism embodies this aspect, too, of a union of rational and intuitive processes. But we have had to stretch the point to make it fit.

One prominent aspect of Quinn's model that is not explicitly present in our analysis of the rational/intuitive union is coalition building and consensus formation. Quinn draws the distinction between "formal-analytical techniques," for elaborating particular solutions, and "power-behavioral aspects," through which a social consensus is constructed around the new strategy. Indeed, one of the very appealing features of logical incrementalism is that a coalition to support a new strategy is constructed in the same time frame in which the new strategy evolves; the supporting coalition develops together with the new strategy. Our source materials for the union of rationality and intuition reflect an individual psychology rather than a social psychology. But Quinn's analysis suggests that we need to re-think the rational/intuitive union as more of a social process, while still preserving the individual-level aspects that have been identified.

Conclusion

In recent years the organizational research literature has tended to reject rationality as a concept in favor of random en-actment, garbage-can models, symbolism, and qualitative meth-ods. Some, myself included, have argued that we should treat managers as poets, storytellers, and mythmakers who interpret the past but who do not or need not organize the present or di-rect the future. These efforts were a reaction to previous, nar-rowly rational models and have been largely successful in open-ing the field to a broader range of theories and methods of inquiry. But such approaches are as incomplete in their own ways as the prior rational approaches were. In this chapter I have argued that it is time to begin asking whether we should attempt an integration of rational and intuitive approaches to organization.

One other recent attempt to reconcile these competing models is Van de Ven's (1982) paper addressing the conflict be-tween rational and random models of administrative behavior. Van de Ven proposes as a third alternative a theory of "reason-able" behavior grounded in the institutional economics of John R. Commons. His analysis shares many of the features of my own, including use of concepts such as performance, "hu-man will in action," timing, and the institutional setting in which behavior takes place. Van de Ven concludes that all three models—rational, random, and reasonable—"should be combined to obtain a more accurate description" of administrative behavior.

I share Van de Ven's basic aim, that divergent models should be integrated, but have taken a somewhat different approach in this chapter.

I have argued, first, that we need to examine how to combine rational and intuitive approaches at the level of primary human processes. On the basis of this inquiry I suggest that a union of rationality and intuition must (1) be incremental over time, taking place through action and performance in the first-hand experience of the actors, (2) incorporate both explicit, concrete details and tacit schemata, (3) feed off and emerge from the misfits, imperfections, and local nuances within an otherwise ordered structure, and (4) result from the actor's subjective encounter with his or her external world. To be exclusively rational is to mediate all one's perceptions and actions through a previously articulated frame of reference; to be exclusively intuitive is to relate to the world without the mediation of such a frame; to join rationality and intuition is to create meaningful frames of reference in the midst of action, over time, out of one's own lived experience. The union of these two distinctive modes of being is needed most when the situation is most chaotic, when old interpretive frames are clearly inadequate and new frames, new structures of meaningful action, are not yet apparent.

I have argued, second, that the primary processes of union can be translated into secondary processes at the organizational level. In particular, I have argued that Quinn's (1982) model of "logical incrementalism" represents a first approximation to implementing the rational/intuitive executive mind within a workable institutional structure. If Quinn's model for managing ambiguous change works at all, I have argued, it works because it embodies the principles of union in an organizational context. It provides a structure within which formal/analytical techniques can interact with power/behavioral processes to produce coherent social action that fits the organization's environment. The match between a rational/intuitive union and Quinn's model of strategic change is not perfect, as I have shown, but it is not a bad approximation.

Obviously more work needs to be done at both levels. Models for managing ambiguity need to be refined so as to incorporate with more fidelity the features of a rational/intuitive union. And the model of union needs to be developed more fully. If we take the incremental aspect of union seriously, then this chapter itself should be seen as merely one step along the path toward reaping the best of both worlds, toward improving managerial action by combining the power of both rationality and intuition through their union.

8

Patterns of Individual and Organizational Learning

Frank Friedlander

When I reflect on my life, I see myself as having gone through sequences of construction, of consolidation, of gradual frustration, and then of upheaval. The upheaval seems in retrospect like a decision toward a basic radical change in my life—leaving the work force to further my education, a divorce, a change in my life-style, leaving a long-held job, changing careers. My experience of organizations is that they go through similar patterns—of building, of consolidating, of increasing frustration, and of radical departure. The departures are into new norms, products, policies, objectives. In these two examples I am not promoting a cyclical theory of growth; I am trying to focus on the basic learning processes that underlie and lead to new paradigms for individuals and organizations. What is the learning (and nonlearning) process? How is knowledge created at these two levels and used by the organism so that it learns? What are the conditions that facilitate and hinder learning?

The main body of this chapter represents the development of several concepts that are key to organizational and individual learning systems. The concepts have been developed inductively (Glaser and Strauss, 1967) and include the following: differences, contact, power balances, conflict, and valuing among subsystems within the total learning system; frustration, defensiveness, continuity, self-confrontation, identity crisis, and reconstruction/integration in the total system. The chapter closes with an effort to link these concepts together to form a framework or theory of system learning.

I will use the term "learning *organism*" in this chapter to include specifically individual and organizational learning. I want to connote through the term *organism* the living, struggling, vibrant character of organic learning. I believe that what I have to say applies equally well to other levels—group and cultural learning—but I will refer to these only occasionally.

This chapter is concerned solely with in-depth learning, or what I shall call "reconstructive learning." In reconstructive learning the organism questions its premises, purposes, values. For individuals these are represented in one's goals, principles, life-style, beliefs. For the organization they are represented by its goals, policies, and norms. Thus, I am not concerned with simpler levels of learning, such as conditioning, in which the goal is to establish repertoires of responses or attitudes. Nor am I concerned with single-loop learning (Argyris and Schön, 1978), in which an organism corrects an error-producing behavior. And finally, I am not concerned with additive learning, in which an organism acquires a new skill that is a refinement of or an advancement on the old. Reconstructive learning calls for in-depth confrontation of old patterns and the development of radically different ones. It suggests the construction of new goals, policies, norms, styles rather than simple modification of the old.

The lifeblood of an organism (an individual, an organization) is its ability to learn. It must optimize its capacity to use and respond to knowledge both within its boundaries and from its external environment. According to the latest Club of Rome report (Botkin, Elmandjra, and Malitza, 1979, p. 6), "Learning and the individual human being—not material resources—are the key to the world's future. . . . The 1980s must become a 'decade of learning' to break the vicious circle of increasing complexity and lagging human understanding."

Learning is the process through which an organism senses and utilizes bits and pieces of knowledge from its external environment and from within its own boundaries so as to make major changes in itself. Changing one's self is not magic—it is simply that significant learning has preceded the change. I believe that any profession concerned with change and development (for example, individual and organization development) must first be concerned with learning. Learning is the process that underlies and gives birth to change. Change is the child of learning.

Change resulting from learning need not be visibly behavioral. Learning may result in new and significant insights and awareness that dictate no behavioral change. In this sense the crucial element in learning is that the organism be consciously aware of differences and alternatives and have consciously chosen one of these alternatives. The choice may be not to reconstruct behavior but, rather, to change one's cognitive maps or understandings. Learning is the process; change is the outcome.

There are many outcomes of learning, one of which is behavioral change. There are many causes of change, one of which is reconstructive learning. Outcomes from learning might be cognitive insight or emotional awareness, at the individual level, or normative and political awareness, at the organizational level. But awareness may result in a choice not to change behavior, structure, policy. Similarly, there are many causes of change other than learning. These include coercion and directed change at the individual level, and mandated policy change and environmental turbulence (for example, from competition or government) at the organizational level.

The need for an organism to learn occurs in response to changes in its internal and external conditions and a sense of frustration, wanting more, or failure in responding adequately to these changes. Learning how it learns may be the first step in adapting its learning process to changing environments or changing internal states. The ability to learn and perform is clearly a major component of adaptability (Terreberry, 1968), and to have this ability, organizations must develop a search-and-learn process as well as a decision process (Thompson, 1967).

I am aware of my value bias (and that of my field of organizational behavior), which sanctifies growth and learning. But I also am aware that there have been long periods in my own life when no apparent basic learning occurred. These are periods of building and consolidating and producing. The chaos of learning is frequently incompatible with being productive, at both the individual and organizational levels. There are times to learn, and there are times to produce. I look back on my days as a university student as a time of productivity more than learning. The goal of obtaining a degree and the path toward obtaining it were clear.

In spite of the abundance of literature describing the turbulent environment in which organizations must operate (Trist, 1969), I doubt that many organization theorists are aware of the repercussions of this same turbulence on individuals. The continual and overpowering interaction of components in our personal environments leads to massive uncertainty, ambiguity, unpredictability—and a vast need for continual on-line learning at the personal level.

Conger (1981), for example, has commented on the variety of interacting factors that have given rise to the modern nuclear family. These include increasingly depersonalized relations between the family and other social institutions, greater age segregation, less economic interdependence of family members, smaller families, greater rigidity in the timing of transitions from one life stage to another, and increased differentiation of the roles and functions of individual family members. Many of these factors, in turn, stem from cultural and technological changes: the invention of television and the speed with which it permits social changes to occur; birth control and the modernization of the kitchen, both of which released women from traditional task roles; the changing male ethic of devotion to career; and so on.

Differences as Initial Grounds for Learning

For an organism to learn, it must be sufficiently heterogeneous to contain differences. These are differences in perceptions, values, preferences, time orientation, plans, expectations,
goals, and so on. They may be differences within the organism
or differences between the organism and its environment. Many
learning theories posit that learning arises from internal differences and conflict. Learning begins with an incident in which
we become aware of something that is inconsistent with or in
contradiction to a current idea. Learning comes from or is motivated by resolving this contradiction. Piaget (Furth, 1969), for
example, found that learning occurs through two related functions: accommodation, the change in an area structure to accommodate new data and experiences not meaningful under an
old structure; and assimilation, the interpretation of environmental data and experiences within the person's existing idea
structure. Learning is optimized when these two functions are
balanced. But this balance is only temporary, for the new idea
structure results in an awareness of new inconsistencies, which
result in new accommodation and assimilation.

The balance process is a way to recognize each developmental stage. It is the process by which inconsistencies are resolved and result in a higher developmental state. Thus, learning depends on the successful incorporation of a new set of
dimensions for understanding the organism's environment, and
the resolution makes salient some new dimensions heretofore
unnoticed.

A similar framework is suggested by Kohlberg (1969),
who is concerned with moral development. Kohlberg claims
that each succeeding developmental stage is motivated by the
timely occurrence of a situation that, in the person's current
stage of development, presents a moral dilemma—it cannot be
handled by the moral framework of that stage.

Silverman (1971) has developed a model of organizational learning along similar lines. In this model people construct
different pictures of their organization depending on the particular functional units they work in. These different pictures of

the organization then create different constructions of the organization's external environment—and various units of the organization begin to respond to the environment in contradictory ways. The internal stress due to contradictions among various pictures of the organization is essential to organizational learning. Opposing pictures lead to conflicting demands made on the organization. Learning can occur only if a restructuring occurs that takes into account these opposing pictures and the values on which they are based. These same phenomena occur at the group level. Maier (1970) has found that differences as expressed through group controversy improve decision making. Groups composed of different kinds of people and groups whose leaders encourage minority opinions make higher-quality decisions.

We see in these theoretical perspectives not only the crucial ingredient that differences form in learning but also two other concurrent phenomena: One is contact between two conflicting ideas, values, or structures, and a second is tension resulting from this contact, which remains until a new synthesis or reality is constructed. I will return to the concepts of contact, tension, and conflict.

The roots of organizational learning lie in differences in representative units within the organization (for example, production versus marketing) or between the organization and its environment (for example, the organization versus government, competitors, clients, unions). It is structural differentiation that allows and encourages the different perceptions and values so essential to existing in an uncertain and changing environment. Differentiation not only allows the organization to maintain and foster contact with differentiated components of the environment, and not only allows these components to maintain the differentiated styles and time orientations necessary for their separate functions (Lawrence and Lorsch, 1969), but also permits heterogeneity in the organization, thus encouraging differences and potential learning.

In this way structure permits or inhibits contact—the interface between differentiated components of a system. It is this function of organizational structure that permits organizational learning to occur.

Similarly, the structure of an individual allows differentiated components to come into contact with each other and result in potential learning. One of the basic themes in Gestalt therapy is to bring into contact with each other clearly differentiated parts of the self (Perls, Hefferline, and Goodman, 1951). Confluence, or the blurring of poorly differentiated components of the individual, inhibits learning by downplaying differences. Gestalt therapy focuses on boundary definitions, dialogue across boundaries, and empowering downtrodden but stubborn parts of the self. Thus, intrapsychic differentiation precedes individual learning, which precedes individual change.

Similar instances occur at a societal level. As blacks differentiated themselves from Caucasians in the 1960s, clearer racial boundaries developed. This was obviously a cultural differentiation (the African heritage) as well as a racial one and resulted in empowerment ("black is beautiful"). The undifferentiated "Negro" now became the differentiated black. Only at this point could authentic contact occur at the black/white interface, leading to the beginnings of learning by the combined black/white system as a whole.

The women's movement has in similar ways permitted systems in which men and women live and work together to become potential learning systems. But only when women differentiated themselves from the undifferentiated flux of people and empowered themselves was authentic contact possible in our male/female culture.

It is interesting to note, in these two examples, that similarities and some degree of integration occurred (among women, among blacks) before differentiation occurred between each of these groups and the larger, less differentiated flux. Thus, integration may precede differentiation, which, in turn, may eventually allow integration at a higher level.

Differentiation also provides the energy for learning. A tenet of general systems theory is that heterogeneity produces energy whereas complete homogeneity leads to entropy. The lack of differences within an organization or an individual results in lowered energy for learning.

Contact, Interfaces, and Connections

Many living organisms, including human beings, are formed by the union of two particular cells, each of which is a whole in itself. Only in conjunction with another cell can a new organism be produced. The continued life of the organism depends on cells connecting. Within an organism, every cell communicates within itself and to all other cells. Furthermore, each cell is equipped with three basic kinds of information: its own special task, the master plan of the finished product, and the knowledge of how parts relate to fill out the whole.

Boundaries have two somewhat contrary purposes. One is to separate, contain, and define the organism; the other is to provide the contact surface for interface with other organisms.

A learning system is born when a link is created between two or more organisms or components. From that link a consciousness is born, and both parties are responsible for that system. We must manage, regulate, and care for that connection. The task is to help the components of that system move from the experience of linkage to awareness to expression of that awareness.

The learning system to which I refer may be an individual (with linkages and contact among the parts), a couple, a work group, an organization (with contact and linkages among its departments), or a system (composed of part of the organism and its environment).

Organizational learning derives from subunit experiences and perceptions and takes the form of sharing these among individuals and across relevant units of the organization. In this sense organizational learning occurs at the interfaces between persons, between organizational units, and between the organization and its external environment.

It is at the interconnection between persons and between organizational units that excitement, creativity, and feedback emerge. These are crucial ingredients of the learning process. It is in these connections that a simple knowledge system is actualized into a learning system.

Knowledge resides within and outside the organization in bits and pieces. When put together in various configurations, these then become a knowledge system. A knowledge system may be a loose network of individuals either totally within the organization or spanning its boundaries, such as temporary task teams, a matrix network, or part of the formal organizational structure. But a knowledge system is not necessarily an effective learning system. All the right parts are there with the appropriate knowledge. But the process of the interchange across the subunit boundaries has not yet occurred. A learning system, in contrast, is a structure composed of resources (knowledge, skills, perspectives) relevant to a particular issue and connected in ways that can optimize these resources in exploring and solving the issue.

Power Differences

Power differences hinder system learning when subordinate components suppress or deny their own resources and expertise, when superior components impose theirs, or when either party distances itself from the other (for example, in order to protect itself). When resources and expertise are suppressed, the raw material for learning—the necessary differences and heterogeneity—is lost. When parties distance themselves from each other, contact is lost. Thus, power imbalances diminish heterogeneity and contact and thereby diminish system learning.

In case studies of the effectiveness of organizational task forces and core groups, continual contact between the task force and the dominant coalition was essential to learning among both (Friedlander and Schott, 1981). The task forces in these studies were study groups that had explored organizational issues and were recommending innovative departures from current policy and process. The dominant coalitions were those at the top of the hierarchy who had politically vested interests in maintaining the status quo. More successful task forces were those that maintained continual interchange with the dominant coalition rather than working separately from it and then presenting study results. The combination of sporadic contact and disproportionate power between the two groups frequently prevented the system from learning.

Power imbalances occur within an individual when one part of the person overpowers another part in a coercive or oppressive way. Each of us is a never-ending sequence of polarities. Whenever we recognize one aspect of ourselves, the presence of its antithesis, its polar quality, is implicit. The polar quality rests as background, giving dimension to present experience and yet powerful enough to emerge as figure in its own right if it gathers enough force (Polster and Polster, 1973).

For the whole system of the person to learn, mutual empowerment must occur between polarized parts. The best-known example of Gestalt polarities is the top-dog/underdog split (Perls, 1970), in which the struggle is between master and slave. The master commands, directs, and scolds, and the slave fights back with passivity or stupidity, with ineptness or pretense of trying unsuccessfully to do the master's bidding.

Many of these phenomena occur in organizations where bosses implicitly seek conformity to their already-established views from subordinates. The latter learn to suppress their deviant views and ideas, and learning for the larger boss/subordinate system is thwarted. Where a manager acts autocratically or suppresses alternative ideas and suggestions from subordinates, potential differences between the manager and subordinates do not occur. Managers who are expected to control their subordinates tend not to understand a subordinate's views or incorporate them into their decisions when the subordinate is different. When the subordinate wants control, control-oriented managers understand the opposing opinion but tend not to use it in their decision. This also occurs where a particular department is less powerful than others, making it difficult for the rest of the organization to learn from it. In both cases it is the larger system that suffers from lack of learning—in the first case the department, in the second case the organization.

Our current research paradigm, in which researchers and subjects represent highly unbalanced power roles, inhibits learning. Researchers define and control the situation, roles, and activities of both themselves and subjects. They then attempt to learn something from this and impart it to their respective community of scholars. There is evidence that the role and activity constraints imposed by the researcher clearly truncate and constrain potential learning and may even warp it (Friedlander, 1968, 1970). The learning system of scholarly research suffers from the unbalanced power relationship inherent in our current research paradigm.

Finally, at a more pervasive institutional level, families in most cultures have well-defined power differentials among their members. Most of us are brought up in families in which one or both parents exert clearly unbalanced power over children. To the extent that this occurs, family structures inhibit learning for the family as a system. Perhaps to compensate, we then send our children off to school for learning—an institution in which the power of the teacher is supreme. It is worth noting that in all these examples it is the total system in which oppressor and oppressed operate that sacrifices its learning.

Contact and Structure Across Time

A very different source of learning is possible when an organism makes contact with who or what it was in the past. Differences, contact, balanced power are again crucial ingredients in creating a learning system that is not simply reminiscing, revisiting, or reunion.

At the individual level a learning structure occurs when a person returns to his or her home town, long-lost lover, or old workplace or spends time with family after a long lapse of time.

A learning system can occur within the individual in which the new or changed person confronts and is confronted by the past person. Differences in identity, values, attitudes, and perceptions arise, causing confusion and tension. The temptation is to empower one of the parts of self in this interaction—to bring only one into the foreground, causing loss of contact. We may put down the past self: "What a crazy family I was brought up in!" Or we may put down the contemporary self: "Things are not what they used to be." "Times have changed." "I could never get through college again."

Groups may also have this opportunity for learning. The high school or college reunion may prove to be an important learning structure for the group or individual. Reminiscing as well as appraising historical progress provides groundwork for the learning but is insufficient.

Organizational learning similarly requires that the organization make authentic contact with its past, neither overcoming it nor being overcome by it. Exploring the differences between its past and present identity and values can provide an integrated sense of its progress and course of action. This, in turn, can lead to recharting new paths for the organization, new goals, and new values.

In most theories of growth and development the seeds for the subsequent stage of development are planted in the prior stage. This holds for theories of individual growth (Erikson, 1950; Kohlberg, 1969), group development (Bennis and Shepard, 1956; Tuckman, 1965; Tuckman and Jensen, 1967), and organizational evolution (Greiner, 1972; Adizes, 1979). And in each theory the values, perceptions, and activities of the organism within a phase are relevant to the issues it faces during that phase. For example, Greiner (1972) holds that each evolutionary period is characterized by the dominant management style used to achieve growth during that period, which, in turn, creates a new set of management issues that must be solved before growth can continue.

Few of these theories, however, suggest that contact and confrontation with past stages may produce incremental learning for the organism. These are theories of development but not theories for development.

Tension, Conflict, and Negative Feedback

Authentic contact between system components that represent differences in values, beliefs, and perceptions quite naturally leads to tensions between these components and frequently to conflict. Earlier I discussed the central role that tension plays in Piaget's, Kohlberg's, and Silverman's theories of individual learning. In addition, Lewin (1951), whose concern was with both individuals and small groups, presented a model of

learning in which old, or frozen, patterns of behavior were un-
frozen through various influence processes. Primary among
these is the introduction into small groups of concerned individuals' ideas for new modes of behavior or beliefs. New approaches,
ideas, beliefs were then introduced (the unfreezing process) and
were established and reinforced (the refreezing process). The
unfreezing process, according to Lewin, implied a tension between present circumstances and an emergent felt need not
being addressed. Dalton (1970), applying this theme to organizational change, found that the unfreezing process began with
the organization's experiencing tension and the need for change.
Former social ties built around previous behavior patterns were
refrozen into new relationships that supported intended changes
in behavior and attitudes. Kolb and Fry (1975) suggest a more
recent approach to learning, emphasizing the personal experience of the learner. In this model the individual goes through a
four-stage cycle: (1) immersion in a concrete experience, (2)
observing and reflecting on the experience of this situation,
(3) forming concepts from this situation, and (4) testing the implications of these concepts in new situations through active experimentation. This testing obviously places the individual in a
new concrete experience, and the cycle begins anew. Major tensions exist in the polarities between concrete experience and
conceptualization and between reflection and experimentation.
Yet both polarities are essential to the learning process.

Conflict and tension in the learning process occur not
only among parts of the individual and between individuals but
between groups and between organizations as well. At each of
these levels it is the difference in values, perceptions, and beliefs
that results in each party's being confronted with its *own*
values, beliefs, perceptions. Neither party teaches the other. The
learning party sooner or later *allows* its own beliefs and values
to be questioned—and only then can potential alternative paths
be considered. The tension begins when the party begins this
allowance process, is most acute when no alternative seems apparent, lessens when two or more paths seem plausible, and re-
laxes when a decision is made on a single forward direction.
Energy from this learning process is then transmitted to taking
action steps in the new direction.

A variety of factors may precipitate self-confrontation and conflict. Predominant among these is negative feedback to the organism from another part of the system. Thus, negative feedback from one person to another may result in self-confrontation, as may negative feedback from one organizational department (for example, production) to another (marketing), from one organization (Environmental Protection Agency) to another (an oil refinery), or from a set of organizations (competitors) to a single organization.

The stress produced by negative performance feedback is an important condition for the organism to learn. Studies of decision making in governmental administration, international economic development, and research and engineering programs led Hirschman and Lindblom (1962) to conclude that organizational learning occurs in response to immediate problems, imbalances, and difficulties more than it does in response to deliberate planning. They argue that the intraorganizational conflicts and tensions created by these immediate problems serve a constructive function in stimulating search behaviors that lead to organizational learning. In a business-firm simulation, Cangelosi and Dill (1965) found that early decisions that produced negative outcomes for the firm were likely to be abandoned or quickly modified. They conclude: "Failure, we agree, leads to change. The consequences of success, we argue, are less clear" (p. 196). In another business-firm simulation, Miles and Randolph (1980) found that greater learning occurred in the organization that received negative performance feedback and consequently experienced greater intraorganizational conflict. The conflict generated by the organization's "poor" performance stimulated dialogue and encouraged members to experiment with their own theories of action, which eventually became the focus of organizational debate.

Whether negative feedback is intrapersonal, interpersonal, intergroup, or intraorganizational, learning may occur if the receiving party fully allows the negative concept to enter into its framework. In some instances the organism may be sufficiently frustrated or failing so that defending against the feedback is less likely. This occurs when a firm's market is evaporating because of competition or when new government regulations place severe limitations on the firm's raw materials, practice, or product. But when an expected promotion is denied to an employee or the nature of work is ungratifying or frustrating, such feedback may have less effect.

The task in resolving these conflicts and polarities is to aid each part(y) to live its fullest while making contact with its polar counterpart. This strategy reduces the chance that one part will stay mired in its own impotence, hanging onto the status quo. Instead, it is energized into making a vital statement of its own needs and wishes, asserting itself as a force that must be considered in a new union of forces (Polster and Polster, 1973). Although Polster and Polster are discussing polarities within the individual in a therapeutic milieu, the concepts apply to larger systems as well. The race riots of the 1960s and the subsequent conflicts between blacks and whites are, for many, resulting in not only a stronger sense of identity for each race but learning for the larger black/white system. Similarly, the feminist movement over the past twenty years and the ensuing conflicts between men and women have, for many, resulted in a new sense of identity for each sex and, one hopes, an improvement in contemporary and future relations between males and females. Finally, the frustration and eventual survival of both the auto industry and the United Auto Workers in this country have given rise to a new set of values and action by both parties, resulting in an unprecedented union/management contract and effort to work together.

Trust and Valuing

Whereas differences and ensuing conflict are essential ingredients of learning, trust and valuing between subsystems are conditions that permit differences to be accepted and integrated into a new formulation or learning. Without valuing, mutual respect, and care between subsystems, differences tend to result in digging in by these components, each to defend its current position. Trust and respect permit exploration of differences. Caring and affirmation allow the confronted subsystem to feel at least partial acceptance. Trust allows the more powerful subsystem to grant power to the less powerful and allows the less powerful to accept this power. In effect, subsystems cooperate in a struggle to have each influence the other with its unique knowledge.

Affirmation permits differences to result in learning at all systems levels. The more units within an organization value each other, the more each can learn from their differences. The more an individual's differing parts can value and trust one another (for example, the tough and tender parts), the more likely that these can be integrated into a new pattern that utilizes the merits of each. Similarly, individuals who value and accept their past are able to integrate who they are now with who they were in the past, without rejection of one or the other. The integration permits the present self to learn from the past self. Only if I value and accept my past experiences and identity can I permit these to confront my present.

Conflict does not, obviously, always result in learning. Nor is it always intended to do so. Thomas (1976) argues that each party's behavior in a conflict situation can be described along two basic dimensions: cooperation, or attempting to satisfy the other party's concerns, and assertiveness, or attempting to satisfy one's own concerns. Five conflict-handling modes are plotted along these two dimensions: Competition is assertive and uncooperative, collaboration is assertive and cooperative, avoiding is unassertive and uncooperative, accommodation is unassertive and cooperative, and compromise is intermediate in both assertiveness and cooperativeness. What Thomas and Kilmann term the collaborative mode is part of the learning process. It calls for an attempt to work with the other party to find some new solution that satisfies the concerns of both. The learning mode implies digging into an issue to identify the underlying concerns of the two individuals and to find an alternative that meets both sets of concerns. Learning between two persons might take the form of exploring a disagreement to learn from each other's insights, concluding to resolve some condition that would otherwise have them competing for resources, or confronting and trying to find a creative solution to an interpersonal problem.

Planning as Learning

Contact with self and self-confrontation can also occur
through a system planning its own future. One of the main purposes of planning is not only to reach into the future with a
higher degree of certainty but, perhaps of even greater importance, to compare an ideal future scenario with the likely future if the present path is continued. This comparison feeds
back and confronts the system's present beliefs and values and
helps it explore its current condition. Michael (1973) sees the
period between now and the end of the century as one of un-
learning and learning anew—one of discovering new norms, new
goals, and new modes of conduct. This is all aimed at making
present life more meaningful by starting now to create and attain desired futures. Much of what we will need to know in
order to reach the future, we will have to discover and learn as
we proceed. Planning is the mode in which we can learn what
we seek to become, how to seek to do so, and the validity of
our present.

I have personally found it difficult to give up my (false)
image of my future until I confront myself and accept my likely
future if I were to remain on my current path. Only through
this confrontation of the future have I been able to confront
my present condition. Du Pont in the early part of this century
was a highly successful gunpowder manufacturer. Through exploring its potential future, it was able to confront its narrow
product line and launch into a number of new products.

Thus, future envisioning enables us to confront the present. Contact between present and the envisioned future enables
learning and altered courses of action to occur.

Identity and Resistance to Learning

Although identity is the source of an organism's sanity,
its preservation is the enemy of learning. Identity is conceived
here as an organization of knowledge among the interdependent
parts of the organism. As conditions change, this organization
of knowledge must also change. Thus, adaptation calls for modi-

fication in identity. Yet identity modification is invariably threatening to the consistency and competence of the organism. The organism will consequently go to great lengths to fend off changes in its organization of knowledge. Learning is thereby inhibited.

A strong sense of self is crucial to the well-being of an organism. A sense of self provides the individual or organization with boundaries, conviction, purpose, values, beliefs, and a guide for action. Furthermore, a clear sense of self allows the person to know how to behave with others in order to receive confirmation and affirmation. Similarly, the image an organization presents to its publics and to its own employees provides it with a sense of mission, values, and boundaries—its guide to action. Corporations spend millions of dollars on public relations to portray particular images to their publics.

One of the major criteria of individual health (Jahoda, 1958) and organizational health (Bennis, 1966) is a clear sense of identity. In order for an organism to develop adaptability, it must know who it is and what it is to do; it must have some clearly defined identity. The issue of organizational identity can be understood in at least two ways: (1) the extent to which the organization's goals are comprehended and accepted by its members and (2) the extent to which the organization is perceived veridically by its members (Bennis, 1966).

But identities may also be tender and vulnerable, so that we build castles around them for purposes of defense and fortification. And sometimes it is difficult to distinguish the castle from what it protects—to separate the identity from its defenses. Defenses then become embedded in the very composition of identity. Harrison (1977) has aptly summarized their function as serving to keep us from becoming confused, upset, and rudderless every time something happens contrary to our hopes. Defenses protect our liking for ourselves and others when we and they fail to live up to our ideas: "Defenses give life as it is experienced more stability and continuity than could ever be justified by reference to the contingency and complexity of real events alone. Defenses keep our relations with others more pleasant and satisfying, protecting us from our own and others' anger, and helping us to go on loving people who are usually less than perfect and sometimes less than human" (Harrison, p. 82).

Defenses, then, are not to be torn from the fabric of the person or the organization but, rather, accepted as parts of its diversity—as one of the characteristics composing it. Yet these very defenses block the learning of the organization or person.

A strong sense of identity involves investment, commitment, momentum—and, paradoxically, rigidity. These all preclude learning because their existence depends on limiting knowledge to that which will reinforce and applaud investment in the person's or organization's established mission. Radical movements cannot tolerate dissenters; cultures discourage deviants through legal means and ostracism; organizations resist knowledge about their performance failures and the social injustices they cause; groups demand conformity; and individuals strive for self-consistency.

Most organizations prefer to apply familiar solutions to new problems (Cyert and March, 1963; Cohen, March, and Olsen, 1972) and are generally reluctant to change their basic strategies (Snow and Hambrick, 1980). A large investment in time, people, money, and other resources is required to develop the distinctive competencies, technologies, structures, and management processes for pursuing a particular strategy. Furthermore, the managerial stress associated with planning and executing strategic change is often a deterrent to major or frequent changes in strategies. Perhaps the greatest obstacle to strategic change is that over time a given strategy attracts and fosters a set of managerial values and philosophies that are wedded to the strategy (Beer and Davis, 1976; Guth and Taguri, 1965; Richards, 1973). Thus, if at all possible, organizations faced with external change or pressure tend to adjust rather than change their strategies.

Miller and Friesen (1980) use the term *momentum* to characterize the great sluggishness that organizations show in adapting to their environments. Organizations often resist change even when their environments threaten them with annihilation (Hedberg, Nystrom, and Starbuck, 1976). This resistance may be due to the pursuit of stability and avoidance of uncertainty (Carter, 1971), the programming of activities and the reluctance to deviate from programs (March and Simon, 1958), the inability to innovate (McGuire, 1963), the incapacity of firms to appraise their own performance (Wildavsky, 1972), executives' narrow and parochial models of external reality (Hedberg, Nystrom, and Starbuck, 1976), and the economies of stability (Perrow, 1972). Adding to the momentum are enduring organizational myths and ideologies (Mitroff and Kilmann, 1976) and political coalitions with vested interests in evolving strategies (Pettigrew, 1973).

Most difficult decisions are not choices about what to do in an isolated event but are choices concerning the fate of an entire course of action. This is especially so when the decision is whether to cease a questionable line of behavior or to commit more effort and resources to making that course of action pay off (Teger, 1980). Should we continue to invest in repairing an auto that has already cost us more than its initial worth? Having already put large amounts of time, energy, and money into a career, should we continue in this path despite frustration and dissatisfaction? When our nation has become committed to a losing war effort (for example, the U.S.-Vietnam experience), should we escalate the commitment or back out? Studies by Staw (1981) and Teger (1980) indicate that individuals tend to escalate their commitment to a losing course of action, in effect throwing good money after bad.

The institution of science itself is subject to a similar persistence. Kuhn (1970) has noted the resistance to paradigm shifts. And Sheldon (1980) argues that this is particularly the case for those whose productive careers have been committed to an older tradition of "normal science." Strengthening such resistance is a feeling of assurance that the older paradigm will eventually solve all its problems, that nature can be shoved into a box that the paradigm provides. Friedlander (1970) cites a case in which once major resources have been invested in a research project that is more than halfway to completion, yet with increasing evidence of an inappropriate set of research questions and methodology, the tendency is to continue on the same path. How can we use the knowledge we obtain from our venture to alter our course so that we can get on with life and learn something more appropriate?

A variety of factors reinforce the organization's identity and thus preclude the possibility of learning. These include the reluctance to shift away from known standards, norms, behaviors, products, and policies that have been effective in the past; the tendency to make ineffective decisions to justify prior ineffective decisions; the reluctance to depart from historical continuity; an insistence on treating shortcomings as failures to be punished rather than opportunities for learning (Michael, 1973); and a tendency to be intolerant of ambiguity and uncertainty (March and Olsen, 1976). In many ways, all these are mechanisms that preserve identity.

Argyris and Schön (1978) cite a number of cases in which an organization's top management refused to listen to or comprehend important negative performance feedback from middle or lower levels. Over time, lower levels learn not to report these less pleasing results. Argyris and Schön have found a variety of organizational norms that inhibit organizational learning. These are represented by some of the following thoughts: let buried failures lie; keep your views of sensitive issues private; enforce the taboo against public discussion; do not surface and test differences in views of organization problems; avoid seeing the whole picture so people do not see how problems are connected; protect yourself by avoiding interpersonal confrontation and public discussion of sensitive issues that might expose you; protect others in the same way; control the situation and the task by making up your own mind and keeping it private and by avoiding public inquiry, which might refute your view.

At the psychological level I might add to ways identity is preserved by a listing of such defense mechanisms as rationalization, projection, repression, and denial. These concepts, though originally developed for the individual, would seem equally applicable to the organization in its effort to avoid the threat of learning and change.

Since identity (of a person or an organization) is an organization of knowledge, it serves the functions of observing (perceiving) and recording (remembering) its experience. One of the characteristics of identity, therefore, is that it serves as its own personal organizational historian. However, it protects itself by revising and fabricating history, thereby engaging in practices not ordinarily admired in historians (Greenwald, 1980). Jervis (1976) marshals a good deal of evidence that decision makers vastly overestimate their own importance as both influencers and targets of influence. Several research reviews indicate that people perceive themselves readily as the origin of good effects and reluctantly as the origin of ill effects (Bowerman, 1978; Miller and Ross, 1975; Snyder, Stephen, and Rosenfeld, 1978; Wortman, 1976).

A number of recent studies have shown that people manage knowledge in a variety of ways to promote the selective availability of information that confirms judgments already concluded (Nisbett and Ross, 1980). People tend to reject messages contrary to their prior opinions, while being accepting of messages that reinforce existing opinions (Greenwald, 1980; Sherif and Hovland, 1961). This dominance of prior opinion as a predictor of response to knowledge reflects a cognitive response bias (Greenwald, 1980). It involves not only selective retrieval from memory of information that supports existing opinion but also active construction of new arguments required to refute novel, opinion-opposing arguments (Greenwald, 1980).

At its extreme, identity plays almost a totalitarian role in maintaining integrity and respect of the organism through manipulation of the organization of knowledge. Orwell (1949, pp. 175-176) notes that the "reason for the readjustment of the past is the need to safeguard the infallibility of the party.... No change of doctrine or in political alignment can ever be admitted. For to change one's mind or even one's policy, is a confession of weakness.... The control of the past depends above all on the training of memory.... [It is] necessary to remember that events happened in the desired manner. And if it is necessary to rearrange one's memories or to tamper with written records, then it is necessary to forget that one has done so. The trick of doing this can be learned like any other mental technique.... It is called doublethink."

And finally, Arendt (1966, pp. 348–349, 388) depicts the need for knowledge control at the leadership level: "The chief qualification of a mass leader has become unending infallibility; he can never admit an error. . . . Mass leaders in power have one concern which overrules all utilitarian considerations: to make their predictions come true. . . . In a totally fictitious world (that is, that of the totalitarian society), failures need not be recorded, admitted, and remembered."

Need to Learn Versus
Needs for Stability and Productivity

Within an organism there is an essential polarity between being learningful and being productive and competent. Reconstructive learning, with all its chaos of changing values, standards, and goals, implies the lack of stability necessary for a sense of competence and productivity. Indeed, learning may well involve the questioning and giving up of old standards of competence and of the productivity and sense of quality that give rise to this competence.

In most organizations this duality is apparent in the "bottom line" goal-seeking mentality, which focuses all energy on productivity and profits—and the more organic planning and adaptive functions geared toward learning. The former is goal-directed and has built-in feedback mechanisms for detecting deviance from this goal. It abhors uncertainty and ambiguity. Goal-seeking behavior calls for single-loop, error-correcting learning (Argyris and Schön, 1978); organic behavior demands double-loop learning in which policy, products, and norms are confronted. A task of management is to integrate this duality—to encompass the back-and-forth movement from one state to the other.

The predominant organizational structure in Western culture is geared primarily for production and efficiency. The mobilization of people and equipment to optimize output calls for a hierarchal structure that lends itself to top-down authority and routinization of task efforts (Burns and Stalker, 1961). Plans and objectives are generally defined at the top, subdivided by function, and directed downward. Such a structure serves to effectively allocate work, control costs, and delegate responsibilities. An inevitable cost of this directive structure is a lack of sensitivity to emergent problems and an underutilization of human resources at lower levels in the organization (Schein and Greiner, 1977). These call for an organization structure geared for knowledge generation and problem solving rather than productivity, control, and efficiency (Burns and Stalker, 1961). Organizations are to an increasing degree using ad hoc task groups for problem exploration, knowledge gathering, and learning. Zand (1974) describes the purpose of these (collateral) groups as to identify and solve problems not solved by the formal organization. The group creatively complements the formal organization, operates parallel to it, and draws its members from it. The outputs from the collateral group are inputs to the formal organization. Friedlander and Schott (1981) have described the interface between such groups and the larger organization in terms of optimizing organizational learning.

In the last analysis, the tension between stability and learning is found in each of us as an individual. There is, on the one hand, a powerful drive to maintain one's sense of identity. We need a sense of continuity that allays fears of learning too fast or being taught against our will by outside forces. On the other hand, each person is, by nature, a purposeful, striving organism with a desire to be more than she or he is now.

We need a clearer understanding of how we can grow and change, even as we remain the same people we always were. My own experience is that there have been long periods of stability leading to (seemingly long) periods of learning. But underlying this seeming polarity, I sense a powerful, coherent flow. That flow is within me as I write this chapter. Perhaps, as Block (1981, p. 261) states, "Amidst change and transformation, there is an essential coherence to personality development."

Transitioning as Learning

Understanding the transitioning process helps in understanding the phenomenology of learning. It links together many of the concepts already presented (for example, awareness, tension, identity, threat, resistance). Like transitions themselves, theories of transition emerge from a variety of phenomena: work with terminal illness, life and career change, and organizational crisis.

Kübler-Ross (1969), working with terminally ill patients, observed four stages of transition: (1) shock, denial, isolation, and disbelief; (2) anger, resentment, envy; (3) bargaining; (4) depression and grief—a mourning of the past, which is already gone, and of the future, which is lost. Hanna (cited in Tannenbaum, 1976), working with people who had gone through key crises in life meanings, found five stages: (1) awareness of limits or frustrations to need satisfaction; (2) loss of meaning of one's life situation—the person cannot understand and accept his or her situation in a way that gives value to suffering; (3) attempts to avoid negative experience, yet a temptation to hang onto the safety of old familiar concepts, however inadequate; (4) a reformulation of life questions and an experimentation with new modes; (5) reduction of pain and discomfort. Fink, Beak, and Taddeo (1971), extrapolating from work with patients in physical rehabilitation therapy, developed a four-stage model of organizational transition: (1) shock, perceived as overwhelming and resulting in perceived threat to the existing structure; (2) defensive retreat with attempts to maintain the old structures, avoidance of reality, and wishful thinking; (3) acknowledgment, with giving up of existing structures, facing reality, self-depreciation, bitterness; (4) adaptation and change, with the establishment of a new structure, a sense of worth, new reality testing, and an increase in satisfying experiences. Tannenbaum (1976) captures the experiences of the middle phases of transition with the following words: *defensiveness, denial, anger, depression, grief, loss of connectedness, loneliness, fear, helplessness.* These are strong feelings associated with having to yield, having to give up something, and having to make peace with the loss, with that which is no longer part of the organism. Ferguson (1980), drawing from theories of life transition and creativity, suggests three phases in transition: (1) Disconfirmation or disequilibrium, in which the organism is faced with a situation that it is unable to deal with using its past repertoire of knowledge. Its internal map does not match the external reality. Yet it does what it has done in the past but with more tenacity and

persistence. (2) Incubation, in which, following the disconfirmation, the organism obsesses consciously for a period of time, but
reorganization occurs at an unconscious level, allowing inner
knowledge to come forward. (3) Reintegration, in which the answer appears as a gift or by magic. "The mystery is inhabited
... the individual trusts an inner guru" (p. 92).

Dealing primarily with people in career, marital, and other
life transitions, Bridges (1980) has developed four key phases of
the transitioning process: (1) disengagement from the context in
which we knew ourselves and the cue system that served to reinforce our roles and patterns of behavior; (2) disidentification, or
losing our ways of self-identification ("I'm not what I ought to
be, I'm not who I'm going to be—but I'm not what I was!"); (3)
disenchantment, or the discovery that in some sense our world is
no longer real—giving up old ways to make way for the new; (4)
disorientation, or a feeling of being lost, confused, not knowing
where one is or where one is going. Bridges notes the difference
between disillusionment and disenchantment: The former is
merely rejection of the old; disenchantment acknowledges the
sufficiency of the old in its time but the insufficiency now.

These descriptions may appear dramatized in describing
learning. Most individuals and organizations undergo this depth
of learning only a few times in a lifetime. More often the terms
little deaths and *little rebirths* are appropriate—the taking on of
new and more appropriate elements of identity, not in total,
but in smaller, more specific segments (Tannenbaum, 1976).

Transitions are obviously difficult periods for individuals
and organizations. Little wonder that most organisms will go to
great lengths to short-circuit significant learning! This may explain why most learning is of a more superficial variety, consisting primarily in error reduction, or single-loop learning (Argyris
and Schön, 1978).

Toward a Theory of Systems Learning

Several major concepts emerge from the previous discussion and are diagramed in Figure 1. This diagram is not intended
to represent a linear sequence of steps but, rather, a set of interrelated concepts linked together through hypothetical connec-

Figure 1. Major Concepts and Relationships
in a Theory of Systems Learning.

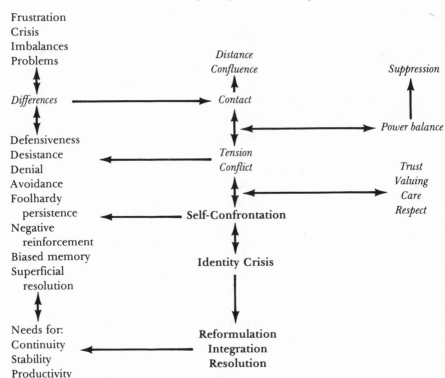

Terms in bold face represent larger-system phenomena.
Terms in italics represent interaction between subsystems.
Terms in regular print represent phenomena occurring both in
    subsystems and in the larger system.

tions. Most arrows in Figure 1 are two-way, indicating mutual
systemic interaction. Several concepts apply to the interaction
between subsystems and are so indicated. Similarly, three concepts apply to the larger system and are noted accordingly. All
other concepts apply to both subsystem interactions and the
larger system.

　　Learning may begin with the organization's or person's
experiencing frustration, crisis, or the awareness of a severe
problem. Frustration may emanate from differences either within the organism or between the organism and its environment.

For example, parts of the organism may respond differently to frustration (for example, declining profits, governmental restrictions, lack of individual success), or the presence of differences may contribute to frustration (for example, differences on what business to be in, internal personal conflicts between contrasting values). Negative feedback or long-range planning similarly presents the person or organization with images that differ from current behavior.

Differences must come into close contact in order for learning to occur. That is, assertion must occur in the interchange between system parts, but so must coordination. Distancing or confluence among parts will preclude the reaching of new ideas, values, beliefs.

Where there are power imbalances between parts of the system, the knowledge resources of system components will not be fully represented or available in the contact. Hence, a power balance is needed in the contact as well as in the tension and conflict that emerge. The presence of two contrasting ideas or beliefs results in tension and conflict, which provide the energy for self-confrontation. A mutual trust and sense of valuing by each subsystem of the other are necessary to allow the contact to result in constructive conflict—conflict in which each subsystem can accept and incorporate the stance of the other. This allows self-confrontation to occur within the larger system. Even though initial differences might have arisen between the system and its environment, it is essential that both of these different perspectives now become internalized within the organism. Such internalization results in an identity crisis for the person or organization. What/who is it and what does it want to become? This differs from the initial crisis, which was seen as an externally derived frustration. Finally, from the identity crisis a new resolution, integration, and reformulation is reached. Reconstructive learning has occurred, possibly with radical changes in the organization's goals, principles, beliefs. These changes bring on a need for consolidation—a sense of continuity, stability, and productivity. And again, continuity, stability, and productivity lead to a defensiveness and resistance to change, fostering the proliferation of differences and frustration.

Throughout this process there are a number of exits. In

addition to those already mentioned (distancing and confluence, suppression of differences through power imbalance), a
variety of behaviors can be labeled resistance and defensiveness.
These include denial, avoidance, foolhardy persistence, momentum, biased memory, and rationalization. These serve the organism's needs for stability, productivity, and continuity.

The Executive Role

The executive role must be to manage the subtle balance
between reconstructive learning, on the one hand, and productivity, stability, and continuity, on the other—both for the executive as a person and for the organization. How can a structure
and a climate be maintained for both learning and productivity?
Under what conditions should the blend be changed, and how
should this occur?

The mentality of most organizations and their executives
is geared to current tasks and goals and to problems that hinder
the attainment of these. Their aim is to optimize productivity
(the bottom line). Stability and continuity of goals, policies,
norms, and structures become (often subtly) of paramount importance. Thus, most executives foster organizational learning
that is primarily error-correcting—to improve the organization's
efficiency in reaching its goals and in maintaining its standards,
image, and policies.

But the executive function is also to lead the organization
in its reconstructive learning. This means to encourage exploration and confrontation of differing viewpoints, to foster structures within the organization that encourage contact between
differing subsystems in which power balance as well as trust and
valuing occur. The executive role is to foster a structure and a
climate for planned transition in which the organization's
knowledge resources are fully utilized.

The executive role in guiding learning is to manage crisis
and frustration; it is to manage differences; it is to manage power, contact, conflict, and tension. It is to navigate the organization through the transitions of self-confrontation and identity
change it must undergo if it is to survive and grow.

9

Managerial Thought
in the Context of Action

Karl E. Weick

This essay is built around a puzzle. In most descriptions of managerial behavior (for example, Kotter, 1982b; McCall, Kaplan, and Gerlach, 1982), managers seem to act thoughtfully but spend no time thinking. If they are thoughtful, when do they do their thinking, and how do they do it?

One explanation is that managers do think, but not while they are on the job. Instead, they think at home, on airplanes, in the john, on weekends. Furthermore, they think by incubating proposals, so that at any moment they are mulling over several issues even though there is no outward evidence that any thought is occurring. Thus, the reason researchers do not see

I am grateful to David Kolb, Richard Mason, Ian Mitroff, Eric Neilsen, and Case Western Reserve University students for help in improving the argument presented at the conference.

managers think is that managers do not think when the observers are around.

The second possibility is that managers have been so successful at reducing uncertainty and at anticipating and preparing
for the future that there are very few occasions when a genuine
puzzle occurs and they actually have to think.

The third possibility, and the one I want to consider, is
that managers think all the time, but researchers have missed
this because they have been looking at the wrong thing. Condi-
tioned by linear, stage models of problem solving and by scientific thinking as the representative anecdote, observers have sus-
pected that thinking is visible in the form of long reflective
episodes during which managers sit alone, away from the action,
trying to make logical inferences from facts. Since observers do
not see many episodes that look like this, they conclude that
managers do not do much thinking.

I want to explore the possibility that thinking is insepara-
bly woven into and occurs simultaneously with action. When
managers tour, read, talk, supervise, and meet, those actions
contain managerial thought, they do the thinking for managers,
they are substitutes for thinking, and they reduce the necessity
for separate reflective episodes. Connected ideas, which are the
essence of thought, can be formed and managed *outside* the
mind, with relatively little assistance from the mind. This is how
managers work, and this is why we are misled when we use reflection as an index of how much of their work involves thinking. Hence, the key issues are, How does action incorporate
thinking? What form does thinking take when it unfolds in a
context of action?

The argument that action incorporates thinking and that
thinking occurs in a context of action will be developed in the
following way. First, an overview of the argument will be presented. Then, three sections will develop three key assertions in
the argument: thinking qualifies activity, thinking provokes activity, and thinking intensifies activity. These assertions will
then be combined into a model that summarizes how managers
behave thinkingly. The chapter concludes with implications for
practice and implications for research.

Overview of the Argument

When managers act, their thinking occurs concurrently with action. Thinking is not sandwiched between activities; rather, it exists in the form of circumspection present when activities are executed. Managers can phone, tour, meet, write, network, and build agendas with variable amounts of intention, attention, care, control, pertinacity. To execute acts more thinkingly *is* to think. It is to create outcomes that are unlikely to be improved by disengaged reflection. It is to add to outcomes most of the increment in quality that would have been added by situation-detached reflection in a quiet place. The basic argument has three components.

First, it is asserted that thinking qualifies action. That is, managerial acts of any kind can be done more or less thinkingly. They can be done with varying amounts of deliberateness, intention, attention, care, control, and pertinacity. It is the *form* of managerial actions that determines how much thinking they incorporate and what kind of environment they create. To answer the question "Do managers think?" we examine the form of their action, not how they spend their time away from action.

The mechanisms by which thinking qualifies action are explicated in the second and third components of the argument. In answer to the question "How does thinking add attention, intention, and control to action?" it is argued that thinking in the form of presumptions energizes action and thinking in the form of meanings focuses action. These two processes produce attention and intention. Control occurs because meanings, presumptions, and actions are interrelated in ways that intensify action and make that action self-validating.

Thus, the second component contains the assertion that thinking provokes action. Something has to lure managers into situations and get them to act in the first place. This lure is assumed to be a presumption of logic. When faced with situations, managers commonly assume that what is about to unfold will have made sense. Sensibleness is treated as a closed issue. All that is left for the manager to do is "run the setting." The important feature of this presumption is that it moves the manager into a setting, stimulates matter-of-fact action; and it is this action, not the initial fallible presumption, that then consolidates the setting in an orderly manner, thereby confirming the initial presumption that it will have made sense (Weick, Gilfillan, and Keith, 1973).

It is important to realize that the content of these presumptions is much less crucial than the fact that they exist in some form in the first place. Presumptions are interchangeable, and their accuracy is less crucial than the fact that they tempt the manager to wade into a situation and act. It is that *action* that then determines the amount of order a situation will exhibit. And this orderliness, in turn, is the outcome that then feeds back to confirm the initial presumption of logic with which the person started.

The third component of the argument is the assertion that thinking intensifies activity. Action takes on more significance, becomes strengthened, and has more consequential effects, the more resonance that is established between it and some explanation. Action becomes more focused when people see what they are doing.

When people say that someone acts thinkingly, they mean partly that the action is coupled with some underlying meaning that explains and adds strength to the action. When some act that in its own right has little significance or meaning becomes linked with an underlying pattern, it becomes more significant. The more significance that is tied to the action, the more impact it has and the more covariation it produces. The more covariation it produces, the more meaningful the situation.

Thinking as Qualification of Activity

Acts done thinkingly have a distinctive form. That distinctive form is important because different forms of action create and implant different events that managers report to be "out there" (Weick, 1979). When managers act as though the world were a certain way, these focused actions often ensure that subsequent data will confirm those initial presumptions

(Manning, 1980, chap. 3). Material from which sense is made is often the product of a person's prior activities.

Thus, to assert that people act more or less thinkingly is not just to say that thought and action are simultaneous; it is also to say that the form of the action truly creates relationships and covariation that did not exist before the action occurred. When managers act thinkingly, they create a different environment than when they act unthinkingly.

Scientific thinking is probably a poor model for managerial thinking, yet, with few exceptions (for example, Barnard's 1938 discussion of nonlogical thinking), theorists encourage this myth by providing steplike analytical formats (for example, Sanderson, 1979), which require that managers take time away from what they are doing to think more as scientists do. I think this approach is counterproductive and wrong. It is reasonable advice based on an incorrect analysis.

The problem is basically that we treat *thinking* as a verb of doing when in fact it is an adverbial verb that requires that some *other* activity must be underway if thinking is to occur. Thinking is a qualification of an activity, not an activity itself. It is a way of acting (Lyons, 1979, 1980; Ryle, 1970, 1971).

Since we are concerned with how managers act, we are concerned with verbs. Many verbs used to describe managerial activity specify autonomous things that managers do: *converse, tour, phone, reconcile, mediate, encourage, fire, sell, buy.* Other verbs clearly are not verbs of doing: *perish, inherit, resemble, possess, outlive, forget, know.*

There is still a third class of verbs that are borderline in the sense that they are treated as verbs of doing, yet they do not stand alone. They are more accurately described as adverbial verbs that qualify some other activity. Examples of these verbs would be *hurry, try, succeed, fail, care,* and *be vigilant.* They do not make sense apart from some further specification of a context and some other activity to which they are appended.

> If told that someone is hurrying, we have
> not been told what he is doing, but only that he is
> doing whatever he is doing at an abnormally high

speed. He may be hurriedly walking or typing or reading or humming or eating, and so on indefinitely. The command "hurry" is only the beginning of a command; it cannot yet, context apart, be obeyed or disobeyed. I label the verb *to hurry* an "adverbial verb," partly because any completed sentence containing it could be paraphrased by a sentence containing a proper verb of doing qualified by the adverb *hurriedly* or the phrase *in a hurry*. I might put the point by saying that hurrying is not an autonomous action or activity, as walking, typing, and eating are. The command "walk," "type" or "eat" is an obeyable command, and not the less so for being pretty unspecific. If I then eat lobster or bread or shoe leather, I am obeying the command to eat. But to obey or disobey the command to hurry, I must do some autonomous X, like eating or humming, . . . for there to be a hurried or unhurried X-ing that tallies with or flouts the understood command, no matter whether the command is specific or unspecific [Ryle, 1971, p. 467].

If a manager watches an ambitious subordinate vigilantly, it makes no sense for us to ask the manager whether he did his vigilating in Spanish, because there is no separate activity that we call "vigilating." If we were to transform the activity into a verb and call it "vigilate," it would be an adverbial verb that could be replaced by the more common adverb *vigilantly*. To say that a manager converses thinkingly is similar to saying that a manager watches vigilantly or drives with care. "Driving with care is not doing two things, as driving with a song is. I can stop driving and go on singing, or vice versa. I can do the one well and the other badly; the one obediently and the other disobediently. But I cannot stop driving and go on exercising traffic-care. In obeying your command to drive carefully, I am not conjointly obeying two commands, such that I might have disobeyed the first while obeying the second" (Ryle, 1971, pp. 467–468).

When we say that an action is done thinkingly, we mean that the act is done with attention, intention, care, interest, pertinacity, patience, initiative, alertness, resourcefulness, cunning, concentration, and self-coaching. For the sake of manageability, this list is shortened to attention, intention, and control. When people act thinkingly, they pay close attention to what is happening (for example, Sproull, 1981), they try to impose order on the setting and their actions in it (for example, Braybrooke, 1964; Carter, 1974), and they correct their performance when it strays from reference standards (for example, Powers, 1973; Glasser, 1981).

When we say that an act is done unthinkingly, we mean that people are acting on impulse, rigidly without sensitivity to surroundings, by rote, mindlessly, as if possessed, without the benefit of one or more senses, without remorse, under the influence of chemicals, during amnesia or blackouts, or while in a state of very low arousal such as drowsiness or a state of extreme arousal that creates extreme narrowing of awareness. In each of these cases behavior does not incorporate thinking. Since these actions are devoid of thinking, people who produce them will need to spend time away from action doing reflective thinking if they want to add thought to what they do.

Managerial activities can be done more or less thinkingly. Most of the thinking that managers do is woven into the act—the act itself carries the wisdom—if the act is done with attention, intention, and control. If people act attentively, that exhausts most of the rationality that can reasonably be applied in the present circumstance. It is conceivable that people could be more rational if they postponed action or thought longer, but that added rationality would not improve the outcome, because it is overdetermined. Thinking can improve outcomes, but only so much. Most of the improvement that thinking can make is already present when action is done thinkingly.

When people use problem-solving heuristics (for example, Jackson, 1975), for example, they are told to *write* a problem description, *sort* those statements into means, ends, and obstacles, and *examine* each statement to see whether it might be *restated* or *discarded* to solve the problem. The content they write is less crucial than the form of their action. It is not so much what they write as how they write it. People can write, sort, examine, restate, and discard with large amounts of attention, intention, and control or with almost none at all. Focused attention is relatively rare, and that is why writing, sorting, and discarding that are done thinkingly usually add most of the improvement to a situation that could be added by a separate act of reflection.

Thinking as Presumptions of Logic:
The Provocation of Activity

Managers fold attention, intention, and control into their action through the mechanisms of presumptions of logic and specifications of logic. Presumptions of logic provoke and energize action. They do so in the following way.

In managerial work, thought precedes action, but the kind of thought that occurs is not detailed analytical thought addressed to imagined scenarios in which actions are tried and options chosen. Instead, thought precedes action in the form of much more general expectations about the orderliness of what will occur.

Order is present, not because extended prior analysis revealed it, but because the manager anticipated sufficient order that she waded into the situation, imposed order among events, and then "discovered" what she had imposed. The manager "knew" all along that the situation would make sense. This was treated as a given. Having presumed it would be sensible, the manager then acted confidently and implanted the order that was anticipated.

Most managerial situations contain gaps, discontinuities, loose ties among people and events, indeterminacies, and uncertainties (Weick, 1982). These are the gaps that managers have to bridge. It is the contention of this argument that managers first think their way across these gaps and then, having tied the elements together cognitively, tie them together in reality when they act and impose covariation. This sequence is similar to sequences associated with self-fulfilling prophecies (Snyder, Tanke, and Berscheid, 1977).

People fill the gaps and discontinuities associated with a novel social setting by anticipating, for example, that other people will be cool and hostile. Although the prospect of walking into such a gathering is not attractive, it is less frightening than walking into some gathering where one has no idea what will happen. The anticipation of hostility glues the setting together long enough for the person to take some action, which, regrettably, often consolidates and focuses the setting so that it actually delivers the hostility that was expected. The manager who receives the hostility treats this as proof that he is able to size up situations and that he has good implicit theories of situations. What he fails to recognize is that the situation was "up for grabs" until he took some action that focused it and gave it specific content.

Thus, the presumptions of logic are forms of thought that are crucial for their evocative qualities. The presumption leads people to act more forcefully the more certain the presumption. Strong presumptions lead to strong actions, which impose considerable order. Weaker presumptions lead to more hesitant actions—which means either that the person will be more influenced by the covariation that is already present or that only weak order will be created.

Presumptions of logic are evident in the chronic optimism often associated with managerial activity. This optimism is conspicuous in the case of companies that are in trouble (for example, International Harvestor, Invsco, Pan Am, Chrysler), but it is also evident in more run-of-the-mill managing. Optimism may be an external manifestation of the belief that situations will have made sense. William James ([1895], 1956) described how the faith that life is worth living generates the action that then makes life worth living. Optimism is not necessarily a blind disregard of grim realities. Instead, it may be the belief that makes action possible, which then assembles realities that become either grim or upbeat.

Presumptions of logic should be prominent in organizations because of the climate of rationality (Staw, 1980). Presumptions should be especially important when beliefs about cause-and-effect linkages are unclear (Thompson and Tuden, 1959). Thompson and Tuden label as "inspiration" the kind of managing that occurs when there are unclear preferences and unclear cause/effect beliefs. It is precisely in the face of massive uncertainty that beliefs of some sort are necessary to evoke some action, which can then begin to consolidate the situation so that explicit inferences about cause/effect linkages can then be attempted. To "inspire" is to affirm realities that are more likely to materialize when they are sought vigorously. That may be the essence of managing thinkingly.

Thinking as Specifications of Logic: The Intensification of Activity

When people act, what they are doing can have multiple meanings. These meanings have decisive effects on action because they influence its intensity and direction, which, in turn, influence the probability that the action will modify the situation in self-confirming ways.

In organizations there are items, actions, documents, details, particulars. There are also generalizations, archetypes, themes, patterns, abstractions, and metaphors that explain these diverse particulars. These are the specifications of logic. When a particular is subsumed under some more general theme, the particular absorbs meaning, but the theme also becomes articulated more fully (Lofland, 1976, p. 62).

The importance of this sequence cannot be overestimated. It is the primitive act of sense-making in organizational life. Presumptions of logic are relevant to this sequence because they facilitate the linking of individual actions with underlying explanations. If, for a particular action, one presumes that there is *a* logic to it, then this presumption suspends doubt long enough for people to discover a specific logic within which the action might make sense. Once the action is linked with an explanation, it becomes more forceful, and the situation is thereby transformed into something that supports the presumed underlying pattern. Presumptions enable actions to be tied to specific explanations that consolidate those actions into deterministic events. These focused actions become stronger forces in the situations where they were first expressed. This greater forcefulness means that more components of that situation will accommodate to, defer to, take account of, systematically evade, move toward, or monitor the acting person. These accommodations produce a more orderly setting whose order is like the underlying pattern with which the action was initially coupled.

The intensification of activity through the establishment of connections between data (observed effects of action) and ideas (underlying explanations for those effects) has been described as the documentary method (Garfinkel, 1962; McHugh, 1968, chap. 4) or the experimental theory of knowing. John Dewey (1979, pp. 174–175) describes the connecting of sense data with concepts, using the example of a physician/patient relationship:

> A physician, for example, is called by a patient. . . . This experienced object sets the problem of inquiry. Certain clinical operations are performed, sounding, tapping, getting registrations of pulse, temperature, respiration, and so on. These constitute the symptoms; they supply the evidence to be interpreted. . . . The observations mean something not in and of themselves, but are given meaning in the light of the systematized knowledge of medicine as far as that is at the command of the practitioner. He calls upon his store of knowledge to suggest ideas that may aid him in reaching a judgment as to the nature of the trouble and its proper treatment. The analytic philosopher, looking on, notes that the interpreting material, by means of which the scattered data of sense are bound together into a coherent whole, is not itself directly sensibly present. So he calls it ideational or conceptual.
>
> Sense data are signs which direct this selection of ideas; the ideas when suggested arouse new observations; the two together determine his final judgment or diagnosis and his procedure. Something is then added to the store of the clinical material of medical art so that subsequent observations of symptoms are refined and extended, and the store of material from which to draw ideas is further enlarged.

Dewey later (p. 178) makes the relevant aside that we would have seen this intimate relationship between action and explanation more clearly if we had not called the patient's symptoms "data" or "givens" but instead had called them "takens." The ill patient is a "given," but the physician has to "take" (select), from that mass of presented qualities, those that may throw some light on the trouble. The qualities selected are tentative until they are linked with an explanation and confirmed by further data. Better clues may have been neglected in the initial selection. Only by continued cycling will less adequate explanations be discovered and modified. As adequacy improves, the pace of activity accelerates, the activity becomes more focused, and this focus imposes more self-validating constraints on the situation, thereby "proving" the adequacy of the explanation.

The underlying explanation need *not* be objectively "correct." In a crude sense, any old explanation will do. This is so because the explanation serves mostly to organize and focus the action. The focused action then modifies the situation in ways that confirm the explanation, whatever it is. Thus, the adequacy of any explanation is determined by the intensity and structure it adds to potentially self-validating actions. More forcefulness leads to more validation and more perceived adequacy. Accuracy is subordinate to intensity. Since situations can support a variety of meanings, their actual content and meaning are dependent on the degree to which they are arranged into sensible, coherent configurations. More forcefulness imposes more coherence. Thus, those explanations that induce greater forcefulness become more valid, not because they are more accurate, but because they have a higher potential for self-validation.

Applied to managerial activity, simultaneous thought and action are more likely among executives because their actions are capable of a considerable range of intensity, the situations they deal with are loosely connected and capable of considerable rearrangement, and the underlying explanations they invoke (for example, "This is war") have great potential to intensify whatever action is underway. All these factors combine to produce self-validating situations in which managers are sure their diagnoses were correct. What they underestimate is the extent to which their own actions have implanted the correctness they discover. They are vulnerable because someone else's actions can alter the situation and unravel the apparent correctness without warning. People overestimate the solidity and stability of their diagnoses when they fail to see the extent to which their own action is responsible for what the situation contains. Managers mistakenly believe they have discovered something permanent when in fact they have created something transient. This error adds to their uncertainty and insecurity because they regard as most factual and solid those very events that in reality are most susceptible to alteration by forceful action. As long as their own action remains the most forceful and deterministic input among the several actors who converge on that sense, solidity is sustained. What they fail to see is that this solidity is an ongoing accomplishment sustained by intense action rather than by accurate diagnosis. If they reduce the intensity of their own action or if another actor directs a more intense action at the pliant elements, then their own solidity is replaced by someone else's. What managers seldom realize is that their action (in this case inaction or weakened action) was as much responsible for the disappearance of "facts" as it was for the original appearance of the "facts."

Figure 1 shows that people act with increased intention, attention, and care as a result of self-reinforcing linkages between presumptions (A), action (B), consequences (C), and meanings (D).

To act thinkingly is to have the connected variables increase. That is, a stronger presumption produces stronger action, stronger covariation, and greater meaningfulness, which strengthens the original presumption. To act unthinkingly is to have the connected variables decrease one another. Doubt weakens the strength of the presumption, which weakens action and covariation, which makes it harder to extract meaning, which strengthens the original doubt.

In either case the initial kick in this deviation-amplifying causal loop is crucial. An increase at *any* of the four variables in the loop spreads, meaning that faith generates a world that confirms the faith. Doubt is similarly contagious. A decrease in any

Figure 1. Production of Thoughtful Action: A Summary Model.

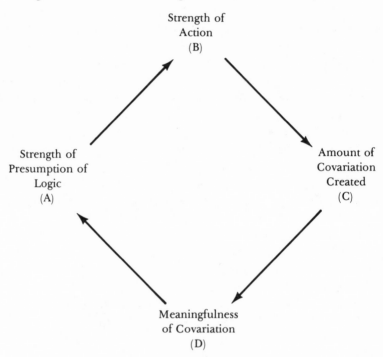

variable produces a decrease in connected variables, meaning that doubt is also self-validating.

Examples are plentiful. A male who believes he is telephoning an attractive female acts warmly, which consolidates a warm response from her, which confirms his original stereotype that attractive women are sociable (Snyder, Tanke, and Berscheid, 1977). A new administrator, suspecting that old-timers are traditional, seeks ideas from other sources, which increases old-timers' suspicion and confirms the administrator's original presumption (Warwick, 1975). People who presume that no one likes them approach a new gathering in a stiff, distrustful manner, which evokes the unsympathetic behavior they presumed would be there (Watzlawick, Beavin, and Jackson, 1967, pp. 98–99). A musician who doubts the competence of a composer will play his music lethargically and produce the ugly sound that confirms the original suspicion (Weick, Gilfillan, and Keith, 1973).

In each case an initial presumption (she is sociable, they are uncreative, people are hostile, he is incompetent) leads people to act forcefully (talk warmly, seek ideas elsewhere, behave defensively, play music poorly), which causes a situation to become more orderly (warmth is exchanged, ideas emerge, hostility is focused, music becomes worse), which then makes the situation easier to interpret, thereby confirming the original presumption that it would be logical.

The model is appropriate for managers because managerial actions are almost ideally suited to create plausible covariation among events. Managerial actions are primarily oral, face-to-face, symbolic, presumptive, brief, spontaneous, and blunt (Kotter, 1982a; McCall, Morrison, and Hannon, 1978; Mintzberg, 1973a; Pfeffer, 1981; Stewart, 1976). These actions have a deterministic effect on many organizational situations because those situations are less coherent than the actions directed at them. The situations are loosely coupled, subject to multiple interpretations, monitored regularly by only a handful of persons, vulnerable to pluralistic ignorance, nonrecurring, and deficient in structure.

Thus, a situation of basic disorder becomes more orderly when people overlook the disorder and presume orderliness, then act on this presumption, and, finally, rearrange pliant elements into a more meaningful arrangement that confirms the original presumption. The form of managerial behavior is more likely to perpetuate than to break this sequence. A manager's preoccupation with rationality may be significant, less for its power as a problem-solving heuristic than for its power to induce action that implants the rationality that was presumed.

Implications for Managerial Practice

The pragmatic heart of this essay is the suggestion that fighting fires, which managers do all the time, is not necessarily thick-headed or slow-witted. Firefighting has seemed like mindless activity because we have used scientific activity as the ideal case for comparison, because we have thought of thinking as a separate activity that stops when people put out fires, because we have presumed that the only time people think is when they make distinct decisions or solve clear-cut problems, because we have not examined activities closely to see how thought might inhere in them, and because we keep examining things as if they occurred in sequences rather than simultaneously.

Managers do reflect as well as act, do disengage from action to make sense out of what is happening. But this "time out" may improve performance, not because of the thinking that occurs but because of what happens to the action that substitutes for thought.

Reflection may be important because it provides relief, relaxation, and diversion. Reflection is more likely to improve effectiveness because it lowers the arousal level below the point at which it disrupts performance (McGrath, 1976) than because it generates specific solutions to problems. Reflection makes it possible for subsequent action to be executed more thinkingly rather than more absent-mindedly. Thus, reflection alters the form of action rather than its content. It slows the action rather than informs it. But aside from its capacity to comfort the manager, reflection is of no greater importance than any other activity. Episodes of reflection enable managers to act thoughtfully during the next time period. The content of the next thoughtful action, however, comes more from the circumstance confronted and from the slowed pace of the action, not from the items pondered during the interlude of reflection.

There is good evidence that managers work in environments where they have to process a flow of information rather than discrete, labeled, bounded problems (for example, Kotter, 1982a). The preceding analyses are compatible with the realities of what managers confront and the tools they have for confronting it.

Thought cannot be attached to discrete, well-bounded problems if there are no such problems in a continuous stream of calls, actions, memos, words, hints, bluffs (Kraft, 1980). Separate analytic activity makes little sense when there is nothing separate, concrete, and labeled to analyze. The absence of bounded problems in managing suggests that models that presume their existence will be of limited value. And models that address how people manage flows through thoughtful action should be more realistic accounts of managerial decision making.

Weiss (1980) has described the sparsity of discrete decisions in managerial action. She argues that decisions accrete and seldom consist in the production of a particular outcome by particular individuals. Decisions are less accurately portrayed as episodes in which people convene at one time to make a decision and more accurately portrayed as small steps (writing a memo, answering an inquiry) that gradually foreclose alternative courses of action and limit what is possible. The decision is made without anyone's realizing it. The crucial activities for decision making are not separate episodes of analysis. Instead, they are actions, whose controlled execution consolidates fragments of policy that are lying around, gives them direction, and closes off other possible arrangements. The decision making *is* the memo writing, *is* the answering, *is* the editing of drafts. These actions are not precursors to decision making, they *are* the decision making. And when they are done more carelessly, casually, or absent-mindedly, the decisions they produce are more foolish.

Decisions that are tied more closely to action are more likely to contain improvisation (Bate and Mangham, 1981, p. 186). As Weiss notes, "Many moves are improvisations. Faced with an event that calls for response, officials use their experience, judgment, and intuition to fashion the response for the issue at hand. That response becomes a precedent, and when similar—or not so similar—questions come up, the response is uncritically repeated. Consider the federal agency that receives a call from a local program asking how to deal with requests for enrollment in excess of the available number of slots. A staff member responds with off-the-cuff advice. Within the next few weeks programs in three more cities call with similar questions and staff repeat the advice. Soon what began as improvisation has hardened into policy" (1980, p. 401).

Managers are said to avoid uncertainty, but one of the ironies implicit in the preceding analysis is that managers often

create the very uncertainty they abhor. When they cannot presume order, they hesitate, and this very hesitancy often creates
events that are disordered and unfocused. This disorder confirms the initial doubts concerning order. What is often missed
is that it is the failure to act, rather than the nature of the external world itself, that explains the lack of order. When people
act, they absorb uncertainty, they rearrange things, and they
impose contingencies that might not have been there before.
The presence of these contingencies is then used as evidence
that the situation is orderly and certain.

In summary, salient features of managerial work are compatible with the suggestions that (1) thinking is seldom sepa-
rated from acting (decisions are not made at specific points in
time, they accrete), (2) acting is continuous, which means
thinking is woven into it (to think is to write memos attentively), (3) people start to act because they presume that what they
are wading into will make sense (significant opportunities lurk
in trivial requests as well as in significant ones), (4) responsive-
ness does set forces in motion that had not been present before
(policy is made through off-the-cuff advice), and (5) although
the pace is exhausting and reflection allows people to regroup,
it is not obvious that outcomes would improve substantially by
the simple addition of more thought.

Implications for Research

The core idea is that thinking is adverbial and operates in
the service of action. The general proposal that people behave
thinkingly has been specified as a set of causal relations among
presumptions, action, induced covariation, and meaning. It is
proposed that action consolidates an otherwise diffuse setting
to the extent that strong, focused action is directed at the setting. Strength and focus, in turn, vary as a function of presumptions and meanings. The key assertion is that intensity is more
crucial than accuracy. Intense actions are self-validating and
carry their own accuracy with them. It is this sense in which
thinking is subordinate to action and accuracy is subordinate to
impact.

Numerous propositions are implied by the analysis; five will be mentioned to illustrate nuances contained within the argument.

First, the argument implies that people think all the time. If that is so, then to account for variance in outcomes, researchers will have to look both at how activities are qualified and at other determinants that have nothing to do with thinking.

Organizational outcomes are sufficiently overdetermined that it is naive to argue that thought and deliberation are their main determinants. Thought can improve outcomes, but it cannot perfect them. Often it does not even affect them. The increment that thought *can* add to outcomes is usually added directly when the actions are executed. There is little more that thought can add, and that is why episodes of reflection are often redundant, make people overly self-conscious, generate solutions that are unworkable, create new crises, and introduce new complications. Outcomes are determined by things like balkanized constituencies, chance, luck, misperceptions, misjudgments, inattention, mislabeling, overgeneralization, distractions, anticipations, fears, memories, energy, inheritance, resources, and temperature, as well as thought. The effects of concerted thought can be offset by any of these factors.

That is not to say that thought is unimportant. But it is to assert that there is a ceiling effect for thought. Thought cannot supply infinite improvements to a situation. It can improve situations up to a point but not beyond. In most organizations there are a sufficient number of other determinants of outcomes, equally powerful, so that thoughtful increments are of modest magnitude. Since thought can make limited modifications of outcomes, and since most managerial actions already carry a thoughtful increment, the likelihood that detached reflection will have an observable effect is lessened.

Second, observers should watch actions as if they were watching thought itself. The person who manages by walking about provokes the question, Was that touring attentive, careful, pertinacious, wily, witting? If so, then that touring was as good as thought can make it.

The implication that we should watch actions differently

can be illustrated by work redesign (Oldham and Hackman, 1980). Work redesign may be successful not because it introduces variety but because it evokes a new pattern of thinking. Redesigned jobs may have their effect because they add strength to presumptions, evoke different underlying meanings, and produce different covariation in the environment.

Third, researchers may be hurting managers when they prescribe lists and steps that managers should use to improve their thinking.

Analytical thinkers and scientists typically set out their processes of interpolation, extrapolation, and reconstruction in a series of steps such that each successive step can be shown to follow in a necessary way from preceding steps. Virtually all books on problem-solving strategies contain these lists and steps. Interestingly, everyday thinking almost never presents a series of steps: "Once the selected or weighted evidence and the accepted generalization are brought together (or in some instances, once the accepted generalization is simply applied to the case in hand), the required continuation or completion of the situation that has provided the occasion to think is simply 'there.' There are no traces of elaborate processes still interposed between data for completion and the completion itself" (Bartlett, 1958, pp. 180–181). This suggests that linear models and step models have only modest relevance to everyday thinking. Even if people tried to implement them, they would find them foreign to what they are trying to do.

People may resist steplike structures because the procedure they prefer is basically holistic in the sense that all steps are considered *simultaneously*. Taken to its extreme, the suggestion by Graham Wallas (1926) that problem solving proceeds through four steps—preparation, incubation, illumination, and verification—may be misleading. (These steps, incidentally, were induced from observations of *scientists*, such as Helmholtz.) What happens with most people is that all four steps go on all the time. At a given moment, one of the four may be more salient, but the three others are commonly being done and may occur in a different order. It is conceivable that when investigators talk about sequences that occur in unexpected orders, they are merely rediscovering that sequence is irrelevant. What is happening is that people are considering multiple things simultaneously, and remnants of each of the four steps are present simultaneously at any one time.

Fourth, recent interest in differences between right- and left-hemisphere brain functioning may be important, not because the hemispheres have different capacities for information processing but because they have a common capacity to influence action that shapes events. Thus, intuitive, nonlogical, right-brain activity may be crucial not because of its capacity for holistic apprehension but because of its capacity to evoke more forceful actions, which create situations that unfold more as they were intuited to unfold. Likewise, left-brain activity, consisting in linear, sequential, analytic thought, may be important mostly as an anticipation of order that lures people to wade into situations that are basically disordered. Having anticipated order and having acted on this assumption, managers frequently are able to create the orderly situation that they anticipated. Rational assumptions hold events together cognitively until people can take action that transforms the imagined covariation into actual rational covariation.

And fifth, the presumption of logic is most likely to stimulate the creation of self-validating environments when key elements of those environments are symbolic (Pfeffer, 1981; Peters and Waterman, 1982) and open to multiple interpretations (for example, when situations are ambiguous, unstructured, novel, complex). As situations become more structured, presumptions of logic may become less influential self-fulfilling rationalities, and action may unfold in a more mindless manner.

Conclusion

What I have tried to show is that we should pay more attention to simultaneity of thought and action and less attention to sequence; we should downgrade the grip that conceptualizations of decision making and problem solving have on the way we approach the more general problem of managerial thinking; we should deemphasize academic thinking as the model we use to understand how nonacademics think; we should consider the possibility that reflection works more because of what it does to arousal levels and less because of what it does to the content of thinking; we should look more closely at the ways managers themselves create the problems and opportunities that face them and therefore have responsibility for what confronts them; we should ask just how managers piece together anarchic settings long enough to take some action that may have some lingering effect; and we should have less hubris about the likelihood that detached thought can produce infinite improvements in outcomes.

The argument, in a nutshell, is the one set forth by a Persian proverb (cited in Fox, 1976, p. 69): "Thinking well is wise; planning well, wiser; doing well, wisest and best of all."

10

Searching for Essence
in Executive Experience

Fred Massarik

Is Phenomenology Esoteric?: A Return to Basics

In this era of pragmatic concern with mundane "realities"—bottom-line results, productivity levels, budget deficits, and fluctuating money supply—is there a place for phenomenology? After all, phenomenology is identified mainly as a somewhat esoteric branch of philosophy. One then mumbles (eyes devoutly turned toward heaven in arcane reflection) something about Husserl, Heidegger, and the noema, whereupon the conversation

I should like to express thanks to my colleagues, conference participants at the Case Western Reserve University Department of Organizational Behavior symposium on the executive mind for their various helpful comments and to express particular appreciation to William R. Woodward, Department of Psychology, University of New Hampshire, for specific constructive suggestions.

becomes totally unintelligible. One grants readily that the classic phenomenological literature is, to say the least, difficult in its logic and organization and resistant to most attempts to render it lucid. Why is it, then, that one may wish to invoke, at this time of major societal change, the ancient ghosts (and we may count Kant and Hegel among them), in the cause of a revival of an allegedly obscure discipline? The answer that I should like to propose is the following: It may well be that a rediscovery and extension of phenomenology is now timely and necessary if we are to make progress in our understanding of "the executive mind"—if we are to appreciate at deeper levels what an executive's life is really all about.

There are a number of reasons for this view, to be considered in some detail in this chapter. For whatever cause, people tend to use the term *mind* with a wide variety of meanings— and, in a sense, perniciously so. Because of assumptions about the term's "common sense" connotations, *mind* may refer to anything from the physiologic brain to an encompassing and diffuse ethos pertaining to the vastness of the total human condition. Eventually one may indeed lose track of what it is all about, while going right along with elaborate study and with complex commentary. Like the proverbial pilot, we may be lost but making very good time.

Here I propose that "mind" is most strikingly manifest in human experience, in what we think, feel, and *experience,* the direct sensory fullness of being human. Thus, executive mind ceases to be either rhetoric or abstraction, nor is it seen as dispassionate "object." It becomes known in our shared quest to unfurl, before the eyes of interested and committed parties, the very fabric of the executive's continuing experiencing, the immediately sensed thinking, feeling, and doing, the essence of being in life. The "raw" but relevant data become the *phenomenon* of ongoing experiencing—thence the concept and term *phenomenology.*

The term *phenomenology* was first introduced by Johann Heinrich Lambert in the middle of the eighteenth century. The German work in which the concept was proposed, the *New Organon,* subtitled "Thoughts Regarding the Discovery and Identification of Truth and Its Differentiation from Error and Superficial Appearance," was published in Leipzig in 1764. Lambert sought to go beyond verbal assertion as such, establishing foundations that we might regard as anticipatory of twentieth-century "attitude research": He spoke of a "transcendental optics" that left room for *degrees of certainty* in assessing a given phenomenon, foreshadowing such commonplace present-day procedures as attitude scaling.

In his time, Lambert's influence extended to Immanuel Kant. Correspondence between the two in 1765 shows that Lambert variously affected Kant's germinal ideas on the nature of truth and appearance. Indeed, at one time Kant considered the possibility of developing a *Phenomenology* rather than a *Critique* of Pure Reason. Both Kant's *Critique of Pure Reason* and Hegel's *Phänomenologie des Geistes* were developed in part on the basis of Lambert's earlier initiatives.

Within a complex dialectic, before Hegel's refinement of this concept, the eighteenth-century contributions of Lambert, Kant, and, most important, Hegel set the stage for a substantial philosophical, and eventually empirical, treatment of mind.

In this context I propose that we move forward with a phenomenology of mind—executive mind included—on the foundations of Hegel's *Phänomenologie des Geistes*—translatable essentially as "Phenomenology of Mind" (1807), thence bridging particularly to the works of Edmund Husserl (1913, 1931). I base this suggestion on the view that Hegel systematically introduced a set of concepts, many now taken for granted, that have proved central to the *empirical* study of mind in a current humanistic and practical sense. In his *System der Wissenschaft: Phänomenologie des Geistes* (1807), Hegel proceeded with a rigorous treatment of such concepts as consciousness, self-consciousness (or self-awareness), reason (but also translatable as rationality or as cognitive style), and mind itself and its alienation and, importantly, with the scientific study of experience.

As noted, "mind" has proved to be an unusually slippery construct. This has been so in philosophy and in psychology, whatever their hypothetical boundaries. Staying with Hegel's example and considering the range of meanings attached to *mind,* one need only examine his congeries of concepts in terms of definitions provided by any good German-English dictionary. Here *Geist* in the sense of mind (or spirit) yields a plethora of synonyms, or, more properly, aspects, translatable as *memory, recollection, attention, awareness, consideration, thought, opinion, attitude, view, conviction, mental set, intention, will, desire, inclination, motivation, intellect, reason, soul, mood, feeling,* and *consciousness,* not to mention *brain* itself.

Charles Hampden-Turner, in his imaginative *Maps of the Mind* (1981), paraphrases, by word and by conceptual diagram, the treatment of mind by a veritable battery of authors, including Freud, Jung, Laing, Lewin, Erikson, Korzybski, Maslow, Marcuse, von Bertalanffy, Bateson, and Levi-Strauss. All this may serve to remind us that the fundamental *meaning* of the concept "mind," drawing on foundations laid by Hegel, enmeshed in vast semantic complexity, and elaborated by many from many perspectives since, cannot be taken for granted. To make progress we need, minimally, to be clear about the concept's chosen meaning and its history in antecedent scientific disciplines. Optimally, the concept can serve as a platform for design of a suitable integrative theory that may add to the understanding of what, why, and how executives think, feel, and act. The executive in action provides a particularly suitable focus for exploration of the rational and the nonrational, of the systematic and the intuitive, and of the Apollonian and of the Dionysian in complexly organized human behavior (Taggart and Robby, 1981).

Recapturing Real Human Experience as Primary Datum

To develop a sound methodology for study of the executive mind, it is necessary as well to develop an explicit epistemology of the meaning of "mind." Such an epistemology, based on historical roots, is essential if we are to develop effective methods to tell us what really goes on in the executive's "mind" and life. The venture before us calls for approaches that go beyond the constraining and often unrealistic and artificial studies that abound in conventional organizational behavior and technical management publications. Here I emphasize concept and method; in addition, some results can also be discerned. Yet, as we examine the history of organizational behavior or, for that matter, of so-called basic disciplines such as psychology and sociology, we find that we are far from "over the hump" in any resolution of what appears to be an endemic controversy.

Hegel and other major figures of much later vintage, such as William James (1890), approach the key concepts from what some might call "mentalistic" foundations. Others in recent literature, notably Hebb (1980), proceed in essentially neuropsychological terms, apparently having no doubt that mind (forget experience) is located specifically (and exclusively) in the brain, their concepts of choice being cell assembly, networks of reverberatory circuits, and so on. And those of us who are enamored of placing emphasis on the term *behavior,* as in *organizational behavior,* tend to follow the notion that it is the external, "objectively" manifest act, rather than the "subjective state," that deserves principal attention—that is, what do executives *do*? And others, perhaps in a spirit of compromise, urge that mental states be "translated" into behavior by operational means, to make them admissible to the "knowable" or, more formally, to the "scientific" (Bridgman, 1932; Lundberg, 1939).

In our concern with operational definition, we are, however, inclined to forget that recourse to such definition only shifts the burden and does not address head on the perennial issue of subjectivity versus objectivity. And further, one needs to consider direct effects of the researcher on subject response— for instance, the "Rosenthal effect" (Rosenthal, 1976).

But the matter does not end there. Clearly we can conceive of *observers viewing observers*; for example, in psychotherapy training the supervisor observes the apprentice clinician's clinical observations. A similar process occurs in academic and journal peer review. And, of course, there are instances of "observers observing observers observing the observer."

It is quickly apparent, as pointed out by Husserl and others, that we face an eternal regress—a never-ending, ever-complicating series of interlocking successive images or "boxes within boxes within boxes," consisting of experiences. Thus, mind is not a "thing" or a given "event" but, at best, human experiences *in seriatim*. If taken seriously, this continuing process— we might call it "cumulative observation"—powerfully draws our attention to the root significance of observed *real human experience* as the fundamental datum of inquiry concerning mind.

In Hegel's terms (1807), attention is directed to "Erfahrung des Bewusstseins," the experiencing of consciousness, with the implication of apperception and reflection on such experience. In this paradigm, experiencing is both a function of *consciousness* of the experiencing mind itself, as it were "within the person" observed, but in turn it affects, and is affected by, experiencing on the part of the "observer" or of any other with whom the self stands in interpersonal relationship.

At a later stage I shall have occasion to speak of the "phenomenological reduction" (Husserl, 1913) as a way of untangling these interlocking experiences. It seems to me that, particularly in Husserl's work, practical approaches for accomplishing this were implicitly present, although then the time was not ripe for their direct implementation. Both Husserl's mode of thought and his concern with abstraction (including, initially, mathematical abstraction) militated against success; his work remained a matter of "thought experiment," rather than practical application. A revised *applied phenomenology* may be able to make use of the concept of phenomenological reduction "hands on," thus connecting to the mainstream of contemporary behavioral science research.

The field of Husserlian application, however, has not remained entirely fallow. For instance, there are Gendlin's contributions, exemplified by his *Experiencing and the Creation of Meaning* (1962). Gendlin's efforts are directed to drawing our attention to the process of "experiencing" as a principal practical approach to the study of the subjective. He notes that experience is "always changing, not equivalent to generalizations, complex and finely determined, irreducible to units of (conventional) explanatory systems, and not the same in participant observer, unbiased observer, or spontaneous participant" (p. 23). It is especially in this context, the role and dynamics of the observer, that one needs to return to the fundamental concepts proposed by Husserl, notably as related to the nature of experience as *given* and ubiquitous and to the *phenomenological reduction* as method.

Toward a Substantial Theory
of the Experiencing Process

In the establishment of theoretic foundations for an applied phenomenology, three strands of influence can be discerned: the *classical*, beginning with Hegel and thence with influences of Brentano (1924) and Stumpf (1912; see also Schmidt, 1924) to Husserl (1913); the *empirical*, including Gendlin (1962), Goffman (1959), Snygg and Combs (1959), Combs, Richards, and Richards (1976), Mahrer (1978), and the Duquesne group (Strasser, 1963); and the *theoretic-practical*, exemplified by Lewin (1951; Leeper, 1943). It is evident that, among those listed, a number, especially those on the empirical side, do not use the term *phenomenology* although their concepts and procedures partake of "phenomenological" positions.

As noted, I suggest that the study of the executive mind is essentially a direct study of certain kinds of *experiencing,* by the executive and concurrently by those seeking to understand the nature of executive mind. With this perspective, the following propositions can be formulated:

- Executive mind itself is *not* a given segment of behavior or a chain of such behaviors; behaviors are overt expressions of processes internal to an experiencing and observing human being, linking to other likewise experiencing and observing human beings.
- Executive mind itself is *not,* in a holistic sense, any given managerial function such as "problem solving" or "decision making." Rather, such functions stem from the same base of experiencing just noted, and they must be understood in the context of this ongoing process.

In view of these positions, I am more inclined to follow William James and his "stream of consciousness" in preference to either formal behaviorism or bland operationalism, paying attention to "people as they are," as experiencing and experienced human beings in the living wholeness. People become known, ideally, by unfolding experienced *processes,* extensive through time and best accessible by longitudinal, not snapshot, approaches. And should we have only snapshots in our grasp, as by cross-sectional observation or by brief journalistic and research report, then we need to be doubly reminded to interpret these fragments within the frames of change in time and of human wholeness.

Management thought is frequently entrenched in an implicit dualism. It is an apparently simple strategy to divide the world into "good guys" (white cowboy hats) and "bad guys" (black cowboy hats). So we are wont to think of mind *versus* body, although we may temper the concept by speaking of "psychosomatic illness" and the like. Similarly, one may refer to rational "versus" intuitive management styles and to right-brain "versus" left-brain modes of thought.

One need not argue that everything is one big, homogeneous "blob" to suggest that apparent dichotomies like these are in actuality holistic in their very essence. Managers do not function in terms of fixed categories or labels. Although one may wish, for *analytic* purposes, to create dichotomies or other categories with apparently "hard" delineations, the continuing process in which an executive is engaged involves a complex and implicit intertwining of many discernible experiences. Some of these may obtain clear delineation at a given time, only to fade into the background later, to revive again, and so on. Thus, rationality and intuition may merge into a patterned whole as the executive goes about his or her business.

The notion that certain executives prefer, explicitly or as demonstrated by their actions, one or another mode of operation does not defeat the conceptual view that executive mind might indeed be best considered as a unified process, linking "external" environments as represented by technological, economic, and interpersonal forces to the executives' "internal" experiencing. Therefore, it is advisable to leave behind the narrow distinctions between mind and brain, between body and mind, and the like, focusing instead on the *whole human being*—in this instance, an executive functioning in a role that (1) is not cut in advance into discrete categories and (2) involves simultaneous phenomena at all levels, accessible through study of the person's full experiencing.

A word of methodological caution: The risk of "throwing out the baby with the bathwater" is ever present. One cannot, of course, study all of holistic executive mind at any one time; one must examine aspects of it in the context of the whole. These aspects, however, although they may be apparently analyzed, that is, studied as parts, need not be regarded as segmented, autonomous part-functions. The total context serves as organizing principle when the aspects, not parts, are examined. For instance, "problem solving" or "decision making" may reflect some aspect of executive mind embedded within the human context that gives it meaning. Here the Gestalt notion of figure/ground serves us well (Ellis, 1950; Köhler, 1947). At a given moment, a particular aspect may be considered "figure," with the remaining wholeness seen as "ground," but emphasis may reverse or shift at a later time.

To "get on with it," we now consider how we can draw on certain aspects of phenomenological thought as a basis for gaining better insight into executive mind.

Studying Real Experience: The "Lebenswelt" Examined

As we proceed with procedures focusing on "real experience," we may consider the generic concept of *Lebenswelt*. This term, rooted in various phases of classic phenomenological thought and recast by Lewin as "life space," essentially is "the world as I experience it now." The Lebenswelt is constituted by the *entire constellation of sensory, affective, and cognitive events observed as subjectively "there" by the person at a given time and place*. The content of the Lebenswelt thus is "raw," direct, and not appropriately subject to dispute by an external observer; it is phenomenally and subjectively "given." It is the total pattern of now-existing experiences at various levels of the person's self. The following are suggestive of these levels of self, which typically are coexisting, simultaneous, and interinfluencing:

- Cognitive/affective experience
- Verbal/nonverbal experience
- Conscious/unconscious experience
- Experience capable of being expressed/expressively inchoate
- Experience clearly structured/undefined

Other dimensions undoubtedly could be added to the list. Whatever its proposed substance, Lebenswelt is fundamentally an intrapsychic phenomenon that is a resultant of both psychological forces within the person and exogenous influences, including environmental and interpersonal. This view is not solipsistic, reducing everything to "mere" sensation; rather, it points to the existential present product of the vast number of factors—personal, interpersonal, group, organizational, societal, and, for that matter, technological and economic—that make us think and feel as we do every moment of our lives.

In treating the concept of Lebenswelt, we face, as often happens, the consequences of the Whorf-Sapir hypothesis (Whorf, 1956): The words and syntax available to our thinking limit the thoughts that we shall think. In this respect, the nature of the English language proves to be a specific constraint. English-speaking scholars are inclined to use the single word *experience* to cover at least two separately discernible processes identified in German as *Erlebnis* and *Erfahrung,* a distinction made by Cairns in 1973 (William Woodward, personal communication to author, 1982). Erlebnis, partaking of the same root as *Lebens-*welt, addresses the notion of ongoing, direct, and lively experience in the sense of "what is happening to me now." Erfahrung, however, is a different kind of experience: It relates to that which we have experienced at some time in the past, something on which we may reflect and from which we may perhaps learn. In Erfahrung the root concept is expressed by the letters *fahr,* carrying the connotation of a "journey in process." Making use of Erfahrung *now* may make it an aspect of Erlebnis, but in principle it is "experience one step removed" from what I am living through.

Whatever the distinction, the question arises how "experience" is rendered accessible to the person experiencing and to an "outsider" who wishes to know the experiencer's Lebenswelt. Here we shall focus on the latter issue with special reference to the *phenomenological reduction.*

Let us attempt, variously following Husserl's precise yet typically complex description, to specify the phenomenological reduction process (PRP) in ordered sequence. In doing so, we realize that we impose a linear discipline on a process that may not unfold in linear fashion; for purposes of discourse, however, it is convenient to do so.

The purpose of the PRP, its goal, is to determine the *essence* of experience. This essence is "the characteristic of being or existence, that aspect of (the experiencer's Lebenswelt) which is the object of belief in an independent present reality" (Spiegelberg, 1965, p. 134).

As the first step, the observer (that is, the phenomenologist) seeking the essence of the experiencer's Lebenswelt suspends all prior assumptions. The observer consciously holds apart the attitude set that he or she normally employs, either in everyday life or in conventional scientific inquiry. Thus, the observer is keenly conscious of her or his value assumptions, observational style, and attitudes, as well as of momentary moods, preferences, orientations, and the like, but these are consciously held in abeyance.

The core of PRP is that the experiencer's Lebenswelt is *bracketed* by the observer; that is, it is held in suspension to clarify the nature of the presented phenomenon *directly experienced by the person* whose Lebenswelt the observer wishes to understand.

In addition, the observer also brackets his or her own self, examining its now-existing structure and dynamics and taking account of them in the process of seeking the essence of the person to be understood. Figure 1 is a diagrammatic representation of *double bracketing.*

In usual parlance, we paraphrase social "observation" as

Figure 1. Double-Bracketing Process.

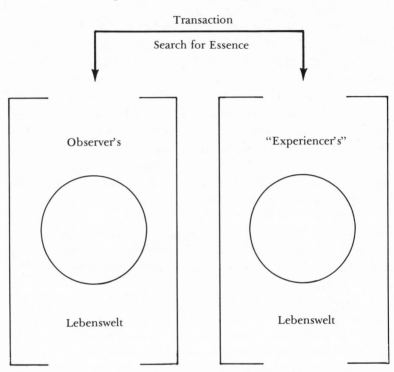

simply "person looking at object." This statement masks, of course, the inherent complexity of person, object, and the transaction occurring. Phenomenological bracketing requires a change of attitude in which *nothing is taken for granted.* Ideally, the person being observed is to be examined in full complexity, from every viewpoint experientially conceivable; only available time and energy limit the process. The observer is instructed to divest himself or herself of all assumptions, although more detailed reading of Husserl suggests that he points primarily to *untested* or *unexamined* assumptions. Accordingly, even though Husserl's writings do not place brackets about the observer as well, his concept of "meditations" may be regarded as partly equivalent. In this process the self is abstracted from the rest of the world and, as personality dynamics permit, examined in relevant context.

In this double-bracketed framework, the observer examines the nature of the observing self as a starting point—the observer's Lebenswelt—and directs attention—in the transaction entering the experiencer's Lebenswelt—to the essential existence of the person observed, having taken into account the self's impact on the transaction.

Phenomenological concepts such as *noema,* relating to the nature of meaning, and the *cogitatio,* relating to identification of the person or event observed, may enter the technical discourse. In practical terms, however, the process of double bracketing can be paraphrased, with focus on the observer, as follows:

> I need to know who I am and what I am and how I feel now as I proceed with observing who is before me. I need to understand my real relationship to the person whom I am to observe and the reciprocal relationship as well. Then, I want to look deeply at all that is before me, at the person and at the person's experience that I want to understand. I want to look openly at every possible aspect of all this, no matter what my "common sense" or scientific "biasing" assumptions may hold. I want to look at all aspects of person and experience as these present themselves, as they *directly appear,* as emergent *"phenomena."* In this way I want to experience the *essence* of that person and event: I want to give this person every possible opportunity to present this essence in our interaction with each other.

Spiegelberg (1965), in his consideration of Husserl's version of the phenomenological reduction, explores in depth the nature of skepticism, including Santayana's approach to analogous issues, and concludes that Husserl alludes to a more revolutionary breakthrough in approach to knowledge than is readily apparent by a simple espousal of personal skepticism. I would argue that this more significant depth of understanding results when *double* bracketing, rather than single bracketing, is proposed. The fundamental understanding emerges *in the inter-action* between profound self-understanding and profound effort to understand the other.

Applying the Phenomenological Interview

One may want to explore the study of executive mind by the application of double bracketing—that is, by a deeply probing, real-life, experiential search for what goes on "within" the observer and what genuinely unfolds in the lives of people functioning in all kinds of roles. The question remains, of course, how one proceeds in implementing the necessary methodology. Every experience is, by its very nature, unique. Any intrusion, whether by questionnaire, interview, or other conventional research instrument, itself creates a *new* experience; the question remains whether this new experience can capture the *essence* of a prior experience that we wish to study. In this connection a reconsideration of the phenomenological interview may be in order.

The phenomenological interview has been described in some detail elsewhere (Massarik, 1981, p. 203). Here I shall briefly review its chief characteristics.

This interview is characterized by maximal mutuality of trust, attaining a genuine and deeply experienced caring about interviewer and interviewee, and a commitment to joint search for shared understanding. Interviewer and interviewee respond to each other as total persons, ready to actively examine and disclose both remote and readily accessible aspects of their lives.

This relationship involves fundamental equality and concurring commitment to the quest at hand. The time frame is fluid, unbounded by the usual constraints of a therapeutic hour or sometimes even by considerations of night and day. Interviewer and interviewee have, within appropriate recognitions of their life constraints, free access to each other; ideas explored on one occasion may be temporarily laid aside, only to be reexamined in changed context later. There is little by way of simplistic question-and-answer exchange; rather, free-form modes of communication and iterative opportunities for review and clarification characterize the process.

Interviewer and interviewee aspire to enter, with shared commitment and mutual caring, each other's experienced "worlds"—their existential Lebenswelten. The interviewer's empathic effort to explore the interviewee's "world" is aided by a sense of reciprocal empathy by the interviewee in which the latter acknowledges the realities of the interviewer's world. Thus, although an important emphasis remains with explication—or, in the German sociological sense, with *Verstehen*—of the interviewee's world, the dynamics of the interviewer are explicitly part of the process. Unlike the conventional interview philosophy that seeks to hold constant the interviewer's impact on the interviewee—a goal of questionable feasibility—this interview style recognizes the inherent humanness of both participants and indeed the genuine relevance of the total interpersonal (as well as nonhuman) environment within which the process occurs.

Accordingly, some conventional strictures of the standard interview fall by the wayside. Here the interviewer functions as self-aware self, directly involved in a commitment to empathic search *with* the person interviewed, in quest for the essence of that person's experience.

Chances are that phenomenological interviewers in their natural habitat are a rare species and that those who "qualify" are a varied lot—some ethnographers, psychotherapists, and television interviewers included. It is not clear whether academic psychological researchers and scholars of management establish a numerically significant presence in this connection. If we leave some leeway, we would include in the list Studs Terkel (1972), Oriana Fallaci (1977), and Robert Lindner (1958), among others.

Because it is necessary to respond to the other with deep awareness of one's own unique perspective, the phenomenological interview unfolds with mutuality and awareness of the interinfluence between interviewer and interviewee. Thus, it resembles not a "vending-machine model" (throw in 50 cents and get a Pepsi) but, rather, the model of a shared voyage: Each aids the other as the journey toward essence proceeds. Instead of pseudo objectivity, this shared exploration is based on jointly discovered perspectives. These, however, neither constitute nor reveal fixed "reality"; rather, alternative "realities"—that is, various specified essences—are uncovered in this double-bracketed mutual search.

The phenomenological interview may be considered in the framework of a typology of interviews (Massarik, 1981). Although it shares certain common characteristics with the "depth" interview, the phenomenological interview goes beyond the latter, particularly in its commitment to openness and unboundedness. Ideally, the phenomenological interview stands particularly high in acceptance, trust, and psychological closeness between interviewer and interviewee, in emphasis on the interviewee's whole "life world" or on major aspects thereof, in attention to concerns shared between interviewer and interviewee, and in awareness of both content and process as the interview proceeds. Importantly, for a given interview, time is ample and eventual allocation is virtually unbounded.

It is evident that there are few ordinary circumstances in which all these criteria can be fully satisfied. However, it is practically possible to meet these criteria in much greater measure than in the typical structured or open-ended interview. A kind of informal corroboration of many "good" interviews that surreptitiously border on the phenomenological is constituted by the "over a cup of coffee" conversations among survey interviewers, recounting what "really" happens—how a "respondent" broke down in tears reporting a marriage breakup, for instance, when the interview supposedly addressed issues of voting preference; or an instance in which interviewee and interviewer began to exchange life stories, common childhood experiences, although the interview was supposed to deal with attitudes toward three shampoo commercials. These topics that seem to give meaning to the interaction may not have been at all irrelevant either in terms of specific interview objectives or in terms of an understanding of the person whose segmented responses ostensibly were called for in the "official" study plan. It is likely that conventional interviewers do a lot of "cleaning up" of what really happens, to maintain an illusion of focus and clarity, presumably demanded by "objective" study procedure. Still, it is possible to develop study designs that follow orthodox sampling requirements—for example, the selection of multistage, random-probability, stratified samples of executives in various industries, company sizes, job titles, and hierarchy positions—while the interview itself is phenomenological in approach.

Finally, we must consider the nature of the data yielded by the phenomenological interview. We must recall that our emphasis is on *reports of experiences* emerging in the life worlds we have studied. It is evident that such experiences do not necessarily follow cut-and-dried logical structures. Although the direct "readout" of experience still remains beyond our ken, it is possible (and here much is available in clinical case reporting, diaries, videotapes, and extensive protocols) to obtain finely detailed *secondary* documentation of *aspects* of experience. Experience in this sense more closely approximates Erfahrung, in contrast with Erlebnis, the former recounting and reflecting on prior direct experience. Of course, this process of recounting and reflecting itself may be viewed as a *new* direct experience in the sense of Erlebnis.

The problem of phenomenological interview analysis is illustrated by research, in process, conducted in connection with assessment of organization development outcomes in a large West German mail order and merchandising corporation. The data collection and analysis portion can be summarized as follows:

1. Interview purpose or *boundary* is broadly defined by interviewer, noting interest in interviewee's experiences in personal, professional, and technical training, provided by company or elsewhere.

2. Interviewee chooses own *entry point* into shared discourse with interviewer, focuses on a given topic, expresses feelings, asks questions of interviewer, and so on. Interviewer *accepts and responds to* interviewee's entry point, comments as appropriate in the context of evolving relationship between interviewer and interviewee.

3. Interview begins to develop *"a life of its own."* Some

topics are raised, dropped, returned to, and elaborated; others are interspersed; new ones are put forth. An often-irregular constellation of commentary evolves as interviewer and interviewee search together to *understand* the interviewee's experience. This does not preclude balanced examination of the interviewer's experience as well.

These various aspects of reportage, revelation, and reflection may be viewed in terms of a series of unfolding *contours*; each contour describes a particular issue or subject matter and the feelings associated with it.

Contours should not be seen as "rigid hoops" but, rather, as continuously moving and changing emphases as conceptualized, for instance, by the thermal lines of a weather map or by the movements of an ameba. To grasp the nature of contours, one literally "goes with the flow," following the shifting concerns (experiences, as Erfahrung) of the interviewee in an effort to make clear their *manifest aspects* and eventually their *essences*.

4. Eventually the interview approaches *closure*. Ideally this occurs as both interviewer and interviewee sense that, at least for the present, the topics within the boundary have been amply explored. There may be a desire for future opportunity to continue the exploration. Or there may be a sense that the task is complete. Additionally, interviewer and interviewee have come to know each other in some deeper sense as human beings, rather than as question-asking/answering machines. We may discern a kind of *closing ritual,* often a brief reflection on what has occurred, exchange of thanks, expression of hopes for other meetings, and the like.

5. For present lack of a better medium, the unfolding events, as outlined above, yield a *protocol.* This protocol may be arrived at by transcript of the recorded conversation or on the basis of the interviewer's elaborated notes or by a combination of both. The chosen procedures remain subject to well-known limitations. Videotape provides an increasingly available, though also selective and constrained, means for documenting phenomenological interview process and content.

Assuming that it is a *verbal* protocol that is at hand, one proceeds to examine its pattern of information in terms of boundary, entry point, contours, and closure at conceptual levels and in terms of various content and feeling categories.

Quite complex data sets result, related to but going beyond conventional content or theme analysis. These procedures derive from concepts described above and make use of *emergent* conceptual categories, as constructed by one or several observers. In turn, word-processing technology facilitates analysis of the verbal data in ways previously excessively laborious or impractical.

In summary, the proposed method provides insight into the experienced life world of any person, including the executive. It is based on an examination of aspects and essences of life by the creation of a special shared interview with focus on a moderately bounded universe of subject matter, salient to the executive.

Reconsidering the Nature of Knowing

"How do you know that you really know?" In a fundamental sense, the answer is "never." The criteria defining "satisfactory knowledge," or if one wishes to follow March and Simon's (1958) approach, "satisficing knowledge," themselves are human inventions related to human goals. It is "good enough" (satisfying/satisficing) to know that *in our culture* a red light, under certain circumstances, means "Don't cross the street." In other cultures or other circumstances, a red light might mean something else. In every instance, it is human purpose that indicates whether what we know is sufficient, whether it is a humanly useful guide to thought or action. By this mode of conceptualization, knowledge is necessarily relative but never complete.

Formal statistical theory defines parameters that, under specifiable conditions, establish probabilities of knowledge about the occurrence of certain events. The statistician bears the burden of making ostensibly correct choices concerning assumptions underlying the use of a particular statistic and the selection of that statistic. Indeed, one endemic problem associated with conveniently available software packages is the potentially inappropriate use of statistics simply because it is convenient to make use of a particular procedure. De facto, the process of human choice is not by any means eliminated when the researcher seeks recourse or refuge in "hard-nosed" data analysis.

The challenge facing the phenomenological researcher follows a different path but again points to the relativity of knowledge. A given human event, such as the responses of the interviewee in a phenomenological interview, may be seen in brackets, but from the viewpoints of a number of phenomenological interviewers, as depicted in Figure 2.

Figure 2. Interviewee in a Phenomenological Interview.

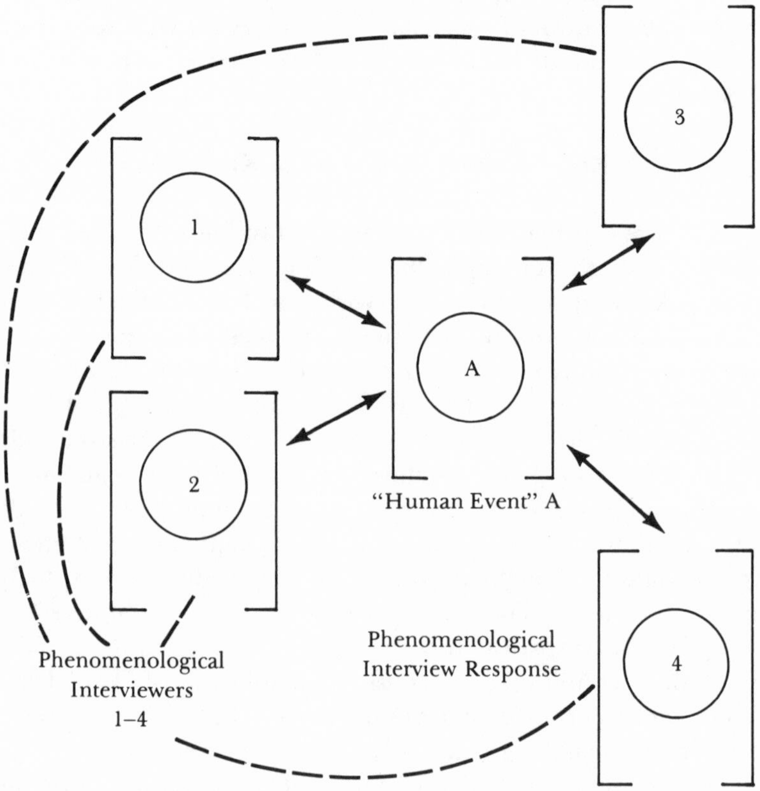

Further, a given phenomenological interviewer may, of course, still respond, following the modes of bracketing, to a number of interviewees, as presented in Figure 3.

Figure 3. Modes of Bracketing and
Phenomenological Interview Process.

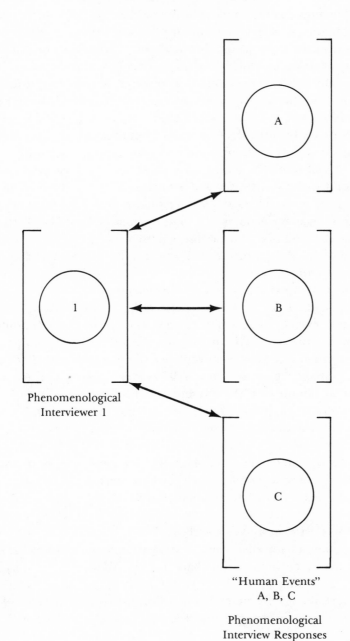

Phenomenological
Interviewer 1

"Human Events"
A, B, C

Phenomenological
Interview Responses

It is evident that both these strategies in accumulating knowledge yield a range of data points that are likely to have both common elements and diverse elements. The issue comes to be one of selection both of phenomenological interviewers and of interviewees, together with an awareness of the range of circumstances in which the varied interviews may occur.

In conventional statistical research, samples typically are chosen at the outset, although more sophisticated designs permit iterative successive sampling, in which results obtained at an initial pass through data are used in guiding subsequent sample plans. The latter strategy seems most appropriate in phenomenological research. With guidelines similar to those proposed in grounded theory (Glaser and Strauss, 1967), one may select, on theoretic grounds, particular persons or situations as initial data points, to explore all aspects and essences. One proceeds to add such data points to examine whether additional new aspects emerge in the observational process as additional cases are added to the data base.

One must see to it that the selection of cases is based on explicit theoretic considerations, rather than resulting simply from convenience or arbitrary choice. It seems to me that many inquiries that are self-consciously labeled "phenomenological" represent nontheoretic convenience samples that include certain cases simply because they fall within vaguely defined conceptual boundaries. An example: If I am studying behavior in bars, do I simply go to the one around the block and to one more down the street "because they are there"? Or am I prepared to specify a more substantial decision rule? Further, if I am to conduct phenomenological interviews of executives, do I simply pick a couple of middle managers who are friends of mine (plus a few of their buddies as well), or do I proceed with a more purposeful delineation of executive and/or organization characteristics as a basis for choice?

The major advantage of iterative selection of cases is that it provides continuous feedback loops of data processed by observers, adding power both to the analysis and to the range of understanding. To defend this procedure against charges of inherent bias, let us note that the bracketing procedure includes not only the principal participants in the phenomenological interview but also external and less "biased" observers, considering the nested principal phenomenological observations. Figure 4 represents this process.

Figure 4. Relationship Between Principal Participants in an Interview Situation and Externals.

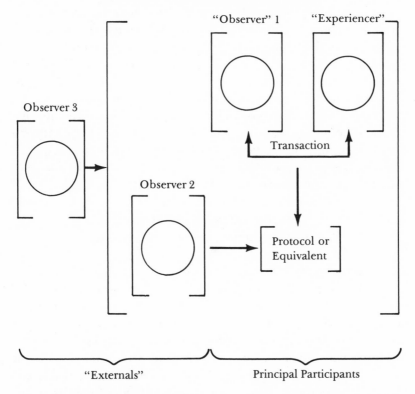

Eventually the process of "consensual validation" may be regarded as one appropriate way station in the odyssey to understanding of the executive mind. Presumably saturation has been reached in the collection and analysis of data: No major *new* aspects of the phenomenon appear after a while, essences have been identified, and there is concurrence among some specified set of observers that certain recognizable dynamics prevail. This stage represents some interim level of agreement concerning the phenomena studied. It is obvious that such agreement speaks only to a *current* level of knowledge and that it is subject to change, but with notice, or to total refutation.

Finally, a brief observation about the *single case*. A considerable literature has made clear that the single case is indeed relevant, sometimes a critically important building block in the development of knowledge. First, the single case may reveal aspects that previously had not been known at all or in a given context. Thus, it provides a basis for subsequent large-scale inquiry. Second, the single case may provide such richness of perceptive detail, as do Freud's case of Dora ([1905], 1952) and other insightful clinical histories, that it assists a wide range of observers in deriving meaningful and applicable conclusions. Finally, the single case may yield an understanding of the internal microstructure of a given event, directly and indirectly infusing meaning into other apparently disparate events. In a metaphorical sense, one may consider that even a tiny grain of sand holographically reflects aspects of the universe.

The Executive Mind Revealed:
Some Phenomenological Observations

It is not the primary objective of this chapter to report extensive research findings. However, to give some sense of results concerning aspects and essences of executive mind, based mostly on U.S. and West German phenomenological interviews and related procedures, I offer the following theories and dilemmas, which emerge from conversations with some executives:

"Happy Firefighting." Dealing with changing realities is exciting, energizing, fun; there is an underlying sense that riding in and out of day-by-day turbulence is essential (in the present meaning of *essence*) to attain concrete rewards (financial or nonfinancial) for efforts expended.

"Grabbing the Brass Ring." Looking for medium-term results . . . that brass ring is not immediately reachable, nor does it appear on a far horizon . . . it is worthwhile to expend energy (although it sometimes feels like going in circles) because that goal *is* reachable.

"A Life World of Ladders." There are tall ladders and

short ladders, and climbing some of them is important. Life is defined by looking upward and, as possible, by climbing upward. Many potential ladders are available; some are inviting and some are irrelevant or perhaps not seen at all. Some of these ladders may be technical, managerial, or familial. Various aspects in this life world of ladders relate to "life goals" and to core values (Buhler and Massarik, 1968; Buhler, 1962).

"If You Can Keep Your Head." The executive needs the ability to stay focused, yet to go with options and quick reversals—reversals that may seem inconsistent to an observer but are regarded as internally consistent. Alternatively, problems arise if a given course of action is "locked in" in the face of changing circumstances in the relevant system.

"The Agony of Primacy." What really matters most? Facing issues of priorities in terms of differential time and resource allocation remains paramount. Often not confronted explicitly, it sets the framework for potential agony: "How can I do it all?" "What should I do next?" "Work comes first, family comes second? how to handle . . . ?" This perennial matter of priorities may be aggravated when collision courses develop among considerations of "firefighting," choice of "ladders," and the like.

"The Agony of Self-Doubt." Beneath the surface of assertive competence, sometimes overlaid with purposeful "image building," the dragons of self-doubt spew their venom. Indeed, the need to *be* competent or to maintain the *image* of competence may serve to enlarge even small cracks in the veneer, with self-doubt either dynamically repressed or resulting in genuine and private agonizing. The relationship to "stress" and to responses often appearing in the "known to self—not known to others" segment of the Johari window (Luft, 1969) becomes readily apparent.

One is reminded of the concept of "life metaphor" as one seeks to organize the essences of executive mind. For Richard M. Nixon and for others with certain views of the political world, the metaphor may be "winning the football game at all costs" and the world as jungle. To some of a more benign nature, it may be "tending one's own garden," and for Antoine de Saint-Exupéry, the author/aviator who perished in a World

War II reconnaissance mission, it was the metaphor of the freedom of fulfilling flight.

Epilogue

I position this present effort as occupying a niche in a *beginning* stage of *an applied and a practical phenomenology,* even though, as observed early in this chapter, the relevant sources date back at least to the eighteenth century. I experienced this sense of historic continuity in the course of a visit to the principal Husserl Archive at Leuven, Belgium, in the fall of 1982. The founding of this archive constitutes a fascinating but separate story. We may note briefly that the archive contains the bulk of Husserl's technical library, including his marginalia on existing material and voluminous working notes.

In this connection, a closing anecdote: Although I am quite proficient in German, my high hopes of reading much unpublished work by Husserl were quickly dashed. It turns out that Husserl typically wrote his notes in shorthand, and not the currently practiced kind, either. Rather, his prolific comments were put forth in *Gabelsberger Kurzschrift,* a fairly obscure German system of stenography. The question now arises: "Do I need to study *Gabelsberger Kurzschrift,* and if so, how will I go about it?" I *am* tempted to give it a try. For what it matters, I guess I look forward to the experience.

In a fundamental sense we each choose our own parable, often obscured by the shadows and fog banks which in part we create and which in part we encounter. It is this chapter's thesis that we need to look at the very basic raw material of daily experience through a new set of eyes and with an affirmed commitment to understanding both what goes on within us and what goes on in the worlds of those we seek to understand. Each may provide enhanced clarity to the other. All this may constitute but a modest modification—a small reorientation in our approach to inquiry. Yet in the long run we might hope that these renewed perspectives will make a discernible difference in enhancing the quality of our knowledge of executive mind as it reveals itself in ever-unfolding complexity and in its emergent essence.

11

Strengthening Management Education

Ronald E. Fry
William A. Pasmore

Our experience of the symposium was the genesis of this chapter. As reflected in the preceding chapters, we were witness to an exchange of ideas that was rich in its intellectualism, diversity of vantage points, and interconnectedness. What made it particularly exciting was the recognition that all the scholars who attended were, for a few days, trying to answer the same questions: How does the executive mind function? How can we understand organizations as expressions of executive minds? Although answers to these and similar questions are still partial at best, the symposium clearly marked a leap forward in our understanding of executive thought processes and perhaps set a new direction for the field of organizational behavior as well. More specifically, the ideas discussed were more cognitive than behavioral, more theoretical than applied, more introspective than descriptive. This could signal the evolution of a new paradigm of inquiry dealing with the unique, enigmatic issues that arise at the nexus of research about persons and research about organizations.

An aspect of the symposium that stood out was how appreciative the contributors felt of executives and the complex challenges they face. This was clearly not an ivory-tower attack on the misguided dealings of well-intentioned but incapable managers. Instead, it was an almost reverent inquiry into the lives and struggles of those who, against the odds, make useful contributions to their organizations. We wish to continue the appreciative spirit begun during the symposium in addressing an area that emerged for us as one deserving special attention by those in attendance and all others in the broadly defined business of executive education.

During the symposium we learned a great deal about how executives currently think and act; we were also stimulated to think of how we might improve our current methods of research to improve our understanding of the executive's world. At the same time we were aware that symposium participants had addressed primarily the *current* state of affairs, without much attention to the ways in which the executive mind *could or should* function. We in the business of executive education and development have a unique opportunity and, in fact, responsibility to improve the effectiveness of organizations and society by shaping the minds of their leaders; but how should we do this, and toward what end? Without understanding how the executive mind works, let alone how it could function more effectively, how can we improve our educational programs? What should we be doing to prepare executives for the unknown challenges of tomorrow instead of teaching them how to answer yesterday's questions? What are the key phases and processes through which the executive mind develops? What skills and abilities do executives need that we should be helping to provide?

These and similar questions prompted us to review how the executive mind is educated and developed currently, with a critical eye on the nurturance of essential cognitive capacities identified during the symposium. Our review indicated to us that executive educational systems are in need of major revision.

The purpose of this chapter is to own up to our role in executive miseducation and to set out some thoughts on how to do things differently. If the capabilities of present and future influential leaders can be improved, then the effectiveness of their organizations should improve as well. If they learn to utilize the talents of their employees in ways that are more productive and more personally satisfying, the quality of working life should benefit. If they can be more aware of the processes through which they acquire, process, and react to information, they and their organizations should become more open to feedback and more capable of responding flexibly to significant changes occurring around them. And if we as educators or experienced executives can better understand how the executive mind develops and influence that process through which the executive mind functions in the ways just outlined, we can play a significant role in shaping the future of American management practices.

To enhance critical thinking on the part of executives will require, first, that we assess the processes and contexts through which the executive mind develops. In so doing we will make clear our view that the development of the executive mind requires simultaneous attention to three independent but interpenetrating dimensions of growth: growth of the executive as a person, growth of the executive in the context of others who provide significant learnings and resources, and growth of the executive in regard to developing mastery over the environment. Our task is to begin exploring the interworkings of these variables in shaping the nature of executive thought processes. Finally, we suggest a developmental process of executive interaction and ways to further this process in educational and work settings.

Development of Executive Individuality

Few would deny that children are ill suited to perform executive roles; but then, some would astutely point out that most executives have lost the ability to gain from the spontaneous creativity that characterized their youth. Something almost indescribable happens between birth and adulthood that transforms the child into a mature human being; in a handful of cases, that mysterious process produces a man or woman capable of exercising the power of executive thought. Others have written extensively about the process of human development, most prominently Piaget (1951), Erikson (1950), and Freud ([1923], 1961). Although these authors use different vocabularies to describe the process of development and each chooses to divide the lifetime of an individual into different segments for the purpose of analysis, each also conveys a common message: As a child grows into an adult, the identity and thought processes of the individual, once quite open to influence from significant others, become relatively stable and resistant to change. The adult is more certain of himself or herself, more self- and less other-directed, and more capable of exercising independent thought. The process of ego and identity development, according to Erikson, continues at least until the teenage years and in some cases far beyond. Much later, the focus of individual energy turns again toward others, in search of resolution to issues of generativity. The quest becomes to teach others what one has learned through life's struggles and to leave behind with others some legacy that will indicate the importance of one's having existed. Although Erikson does not refer to the motivational theories of Abraham Maslow (1943), if he had, he might have noted that the early years tend to be devoted to issues of survival and security, the middle years to social and ego development, and the later years to self-actualization. The executive minds we wish to understand are typically moving from middle to later years in age and are busy seeking resolution to generativity issues.

The implications of these processes of personal development for executive education are, on consideration, straightfoward. Budding executives in their early years learn in settings that intensify their need for direction from others and their dependence on others as teachers of knowledge and values. In the classroom, teachers determine what material is to be learned, how it should be learned, and how learning must be demonstrated. Parents convey expectations, encourage good behavior, and punish that which deviates from their standards of acceptability. Coaches or piano teachers outline methods to be used in mastering skills, which are to be repeated time and again until the desired behavior can be performed almost unthinkingly (as contrasted with thoughtfully, as Weick suggests in his chapter in this volume). Likewise, in work settings, superiors outline the tasks, methods, and standards for behavior that will lead to promotion. Hence, during the young executive's formative years, when he or she is most open to influence from others about learning and thinking, the teaching done utilizes methods that not only ignore but actually militate against the exercise of independent or creative thought.

Ferguson (1980, pp. 282-283) comments on the impact our current educational systems have on the development of the adult mind: "As the greatest single social influence during the formative years, schools have been the instruments of our greatest denial, unconsciousness, conformity, and broken connections. Just as allopathic medicine treats symptoms without concern for the whole system, schools break knowledge and experience into 'subjects,' relentlessly turning wholes into parts, flowers into petals, history into events, without ever restoring continuity. . . . Worse yet, not only is the mind broken, but too often so is the spirit. Allopathic teaching produces the equivalent of *iatrogenic,* or 'doctor-caused,' illness—teacher-caused learning disabilities. We might call these *pedogenic* illnesses. The child who may have come to school intact, with the budding courage to risk and explore, finds stress enough to permanently diminish that adventure."

Toffler (1980), in a similar vein, accuses our current standardized, lock-step, "one right answer for every question" educational systems of preparing individuals to serve as obedient, unthinking drones of second-wave industrialists. Free thinking, experimentation, and challenging authority, according to Toffler, are intolerable behaviors in a machine-oriented society in which every person (cog) has his or her proper place and function. In Toffler's view, educational systems are *designed* to stamp out creativity and unstructured problem solving in favor of teaching punctuality, the virtue of consistent attendance, and deference to authority.

To the extent that our current educational systems produce the effects noted by Ferguson and Toffler, we are indeed inducing pedogenic illness among those who aspire to become executives. Clearly, the requirements of executive thinking transcend those of obedient drones; instead, executives need to be able to think creatively, to synthesize, to extrapolate, to dream, to experiment, to deal with messy problems which may have no solutions but which, for certain, there is no single right answer. Just as clearly, our current educational systems are not likely to provide the atmosphere in which executives need to learn how to think. To make matters even worse, educational methods do not adjust themselves to the personal development of students. Management programs at the undergraduate and even graduate levels continue to use methods that emphasize single answers, passive learning, and individual accomplishment. Meanwhile, for most young adults, the need for direction from authority figures has been replaced by the need to develop an identity and a sense of independence. In addition, students in their early twenties and thirties are still very much concerned with developing important interpersonal relationships. Neither of these needs is satisfied by their management education experience. Hence, even if the content of courses is meaningful, it is difficult for students to accept or to integrate with the important developmental issues in their lives. Students finish their education largely unprepared to work. They are left to learn from others to think independently, to transcend dogma, to stretch their limits, to ask questions of consequence, to take risks, to break frames, to help others develop, to continue to grow. Even programs designed specifically for executives suffer from the same problem; they frequently use elementary school pedagogies with students who not only are beyond being passive learners but who are most critically concerned with issues of their own generativity. They need to learn how to influence others in ways that result in appreciation rather than disregard, to manage the environment of an organization in order to guarantee its continued survival, and to manage their own transition from follower to leader. To address issues of interpersonal competence and environmental mastery not currently being adequately addressed in managerial education, and to readjust pedagogies to the developmental needs of adults, a new paradigm for executive education is urgently and vitally needed.

At the same time it should be recognized that our educational institutions are not alone in the need for reformation. As almost all executives would attest, much of their most significant learning occurs *after* they receive their formal education. In fact, while most executives would acknowledge the importance of their formal education in helping them to gain access (that is, credentials, common language) to the corporate ladder, few would endorse their alma mater as a purveyor of executive skills. Such skills, at least currently, are largely learned on the job. Unfortunately, in spite of the efforts of some companies to provide "how to" managerial training for their junior executives, most do a fairly poor job of creating real learning environments conducive to risk taking, experimentation, and development of interpersonal competencies. Rather, what most of these "high potentials" receive are projects to complete in distinct functional areas, not allowing for the appreciation of the "big picture"; assignments that change every twelve to eighteen months, making it fruitless to develop significant relationships; and continued reward for short-term results. Maccoby's (1976) work on the development of approaches to the game of "making it" as an executive in an organization is brutally descriptive of the struggle for survival in the corporate hierarchy; Whyte's (1956) earlier work on the "organization man" is also illustrative of the lengths to which people will go to secure a place for themselves among the carpeted offices of executive row. Both these authors indirectly elucidate the conditions under which executive learning and development are expected to occur. Is it any wonder that executives who constantly experience themselves at risk in cutthroat battles for career survival in organizations where those who make it to the top are the exception rather than the rule remember little of their human relations courses at school? Instead, what they remember, and repeatedly practice, is how they learned to relate to others in courses that fostered a competitive, grade-oriented, self-sufficing survival attitude. Where are they to learn values of cooperation in the service of the whole, to ask new questions, to anticipate problems not yet experienced, or to practice the delayed gratification required to bring about long-run improvements in performance: the requisites for generativity?

The contrast between American and Japanese methods of developing executive talent within corporations, as pointed out by Ouchi (1981) and Pascale and Athos (1981), is revealing in this regard. Japanese corporations promote very slowly and only after extended experience in working as a team member with peers has been provided. Thereafter careers are guided through lengthy service in each major function to ensure that the executive develops an appreciation for the entire business and the interdependency of his or her role within it. More important, attention is paid to developing executive skills of thought and action through small-group interaction in a climate of employment security at a time when the individual, as a fully developed adult, is prepared to learn about organizational issues through relevant experience. In contrast, the educational programs of most American universities must be viewed more as prep schools than as developers of executives. Likewise, American corporations operating on the principle that the fittest will survive (or, if they do not, that talent can be hired in from outside) seem to be dedicated more to providing the arena for gladiators to do battle than to shaping executives of the future.

A major belief of ours, which follows from the works of Argyris (1957), Schein (1961), Jourard (1973), and Harris (1969), is that a climate of trust or psychological safety is required to enhance the potential risk taking that is necessary in learning through experience. Since experiential learning methods are best suited to the developmental needs of adults (Kolb, 1983), it follows that *the powers of the executive mind are best developed in a nonevaluative climate of safety.* Our educational institutions sometimes provide that climate but fail in most cases to teach individuals experientially at times in their lives when they are receptive to such learning. Rather, they focus on mastery of language, symbols, and models; analyses of abstract cases; and communication through writing. Corporations, in contrast, provide opportunities for experiential learning but seldom in a climate of safety. Individuals are thrust into situations with others where they must make behavioral choices while constantly being evaluated by superiors. Clearly, the two settings could benefit from a merging of strengths, although this is currently rare. Thus, when adults in this country are ready to learn, their time for formal learning is usually behind them, and what they *do* learn from experience in a competitive setting that threatens their individual development is often not that which we would characterize as worthy of the adjective *executive*. Here, then, is one of the important questions for executive educators: *when and how to create an environment conducive to learning from experiences with others in a fashion that does not threaten the developmental goals of the adults involved.*

The Executive Mind in the Context of Others

As noted previously, the development of the executive mind is not simply a question of personal development but of interpersonal development as well. By definition, organizations are cooperative systems designed to do work that individuals could not accomplish working alone (Barnard, 1938). Regardless of what we may hear about its being "lonely at the top," the executive never acts alone. Boards, advisers, staff, subordinates, peers, secretaries, spouses, children, and others all counsel the executive on his or her decisions and carry out executive orders. Observations of executives reveal that they spend the vast majority of their time interacting with others, either in meeting with them or in communicating to them (Mintzberg, 1973a). Hence, how well the executive manages relationships with others politically and interpersonally is a primary determinant of his or her success.

The implications of this conclusion for the development of the executive mind are twofold. First, it should be apparent that *even after successfully negotiating the obstacle course of individual development, the executive may still be unprepared to interact meaningfully and effectively with others.* The development of conceptual skills and concomitant ego identity is not entirely independent of acquiring abilities to relate to others, but it is very nearly so, as observed by Kolb and Pondy in their chapters in this volume. Perhaps, as it has been said, we must first love ourselves before we can love others; however, loving oneself provides no guarantee that one can love another. As noted, to the extent that our educational systems and organizations do prepare executives to interact with others, the focus is on survival of the fittest through competitive tests of abilities. Particularly in graduate management education, students are rarely placed in situations in which their performance assessment depends on the success of their interactions with others. As Levinson (1970) pointed out some time ago, MBO is failing in some organizations because it neglects the interdependent nature of work in assessing individual performance. Is it any wonder that executives continue to endorse reward systems that are tied to the belief that individuals are solely responsible for the success or failure of their efforts, when they have themselves always been subjected to the same misguided treatment and have been concerned with self-esteem and ego development in managing their lives?

What is needed is a shift in management education pedagogy and organizational climates that raises the importance of successfully working with others to the same level as that currently granted to the mastery of disciplinary content. Current offerings of one or two courses in organizational behavior in most programs are not enough to overcome the competitive "kill or be killed" mentality that many students bring to the classroom. Those courses or training programs that do focus on interpersonal relationships or experiential learning are often perceived as unimportant diversions* from more critical work, taught by handholding professors who do not understand the dog-eat-dog reality of life after graduation. Without a *major*

---

*That these experiences be diversionary is important, as we shall suggest further on. It is the fact that the diversion is not seen as important or provocative that defeats its purpose.

shift in pedagogy that cuts across disciplines and removes attention to interpersonal relationships in special courses from the "nice to think about once in a while but probably unrealistic" category, we will continue to produce interpersonally unprepared executives who try to gain cooperation through intimidation and later question why they are not liked or respected by those they must rely on for their success and generativity as organizational leaders.

Another implication of the conclusion that managers exist in a fundamentally interactive context is related both to the immediately preceding point and to our earlier thoughts on postgraduate executive development. Graduate education typically occurs at a time when one's ego development is more paramount than is one's attention to the development of critical thinking or interpersonal relationships. Additionally, we pointed out that pedagogical methods currently in use tend to militate against the development of executive thinking rather than stimulate it. For both these reasons, we concluded, executives are forced to learn their trade later in life in a hostile organizational environment that makes the learning process extremely difficult. The point to be made is that, given the interactive nature of the developing executive's world, the quality of executive learning that takes place will be directly related to the quality of the executive's relationships with others. More precisely, *both the rate and the eventual level of learning achieved will be a function of the executive's ability to enter, develop relationships within, and manage groups of significant others.* These groups include peers, subordinates, superiors, and representatives of other constituencies who affect the outcomes of organizational tasks. Here we are speaking of skills in group facilitation that transcend the ability to carry on casual conversation over lunch or to run through several announcements and answer questions before a collection of one's staff. We are speaking of skills necessary to create group experiences that foster a climate of learning from one another's experience and collective task force. Almost all executives could expound on the pros or cons of using groups, but we suspect hardly any would be aware of theories of group development like those of Bennis and Shepard (1956)

or Srivastva, Obert, and Neilsen (1977) or Fry, Rubin, and Plovnick (1981), let alone be able to articulate the leadership abilities needed to develop group cohesiveness, teamwork, trust, and
the like.

In our experiences with executives and executive groups,
we have observed the misuse of groups more often than not: the
decision to form a committee, team, or task force, for example,
because the task requires interdependent thinking and action
without attending to the fact that such group work requires a
level of interaction and mutual trust that cannot occur within
the time frames given most groups to accomplish their tasks. In
most meetings we have attended in organizations, it is apparent
that, even with a prior history of meetings, the majority of persons in attendance are still struggling with early-phase issues of
group development. They are dealing with needs to be included
or accepted by significant others in the group, or, in the case of
those in secure and/or higher positions in the hierarchy, they
are vying competitively for influence. Few groups we have observed resolved these issues sufficiently to promote mutual inquiry, healthy conflict, leading to organizational learning as
described by Friedlander in his chapter in this volume, divergent
thinking leading to problem finding as described by Kolb in his
chapter, or the realization of common (rather than individual)
fate necessary for true collaboration.

It is noteworthy that the same misuse of groups occurs in
our management schools, often by organizational behaviorists
themselves. Under the banner of experiential learning, we form
student teams to experience and/or discuss some dilemma, topic, or case, under the presumption that they will see and experience the benefit of group work. Yet time and attention are seldom given to truly develop those groups so that the level of
interaction truly stimulates new knowledge either about oneself
or about the topic under discussion. They are one-time affairs
or, at best, momentary diversions, seldom in synch with the
overall norms and climate of the graduate program. At the same
time, our current experiences with some executives may contain
clues for overcoming this abuse of group methods. It is not a
surprise to us that graduates of concentrated executive man-

agement programs often report that the most useful single aspect of the program was "getting to know their peers in their study groups." We believe this occurs when members of these groups live with one another (experiencing one another wholly rather than in one or two class sessions), when all course work necessitates interdependent thinking, when learning from their experience before and during the program itself is valued, and when programmatic steps are taken to create a climate of personal safety and mutual trust. Without these arrangements the risks associated with experimentation and possible failure are simply too great for most persons to overcome. In work settings executives are in the best position to do something to change their environments to promote more intense periods of working together, interdependent task definition, climates of safety and trust, and so on. Yet because they lack the skills and experiences to do so, the minds of the next generation of executives, as well as all others around them, will probably continue to be underdeveloped. How will American organizations become smarter when our current organizations and systems of executive education create conditions antithetical to learning? Where will Weick's "acting thinkingly" occur if the level of interaction going on does not promote new questions, risk taking, framebreaking, discovery, and the like? We thus arrive at a second question in need of inquiry: *how to provide experiences that train and develop executives to appreciate and work in highly developed group settings.*

Executive Mind and Complexity

In addition to being interpersonal, the executive's total world is complex. Addressing educational needs to cope with this complexity is the focus of this section.

That the environment of most organizations is becoming more complex should be evident. Changing world markets, advances in technology, resource scarcities, increasing governmental regulation, and changes in work-force demographics and values are but a few of the current causes for executive concern. The books by Ackoff (1974), Toffler (1980), and Ferguson

(1980) are among many carefully considered works that point to critical trends that will demand changes in the way we live, work, communicate, and think in the near future. Massive unemployment, population shifts away from the traditional manufacturing centers, inability to compete in international markets, demands for equality by women and minorities, ineffective attempts to control government spending, unprecedented divorce and crime rates, threats to the stability of the Social Security system, incredible inflation in world currencies, and massive military buildups are trends that shout for attention and response. However, we also are aware of higher-than-ever levels of education, new technological breakthroughs, medical discoveries that will enhance and prolong life, more controlled population expansion, more nearly equal opportunities for all, and efforts to develop new, reusable forms of energy. How is the executive to make sense of all this and more? And, more important to our current thesis, how does the executive develop thought processes that eventually allow this sense-making to occur?

Ashby's (1952) law of requisite variety states that for a system to survive, it must be capable of adapting to changes in its environment; to do so requires that somewhere within it the system must possess a wide enough variety of behaviors to provide an appropriate response to each significant change. Hence, as the environment of a system becomes more complex, meaning that the environment is changing more rapidly in ways that could threaten the system's survival, the system must also become more complex internally in order to continue to adapt. Organizations as open systems (Katz and Kahn, 1966) must therefore try to match their internal variety of behaviors to the complexity of the environment in which they operate. By virtue of their positions, executives are primarily responsible for ensuring that varieties of internal capabilities are developed in those areas most crucial to the organization's survival.

As Emery and Trist (1965) have pointed out, the task of responding to changes in the environment becomes more difficult as the environment becomes more complex and uncertain. This means that executives must devote much of their own attention, as well as more organizational resources, to preparing for and managing change. To the extent that executives become more capable in this regard, their organizations should become more successful over time. But where do they develop this capability?

In most management curricula, a single course on business policy is taught as a capstone to the program. Through several case analyses, this course attempts to integrate the student's separate learnings in the various disciplines. This type of course does not address the issues of environmental sensing and change addressed here. At best, capstone policy courses refresh students' learnings of programmed, algorithmic methods of problem solving using data already geared to highlight problems that fit these methods. At worst, they misuse groups by gathering students to work on a project at a level of interaction where they cannot make sense of complexity, and they instill a false sense of confidence in students, who are made to believe that, armed with the algorithms they have been taught, they can solve all problems. Later, if data need to be collected to determine what the problem is, students often do not know how to begin; and if somehow they succeed in data gathering but the data do not fit the familiar solution, the tendency is to abandon the problem altogether and search for another, neater one. Even if the policy course were taught earlier so that students could be more aware of the need to integrate their learnings in order to respond more holistically to real, complex problems, where in the curriculum are students prepared for and allowed the opportunity to interact in ways that allow them to investigate a problem which as yet is undefined and for which a new and unique means of analysis and solution must be found? As Livingston (1971) suggests, the answer is not in current business school education. The most important problems executives face defy specific definition or have no solutions, or they would already have been solved by others. Those problems that others are unable to solve are the ones that eventually ascend the hierarchy to alight on the executive's desk. Whether the executive attempts to master the environment or ignores it makes no difference in this regard; problems of true significance will find their way into the organization and head straight for the brain cells of the executive office like some vicious neurological disease. Old treatments, familiar routines, tried-and-true solutions simply will not work in combating problems of this nature. The executive's only hope for survival lies in developing requisite variety.

The development of requisite variety requires creativity and innovation; breaking with tradition; venturing out on thin ice into unfamiliar territory; risking critical abuse by all who value the false security of tradition; putting one's career and one's organization on the line. It requires a long-range perspective that fosters an investment mentality; the maturity to forgo immediate gratification for the sake of investing scarce resources in research and development; a tolerance for ambiguity that results in encouragement rather than punishment of those who break the rules; an appreciation of the need to rise above the turmoil of day-to-day distractions to listen to the music of the world around you; the fortitude to make unpopular decisions to abandon the old to prepare for the new. Finally, these skills require trust and respect in others born from the ability, as Massarik posits elsewhere in this volume, to embrace the total meaning of the experience of oneself *with* others.

Nowhere, to our knowledge, are executives taught how to do these things or put in an environment to experience these things in relative safety. Most executives, it would appear, operate from a basis either of theories-in-use derived from prior, less complex experiences or of intuition born from fixed, limited frames of reference or ways of viewing the world. Our third challenge therefore centers on the notion of requisite variety for the executive mind: *how to develop the capability in executives to create and think in alternative frames of reference so as to handle the complexities they face.*

Having taken our management education programs to task for not contributing to certain needs we see in executive functioning, we are obliged to direct ourselves toward some answers to the challenges we have posed. We have cited three issues in need of attention in the development of an executive mind through educational efforts:

1. Executives, as adult learners, can learn only in situations that value their experience and do not threaten basic developmental issues they are dealing with in their lives.
2. One of the most important things executives need to learn and experience is how to create, and interact in, highly developed groups that are vehicles of learning and problem solving.
3. Executives need to develop skills in breaking old theories-in-use or frameworks and discovering new ones in order to manage complexity.

Taken separately, each does not necessarily appear troublesome. But we have argued that current educational efforts, by and large, are conceived and conducted so as to be unable to meet these needs, taken together. We now wish to suggest a way out of this condition by reframing our own experiences with executives in educational programs. It is from the very set of experiences we have faulted that we also find some learnings that help resolve these issues.

Toward a Developmental Model
of Executive Interaction

We have come to the basic assumption that interacting is a significant part of the functioning of the executive mind—that only through interaction with others will executives be able to resolve generativity issues in their personal development, develop and maintain relationships necessary to learn from experience, and be able to create new, shared visions of problems or actions to be taken in the face of overwhelming complexity. When we reflect on our experiences with executives in educational settings and study the interaction that occurred, we can begin to postulate ways the executive mind develops.

We see five basic types or levels of interaction occurring in our work with executives, in and out of organizational settings. Some forms occur more frequently than others, and some appear to require the prior experience of others. Certain forms of interacting do not typically occur in the "miseducation" that we believe goes on in our business schools; other forms occur often in both work and school settings. As we shall propose, the less frequent, higher levels of interacting may be solutions to the major issues discussed earlier.

Single-Frame Interaction. The most basic form of interaction is essentially one-way communication, or monologue. It is a most familiar type of interaction in classroom and work setting. Lectures, briefings, presentations, reports, and so on for the most part constitute one person speaking from his or her frame of reference to another or others. Such interaction is single-frame because the goal is to merely communicate one's own sense of meaning to another, not to change it, to debate it, or to reframe it. The sender is concerned with transmitting that which she or he feels is important. The receiver's concern is *"What do I have to know or remember?"* If questions are solicited, they are used for clarification to make sure that what was said was what the sender meant to say, rather than to test for understanding, acceptance, or agreement by the receiver(s). When we as teachers or when managers end a monologue with "Are there any questions?" it is as if to say we only want to hear whether something we said was unclear so we can make sure it is clear and accurate. If we really wanted to know whether others understood, agreed, or had additions or how they felt about an issue, we would ask them so more directly. Oftentimes what can be delivered in a single-frame fashion can just as well be written, taped, or otherwise communicated in non-face-to-face modes. We see this happening in videotaping in our graduate management programs, in office automation at the workplace, or in the use of memos and written directives in most social institutions. One consequence is an increased psychological distance between people who are learning or working together. This depersonalization of interaction tends to limit opportunities for interacting at other, more intimate levels.

Single-frame interaction can serve as an important building block for other forms of interaction more necessary for executive thought and action. We have observed that giving our adult learners an opportunity for "monologues" early in a learning experience serves as a "roll call" that helps them to join into the new situation, class, or exercise without threatening their self-esteem already developed through their work experience and maturity. Rather than expect an adult learner to immediately challenge or debate the teacher or a fellow classmate, we have seen the need to just let people talk "at" one another, publicly, as if to say, "I am here, I have worth and significance." Is this not what we as teachers try to do with our opening lectures when we begin our courses?

Multiple-Frame Interaction. A second form of interaction is a two-way conversation or dialogue between two or more persons, each speaking from his or her frame of reference. At this level, however, the concern is more than just stating one's opinion or ideas for another to hear, as in a monologue. Whereas single-frame interaction communicates one person's sense of things to others and asks them to absorb it wholly, the dialogue, or multiple-frame interaction, puts two or more positions on the table so similarities and differences become clear. The concern of the receiver shifts from recall or clarity in single-frame talk to agreement and fit with one's own sense of things. Typical multiple-frame interaction occurs in classrooms when the instructor leads a case-study discussion and interacts with different students in the room. An opinion or idea is offered, a response is given, the degree of agreement is noted, a new idea or question is offered, and so on. There is no collective action or emergent new frame of reference shared by all. Each party is left to agree or not, conclude or not, as an individual. In work settings, the same occurs when a manager seeks advice and counsel from his or her staff, who may represent different functions, disciplines, or constituencies. Each reacts to the manager's framing of the situation from his or her own sense of it. The manager concludes whatever he or she chooses, based on perceived degree of fit, agreement, and so on. Like monologues, such dialogues can often be carried out in written or other non-face-to-face forums, thereby decreasing opportunity for personal contact and relationship building.

This type of interaction is nonetheless important to our understanding of the developing executive mind. Like single-frame talk, this too serves to create opportunities for truly joint or collective action through consensus processes. It is hard to imagine the latter ever occurring unless parties at least interact at this level so that they each have a sense of the degree of agreement, fit, or common knowledge that exists between them. Multiple-frame talk also begins to create common language, terminology, symbols, and definitions among people so that, if required, the possibility for influencing one another or seeking consensus is enhanced. When conducted face to face, relationships begin to be formed as each party experiences how his or her frame of meaning and style of communicating it fits with and is accepted by others.

Although both single- and multiple-frame interaction are commonplace in management education programs, neither is sufficient to allow the interdependent work that we have argued executives must experience. It is the presumption that groups can in fact reach consensus, innovate, find new solutions to old problems in an aura of single- and multiple-frame talk that leads to the misuse of groups cited earlier. This is a point at which many graduate educational programs fail to develop the executive mind—by not promoting and developing skills in further forms of interaction necessary to achieve these collective outcomes.

Frame-Linking Interaction. A third form of interaction occurs in face-to-face talk which is problem- or outcome-focused and in which the parties to the discussion are interdependent. Beyond sharing and agreeing or not to frames presented, attempts are made to influence one another enough to bring together individual frameworks or positions. In addition to needing some common language, listening skills, and terminology from the prior two forms of interaction, this kind of discussion requires some group task and maintenance skills (Schein, 1969) and some problem-solving skills. In work settings, frame-linking interaction is often what typifies participative strategies or integrating mechanisms (Galbraith, 1977) such as task forces, committees, or project teams. The various positions, knowledge, ideas, and experiences that make up the frames of reference of two or more persons need to be put together in order to derive a plan, set of recommendations, new structure or procedure, or whatever. Frame-linking is then the process of connecting like thoughts, cutting away differences, and adding together ideas in order to arrive at an outcome acceptable to all parties. Although frame-linking talk is interaction in the service of some task that requires it, participants are also dealing with personal needs for influence and control. Whose ideas or frames win and lose in the process is an undercurrent of this kind of interaction. This is a significant step toward more intimate interpersonal relationships. It is the first form of interaction presented that contributes much to bonding in any way. Herein lies another shortcoming or missed opportunity in most educational programs and pedagogies in that they seldom construe assignments or allow for structures so that the learners can interact in frame-linking ways. Most often such interaction occurs between a learner and the teacher in written form, so that linking between the two is limited. When educational programs do use appropriate pedagogy, such as study groups, they tend to ignore skill development in managing groups, they still reward individual performance, or they tend to form short-term, transient groups that must first engage in single- and multiple-frame talk to create enough safety and legitimization in order to really address a common task in a frame-linking fashion. Consequently, it often happens in our schools, as well as in group efforts in organizations, that we at least expect frame-linking to occur but instead get the result of single- or multiple-frame interaction: fairly mediocre ideas which few are committed to and which reflect little, if any, modification after initial presentation.

A major contribution of frame-linking interaction is that it is made up of experience-based input. As the parties strive to link together ideas and individual opinions based on experiences, the individuals are at the same time legitimized for their experiences and able to examine their experiences in view of others' reactions to them. This adds to one's sense of esteem and to knowledge of others' resources. The kind of experience reflected in this level of interaction is usually abstract, empirical information about past events, presented in a rational, logical fashion. We have found that this sharing of experience, like the roll-call phenomenon noted earlier, is critical to adult managers' ability to learn. If denied the opportunity to link our academic framework to their experience, or theirs to one another's, they show resistance to learning any of our theories or technologies, no matter how well supported by research findings. The simple step of timing a theory input or presentation after managers use their own experiences in frame-linking interactions seems to result in more interest in the learning process than when we present it first and assign them to apply it (single-frame mode), as if to say that their experience in any particular topic area is irrelevant.

Frame-linking interaction, then, is where we observe managers and executives engaged in problem-solving discussions, trying to put together different points of view, perspectives, and ideas. This is expected to occur frequently in work settings, and its frequency is likely to increase, given current trends toward more participative strategies of management. It may not occur as much as needed or with as high-quality results as needed, because managers are seldom trained in ways that allow them to experience much of this, let alone in actual skills to conduct such interaction.

Frame-Sharing Interaction. One consequence of frame-linking interaction is that parties to it have increased experience with one another in one another's presence. Attention to and exploration of what that shared experience is and means constitutes frame-sharing interaction. This form of interaction is focused on making collective sense of the setting or process the parties are currently engaged in. The critical source of information is the way people experience the immediate situation during interaction, not abstractions of past experiences. Common language and terminology is less important than in the modes previously discussed, and skills in giving and receiving feedback become paramount. This type of interacting is necessarily face to face and is self-regulated by the participants, rather than constrained by some task or project requirements (as in frame-linking). We note here that our need as teachers to remain in control at all times in our educational programs precludes this kind of interaction. When we have let the adult learners go and encouraged them to give feedback to one another, to discuss the way a course is progressing, or to determine what is going on at present or what they should discuss next, they have consistently exhibited a self-regulatory ability as a community or large group (given that certain degrees of the previous three modes of interaction have occurred).

Frame-sharing contributes to relationship building. It creates psychological closeness and confronts issues of influence and intimacy by exploring how each party interpreted a situation the parties experienced together. In this context what matters is the interpretations and discussion of them, not the facts, solution, or answer to any question posed for external sources (see Weick's article in this volume). Hence, we seldom see frame-sharing in organizations because it appears unrelated to accomplishing any task. When we do see it, it is often at special retreats or "bitch sessions" and takes the initial form of complaining or venting pent-up emotions about how some experienced others. In educational settings we often strive for frame-sharing by creating common experiences through simulations, roleplays, or group exercises and then providing time for "process sessions" to make sense of those shared experiences. It is doubtful that these situations fully achieve frame-sharing unless they are frequent, with a permanent group, and are truly felt to be important, relevant experiences by the participants. Like the staff retreat once a year for a weekend in a resort area, if the situation is viewed as a diversion, one can choose to cope with it rather than engage in it. Similarly, we find many executives in our courses coping with opportunities we have designed for frame-sharing rather than engaging in them. Such opportunities are too few or too ill timed to be seen as important by the adult learner.

Underlying these observations is the fact that this level of interaction does require personal risk taking and experimentation. These behaviors, in turn, require relationships that have developed beyond questions of acceptance, respect, and who wins or loses to levels of mutual trust and appreciation of how one's self-worth is enhanced through experiencing something with another. To develop the ability to create such relationships, to be a risk taker in order to grow personally, and to create a sense of common fate among coworkers would seem to be necessary ingredients of the executive's repertoire (see Bennis's chapter in this volume).

Frame-sharing interaction is necessary to the executive to maintain and develop interpersonal relationships with significant others in the organization. It is also necessary in order to create a sense of common fate or shared meaning from which others can carry forward without the executive—the generativity issue discussed earlier. That cannot occur if the relationships remain bonded by loyalty to the chain of command. Truax and Carkhuff (1967) have well documented the fact that relationships that provide for effective mentoring and coaching are based on mutual respect, trust, and a sense of shared understanding of one another, regardless of title, training, or expertise.

Frame-Breaking Interaction. The ultimate contribution of the executive mind, we believe, lies in the ability to rise above the immediate situation, go beyond current definitions of problems, and think past current solutions toward new visions, new conceptions of issues, and new questions. As Bennis in Chapter One finds in his sample of executive leaders, they often possess the ability to project themselves above their own situation, as if from a helicopter, and then look down on it from an entirely different perspective or frame of reference. Such frame-breaking does not occur in isolation. It is, rather, the consequence of interacting with significant others who provide nurturance, challenge, and safety for the executive to dare to pose a new framework. Whereas frame-sharing requires the parties to reflect on what and who they are, frame-breaking requires reflection on what they are not. Argyris's work in this volume suggests that this is often a consequence of realizing that one's theory-in-use does not correspond to what one has espoused. The discovery of one's theory-in-use through others' experience of oneself and awareness of new theories to experiment with are outcomes of frame-breaking interaction.

Frame-breaking interaction is required for one to possess the variety needed to perform in executive positions. It is more than offering one more alternative solution by adding together existing perspectives (frame-linking); it is more than thinking out one more year in the future with the tools and data already at hand. This form of interaction represents the identification and realization of new knowledge and truly innovative ideas. Berger and Luckmann (1966) suggest that only "interruptions" in one's modus operandi create opportunities for new exploration of meaning among oneself and significant others. It is the "interruption" that best connotes our meaning of frame-breaking. A teacher or manager may "disrupt" an exercise or meeting with a provocative, off-the-wall comment or question, but it is doubtful that this results in frame-breaking unless the relationships in the room are highly developed and secure and share a history of frame-linking and frame-sharing interaction. We suspect that few, if any, such situations in our graduate management classrooms or corporate environs meet these requirements.

In the rare instances when we have observed frame-breaking conversations in an educational setting, they have occurred through a progression of interacting in all the previous modes presented and then finding that the adult learner suddenly acts as if nothing were so important as is, in Massarik's terms (see Chapter Ten), fully embracing the experience of his or her self in the context of others who are present. Pragmatically, what we have observed as outcomes of this are sincere solicitation for help from one's peers, executives teaching each other, learners reporting "aha" experiences related to a new interpretation of their experience with others, and self-directed behavior to influence the immediate learning situation. One last consequence of frame-breaking interaction is a shift in criteria for accountability. Rather than hearing the typical challenge to apply something to the "real world" or to justify how the adult learners are getting their tuition dollars' worth from each minute of class time, suddenly the bottom line becomes intrinsic and related to their sense of the importance of the moment at hand. This may be the essence of how a person appears able to "seize the moment"—that the person has progressed through levels of interaction to a point at which seizing the moment is breaking a frame that has been shared heretofore with significant others, thus interrupting the knowledge base in use at the moment and thereby requiring others to exemplify and explore new meaning and transition from old ways of thinking.

In our scheme, then, frame-breaking interaction is a goal,

the ultimate developmental stage for the executive mind. We have sought to reframe our experiences with executives and other adult learners to suggest some clues to when and how the executive mind develops. It is useful to acknowledge that we see little interaction beyond frame-linking in most schools of business and management. Likewise, when we work in organizations, it appears that we are "used" to sanctioning events that try to reach frame-sharing or frame-breaking levels of interaction. The challenge to those in positions to mold future executives is obvious.

It is also important to understand that groups potentially embrace all the forms of interaction we have discussed. It is sad that the commonly accepted view of the futility of group efforts is based on experiences in groups that may never have worked in a frame-sharing or frame-breaking mode. Current and future executives must be able to experience the consequences of working with others in these two types of interaction. Graduate schools and management development programs can offer this opportunity if they experiment with different pedagogies and structures. Permanent study groups, focus on group process, self-directed learning by means of groups, assignments that are done in a group and rewarded on a group basis, groups teaching other groups, and residential settings where learners live together are a few such changes that we have seen produce beneficial results.

Finally, this developmental notion of interaction is not to be confused with another call for effective communication. Our concern is for imparting new skills in executives so that they can attend to their experience of the communication that goes on, not just to its result. It is the difference between leaving a meeting clear about what was decided and leaving knowing exactly how others experienced you in that meeting. Both are important. The latter is what distinguishes the executive mind.

For some people, reading this chapter should be an experience in multiple-frame interaction and nothing more. For others, whose own experiences may be cast in a new light by hearing some of ours, this could be a frame-linking experience. To do any more requires that we engage with each other in face-to-face contexts, such as the symposium that this volume is based on, to create some frame-sharing and possibly frame-breaking discussion.

We, like the organizations described by March and Simon (1958), are prone to search for solutions to new problems in familiar places. The purpose of this chapter has been to point out that developing the executive mind will require new approaches, perhaps in new settings, that develop knowledge and skills that in some cases do not yet exist. Exactly what approach is necessary to embark on is not clear at this time. Perhaps continuing education involving a network of executives, scientists, representatives of government, and other critical thinkers could produce a new framework for viewing and developing the executive mind that results in something more than a beefed-up M.B.A. for older managers. In other areas we simply need to create new opportunities for developing executives to learn in ways that are growth-promoting rather than regressive about things that are important even if they are not well understood.

Organizations also need to change. Young executives need to be rewarded for taking risks and making mistakes in the process instead of simply following orders. A career without failure is a career lacking opportunities to break old frames, challenge outdated methods, explore new possibilities, or exercise creativity. At the same time, organizations need to recognize the interdependent nature of both success and failure by assigning and evaluating work on group projects. We may have something vitally important to learn from the Japanese about promoting slowly, emphasizing teamwork, and training young managers as generalists rather than specialists. Particularly during the early portion of the executive's career, when developing relationships with others is a focal personal need, increased continuity in group membership may be beneficial.

In addition, organizations must place executives in roles that require them to understand and deal with the environment in its full complexity. Executives need to learn that environmental problems are not resolved sequentially but, rather, holistically; that solutions to some problems make matters worse in other areas; that flexibility is more important than following steps that have worked in the past; and that managing the environment means being prepared to take actions that may never be required.

Finally, executives need to learn how to develop others; to help others learn how to learn; to share their knowledge without letting their intentions become orders; to work with groups as equals as well as leaders; to be open to influence from those who question the most basic truths; to encourage creative thinking; and to inspire others to make the same commitment to organizational success that they did when others trusted them to make important decisions. This is the essence of a functioning executive mind.

12

Improving Executive Functioning

Suresh Srivastva

Executives are ordinary people doing some extraordinary work. They are precise, clear, and articulate human beings who usually preside over situations that are ambiguous, complex, and full of uncertainty. However, organizational experience indicates that what one hears is not what was said, what one sees is not what was presented, what one promised is not what was delivered, what one feels is not what is expressed, and what one thinks is not what has happened. Because such observations are commonplace, this volume is an effort to understand the process that pervades the functioning of the executive and the ingredients that support his or her ability to manage the predicaments arising out of personal as well as situational aspects. In the performance of their responsibilities, executives are intertwined with the situation and the environment of the organization as a workplace. This volume is an illustration of rich ideas that permeate the intertwining processes of envisioning, experiencing and sense-making, and knowing and enacting that the executive mind entails. Executive mind, therefore, has been described here as a bridging mechanism between what an executive does as an executive and how the person in the role of an executive melds with the task of an executive.

This conclusion has two main objectives: one, to highlight major ideas in the volume and to discover some common and uncommon themes; and two, to present some thoughts that describe the nature of executive functioning and the processes of human activity that drive such executive functioning. In addition, this chapter is intended to advance an applied perspective to assist the executive in making better use of the many learnings that can be derived from this volume.

Embracing the Executive Mind

The authors who have contributed their thoughts to this volume have immense respect for the challenges executives face. Nearly every chapter makes reference to the difficulty of dealing with decision making under conditions of fundamental uncertainty, amid conflicting demands from others, in less time than would be desirable. Hence, a shared perspective is that of the executive as a person of strength and integrity, capable of acting thoughtfully, thinking dialectically, acknowledging contingencies, demonstrating bravery and persevering honorably in the face of challenges that others might find overwhelming. This is not to say that the authors view executives as superhuman or as incapable of making mistakes. On the contrary, several of the authors point out that it is only by recognizing their own fallibility that executives are able to avoid making decisions or taking actions that are unrealistic rather than idealistic. There is a clarion call here for greater self-awareness, particularly during periods of success, when theories-in-use may go unquestioned until some irrevocable catastrophe makes them obviously untenable.

Another commonality among the authors is the attention paid to executive thinking as mindful, active, consequential, and farsighted. Executive thinking is not done so much for the sake of the executive himself or herself as for the benefit of others. Because executives seldom execute, their thoughts must be formulated and expressed in ways that inspire others to act in accordance with them over long periods of time. The variables that enter into executive thinking are variables that, for the most part, can be changed only very slowly and deliberately. Executives' own lifetimes may be too short to allow them to witness the fruition of processes put into motion early in their careers. They are therefore viewed as unselfish dreamers but, at the same time, as very much in touch with their own needs and desires as well as reality. From this internal dialectic between what is and what could be emerges a union between rational and emotional modes of thinking that produces actions which both appear logical and are bestowed with passion. The executive's supreme success is experienced not when leading but when being carried along by others toward the dream he or she wishes to fulfill.

Although the authors are in agreement on what executives strive to achieve, they are less unanimous about how executives go about their pursuit. Processes of sense-making, for example, are alternatively explained as being based on experience, socialization, myths and fairy tales, failures, successes, confrontation of differences and actions themselves. It may be that each of these explanations is partly correct and that we simply need more elaborate contingency theories to understand how the pieces of the puzzle fit together. Clearly, the thinking put forth in this volume brings us nearer to an understanding of the functioning of the executive mind. Still, processes of sense-making versus interactive apprehension, security versus self-doubt, perseverance versus openness to new data, problem solving versus problem defining, reality testing versus reality transformation, and environmental mastery versus environmental management remain points of disagreement that beckon further inquiry and dialogue.

It is apparent in almost every chapter that the authors are calling for a new appreciation of the tools used by executives to help shape their decisions and guide their behavior. The transformation of reality, the imparting of values, the mastering of time, and the envisioning of the future are processes seldom aided by reports filled with data describing past events. Regardless of the sophistication of analyses produced by others, with or without the help of automated computing systems, the fundamental and most essential responsibilities of the executive will continue to require intuitive attention. Data that argue conclusively for one course of action can and sometimes should be ignored if another course of action seems more appealing to the executive, even when the reasons for the preference are not completely clear.

No amount of formal training or experience in a particular functional discipline can guarantee that an individual will develop the tools of the executive mind, and no amount of money spent on experts or specialists will comfort the executive in the final moment of decision. The world in which the executive lives, works, and thinks is now and will always be an inherently uncertain and irrational one, in which the shortest distance between two points is seldom a straight line. In such a world tools based on the false realities of management science, past experience, or market intelligence can be at best crutches and at worst deceiving mirages of truth in a desert of imperfect predictability. Tools of humanity, intuition, emotion, and sentiment offer the only real hope for survival in the long run.

Although experts may be of little help to executives in making certain fundamental decisions, this is not to say that others do not influence the executive. The presence of others, both imagined and real, helps formulate and reformulate the executive's thoughts about critical issues. Past mentors and role models, current compatriots and adversaries, and even future candidates for their own replacement influence the ways executives make sense of the world around them or act on the theories they have developed. The management of relationships with others to ensure the optimal pattern of mutual influence is yet another common theme that pervades all chapters.

Finally, it should be noted that the authors raise nearly as many questions about the executive mind as they try to answer. What do executives actually think about as they make major decisions? How aware of themselves are they, and how capable are they of acting on that awareness? How do executives decide when to stand pat and when to bend, when to accept reality and when to change it? How much thinking precedes action and how much follows it in the process of experimentation and sense-making? What are the most effective ways for executives to convey their dreams to others? Is it the person or the moment that makes a particular executive great? Can qualities of executive greatness be developed through some form of education or training? How can we influence the levels of self-awareness, dialectical thinking, and mindful action among executives? Can executives be better matched to situations that fit their unique abilities? These are only a few of the questions that deserve additional research as a consequence of this volume. But how are such questions to be answered? How can scientists use their own minds to study the minds of others without somehow introducing their own biases or limitations in the process? This volume provides several insights regarding these questions.

The thrust of thinking represented here, however, is that the executive mind cannot be studied at a distance or through the residues of actions that result from earlier thought processes. Instead, the mind must be studied both *in situ* and *in vivo*; to do less would lead to useless speculation at best on the nature and form of such continuous, evasive phenomena. Research of the kind advocated here would be intensive, immediate, and eclectic without being overly intrusive. It would emphasize the bonding of relationships between the researcher and the executives studied at a level of depth heretofore reserved for the study of psychotherapy. In this case, however, the focus would be on the healthy development of creative capabilities that allow the executive to function effectively rather than on some element of pathology. Moreover, in contrast to the study of pathologies, the study of executive thought processes would necessarily occur as the executive is performing the functions under investigation. Reflective office visits would clearly be inadequate to capture the richness of mindful action in its nascent form.

Research of this nature is difficult to perform, but the

learnings to be gained are worth the effort, as the chapters in this volume attest. The knowledge gained through such efforts is essential to our more complete understanding of the executive mind and will provide further guidance to executives themselves in meeting the absolutely critical challenges they face.

Enacting the Executive Mind

The enacting process of an executive mind is isomorphic with the situation in which the task is performed. One part of the process is task-centered, external to the person of the executive, and located in the situation or the environment. As another part, simultaneously, the person of the executive goes through a continuous activity involving his or her learning modalities, ideas, thinking, concept of time and space, and phenomenological self-awareness; this part is internal to the executive. The task of bridging the task-centered and person-centered activities falls on the processes of the mind, as has been described in this volume. Figure 1 diagrams the relationship between these concepts.

The nature of task-centered functions has been the major concern of scholars and executives, and it has been analyzed in various modes. This volume provides a direction based on the understanding of underlying behavioral as well as organizational process. The executive function described here is a meaningful summary of the executive functions in that it is all-pervasive among organizations regardless of their particular characteristics. These functions prevail in private-sector, public-sector, project-oriented, non-profit-oriented, product-oriented, service-oriented, and other kinds of organized institutions.

Executives perform four distinct but interrelated functions as a part of their organizational responsibility:

- *Rule-making functions* provide for initiating responsibilities for defining the nature of the task, setting directions for the organization, developing prescriptive and proscriptive aspects of conduct at the workplace, and in general setting the boundaries for organizational life.

Figure 1. Interrelationships Between Task-Centered and Person-Centered Functions and the Bridging Process of the Executive Mind.

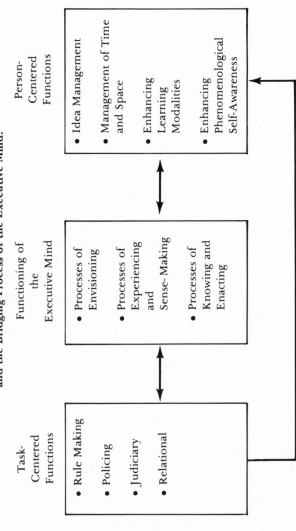

Task-
Centered
Functions

- Rule Making
- Policing
- Judiciary
- Relational

Functioning of
the
Executive Mind

- Processes of Envisioning
- Processes of Experiencing and Sense-Making
- Processes of Knowing and Enacting

Person-
Centered
Functions

- Idea Management
- Management of Time and Space
- Enhancing Learning Modalities
- Enhancing Phenomenological Self-Awareness

- *Policing functions* involve checking, reviewing, and implementing basic agreements, developing reward systems for performance, providing control mechanisms for information, and paying attention to the developmental needs of persons and the organization.
- *Judiciary functions* obligate the executive to be involved in conflict resolution, maintaining equity in the organization, eliminating capricious and arbitrary decision-making processes, and guaranteeing that the organization lives within due process of rules and law.
- *Relational functions* make the executive responsible for building consensus around ideas and tasks, providing support for the personal growth of workers, developing processes of work that are humane, and deliberately enhancing the quality of life.

This volume has been explicit about the functioning of the mind; the compelling question that remains to be addressed is what this volume says about how such functions can be better understood and performed. It is useful here to be more prescriptive and analytical and to draw on the chapters for the answers to this question. The person-centered operations or functions proposed in this volume include *managing ideas, managing time and space, enhancing learning modalities,* and *enhancing phenomenological awareness.* The volume suggests that understanding the interaction between the task-centered and person-centered functions will magnify the processes of the functioning of the executive mind, which include envisioning, experiencing and sense-making, and knowing and enacting.

Operationally, managing ideas implies a more active stance in regard to idea generation and enhancement than has perhaps been the case in most organizations. Rather than wait for ideas to be somehow discovered at lower levels of the organization and float upward, the executive must be more involved, proactive, challenging, and facilitative in the idea-management process. The executive needs to point toward areas in which ideas are sought, clearly identifying ends to be achieved without unduly restricting the equifinality of different means. Then, once sufficient energy for idea generation has been provided, the executive must ensure that adequate resources and freedom have been provided to nurture the creative process. Once ideas are formulated, the executive must guard against premature idea evaluation in order to ensure that each receives fair attention among persons with heavy investments in maintaining the status quo. Finally, the executive must guard against groupthink behavior among subordinates, in which poor ideas are supported out of a belief that the executive favors a particular solution, and those who support it, over others. This can be done by encouraging the natural expression of differences, demanding that counterpositions be studied, and reserving personal judgments. Once an idea is selected, the executive then must provide the energy and resources for its development through his or her statements and actions. Thereafter continuous participation, rather than laissez faire delegation, is required to ensure that critical ideas do not die on the hierarchical grapevine. Throughout the process of idea generation, selection, and management, the executive must be comfortable with ambiguity, encourage active experimentation, and accept disagreement as healthy. Finally, the executive must constantly strive to minimize the risk that subordinates always feel as they seek to abandon the familiar and embrace the new.

In regard to rule making, idea management implies that the executive should encourage ongoing examination of processes and procedures used by organizational members to accomplish their tasks. If rules are needed to help channel behavior in more productive ways, they can be developed, implemented experimentally, and evaluated for longer-term acceptance. If rules, however, are found to be constraining creativity, productivity, or change, they can be studied, evaluated, and eliminated if necessary.

With regard to policing functions, idea management means seeking better ways to reward behaviors against objectives, developing opportunities for enhancing understanding of missions and values, and sharpening the content and immediacy of feedback mechanisms used to shape behavior. In a similar fashion, judiciary functions can be enhanced if those involved in conflict or feeling the brunt of organizational inequities can be involved in processes of idea generation, selection, and implementation to improve due process systems and clarify decision-making criteria.

Relational functions are supported by idea management, as the process itself can greatly enhance relations between superiors and subordinates and among peers. The executive's personal efforts to create conditions in which creativity and risk taking become the norm rather than the exception can have real payoffs for the organization over the long run.

In managing ideas the executive may call on his or her ability to control time and space. By this we mean that the executive can set the frame of reference for idea generation, selection, experimentation, and implementation by controlling either the time referent (past or future) or the space (all or part of the organization or environment) in which ideas are played out. By recognizing that the past is part of the present, the executive can call attention to certain values or traditions to be preserved in making current decisions; by outlining his or her views of the future, the executive can influence the constraints or focus of current idea-seeking activities. Through telling stories and myths, relating personal experiences, selecting language thinkingly and knowingly, and in other ways personally setting parameters for discussions, the executive can actually define the reality of the situation to which others are asked to respond. Likewise, by manipulating where ideas are sought, where they are presented, where they are evaluated, and where they are implemented, the executive controls outcomes of the idea-management process by actively and purposefully shaping the context that constrains which outcomes will later be viewed as workable. Encouraging competition between two locations, each testing an idea for improving productivity, is a simple example of using space to enhance idea evaluation.

Time and space can be manipulated by the executive to either tighten or loosen rules as desired. Policing functions, including reward systems, can be greatly influenced simply by altering the frequency with which policing activities occur or the physical distance between superiors and subordinates. Judiciary functions are affected by both time and space as it is discovered that what is "right" depends on one's temporal frame of reference as well as the level, location, or closeness of the defendant in relation to the prosecutor. Finally, no process of consensus building, personal growth, or enhancing the quality of worklife can even begin without explicit attention to the temporal and spatial referents of the actors involved, which again are subject to executive control. Each of these examples could be expanded on and magnified many times, the point being that the executive has much to gain from greater awareness and skill in managing the ways in which time and space influence behavior.

The management of ideas and the mastery of space and time are not the only tools over which an executive should gain better control as a result of having read this volume. Ideally, the executive will also have been confronted by numerous statements outlining his or her responsibility for enhancing personal and organizational learning. Because change is a constant feature of the environment of most organizations, today's solutions will quickly become inadequate in responding to tomorrow's problems and opportunities. To be prepared to take full advantage of those opportunities and to guarantee continued organizational survival and personal relevance, the executive must actively encourage and personally participate in programs, routines, and events that enhance learning. The law of requisite variety states that in order to respond to a crisis or opportunity, a system must have within its repertoire the skills to do so. Unfortunately for many systems, crises and opportunities represent unexpected events for which skills were not previously needed and therefore not developed. The *only* way to guarantee that systems will be prepared for future contingencies is to ensure that they engage in processes of learning that will develop skills to meet those challenges, even if the skills can find no current application. Usually the decision to acquire or develop surplus knowledge is one that is preserved for the executive; others are too busy trying to get current tasks done with as few resources as possible. Learning, like preventive maintenance for machinery, is an investment in the future of an individual or organization;

the decision to invest in learning may prove to be the most important single decision the executive makes. Nor is making that decision the end of the executive's responsibility in this matter; the executive must thereafter ensure that conditions are created that enhance learning for others, such as reducing the risk of experimentation, providing resources for new ventures, rewarding learning as well as action, and challenging the limits of learning that has already occurred. In fact, the executive might exercise his or her rule-making function to ensure that learning becomes ingrained in the experience of every organizational member and unit. Then the policing of the learning process can be carried out by revising reward systems and criteria of success. The judiciary function will be affected by organizational learning as questions of right and wrong are explored for the truth in both points of view that can contribute to a more complete and realistic portrayal of the situation. Certainly the nature of the relational function in the organization will be transformed when learning becomes a part of interactions rather than simply maintaining a focus on the status quo. In actuality, organizational events are full of opportunities for learning that can enhance both the organization and the individuals within it. It is largely up to the executive to set in motion a process that will enhance the degree of learning attained in each day of the organization's existence.

Finally, the executive may learn from this volume to approach the task of executing the four executive functions phenomenologically rather than distantly. By this we mean that the executive must become more aware as an actor, more in tune with his or her experiences and reactions to those experiences, more in touch with the basic values that guide decisions, more capable of understanding his or her behavior as a function of the influence of both the past and the future—in short, more knowing of self. The authors of this volume make it clear that the power of the executive to make sense of situations, to help others to do the same, to influence their environment, to achieve success, and indeed to accomplish virtually any objective desired is directly related to the ability of the executive to use himself or herself as a tool for interpreting the situation and determining what is to be done. Awareness of self is a prerequisite to conveying to others the values, reasoning, beliefs, attitudes, and dreams that they can use to shape their own thinking and, in so doing, to execute executive orders. Lack of such awareness decreases learning for self and others, provides unclear boundaries and instructions, leads to arbitrary and potentially disastrous decisions, and creates an environment adverse to idea management, risk taking, and growth.

With knowledge of self, rule making becomes less idiosyncratic, more facilitative rather than restrictive, and most important, more open to influence and change. Policing functions become developmental rather than punishment-centered (which executive in touch with himself or herself would not admit to having made a few mistakes along the way?); judiciary functions will be performed less mechanically and coldly; and relational functions will be full of sharing and personal contact rather than devoid of emotion and caring.

It is to this last challenge, that of knowing oneself, that this volume has been most directed. As the authors themselves discovered, one cannot think about the executive mind without thinking about oneself; moreover, in so doing one cannot help becoming more aware of one's own thought processes, values, and behaviors. If this book has accomplished nothing else, perhaps it has caused us to think about ourselves in some new ways that will allow us to make more conscious choices in the future about the way in which we will either live in the world around us or try to change it.

References

Ackoff, R. L. *Redesigning the Future: A Systems Approach to Societal Problems.* New York: Wiley, 1974.

Ackoff, R. L., and Emery, F. *On Purposeful Systems.* Chicago: Aldine-Atherton, 1974.

Adizes, I. "Organizational Passages." *Organizational Dynamics,* Summer 1979, pp. 3–25.

Alexander, C. *Notes on the Synthesis of Form.* Cambridge, Mass.: Harvard University Press, 1967.

Arendt, H. *The Origins of Totalitarianism.* (3rd ed.) New York: Harcourt Brace Jovanovich, 1966.

Arendt, H. *The Life of the Mind.* New York: Harcourt Brace Jovanovich, 1971.

Argyris, C. *Personality and Organization.* New York: Harper & Row, 1957.

Argyris, C. "Double-Loop Learning in Organizations." *Harvard Business Review,* 1976a, *55*(5), 115–125.

Argyris, C. *Increasing Leadership Effectiveness.* New York: Wiley-Interscience, 1976b.

Argyris, C. "Leadership, Learning, and Changing the Status Quo." *Organizational Dynamics,* Winter 1976c, pp. 29–43.

Argyris, C. *Reasoning, Learning, and Action: Individual and Organizational.* San Francisco: Jossey-Bass, 1982.

Argyris, C., and Schön, D. A. *Organizational Learning: A Theory of Action Perspective.* Reading, Mass.: Addison-Wesley, 1978.

Ashby, W. *Design for a Brain.* New York: Wiley, 1952.

Barnard, C. I. *The Functions of the Executive.* Cambridge, Mass.: Harvard University Press, 1938.

Barnes, L. B. "Managing the Paradox of Organizational Trust." *Harvard Business Review,* 1981, *59*(2), 107–116.

Bartlett, F. *Thinking.* New York: Basic Books, 1958.

Basadur, M. S. "Training in Creative Problem Solving: Effects on Deferred Judgment and Problem Finding and Solving in an Industrial Research Organization." Unpublished doctoral dissertation, University of Cincinnati, 1979.

Bate, P., and Mangham, I. *Exploring Participation.* New York: Wiley, 1981.

Beer, M., and Davis, S. M. "Creating a Global Organization: Failures Along the Way." *Columbia Journal of World Business,* 1976, *11,* 72–84.

Bennis, W. G. "Defenses Against 'Depressive Anxiety' in Groups: The Case of the Absent Leader." *Merrill-Palmer Quarterly of Behavior and Development,* 1961, *7,* 1–30.

Bennis, W. G. *Changing Organizations.* New York: McGraw-Hill, 1966.

Bennis, W. G. *The Chief.* New York: William Morris, 1984.

Bennis, W. G., and Shepard, H. A. "A Theory of Group Development." *Human Relations,* 1956, *9,* 415–457.

Berger, P. L., and Luckmann, T. *The Social Construction of Reality.* New York: Doubleday, 1966.

Berlin, I. *Personal Impressions.* New York: Viking Press, 1980.

Berne, E. *Games People Play: The Psychology of Human Relationships.* New York: Grove Press, 1964.

Berne, E. *The Structure and Dynamics of Organizations.* New York: Grove Press, 1976.

Bettelheim, B. *The Uses of Enchantment: The Meaning and Importance of Fairy Tales.* New York: Vintage, 1977.

Bion, W. R. *Experience in Groups.* London: Tavistock, 1959.

Blackburn, T. R. "Sensuous-Intellectual Complementarity in Science." *Science,* 1971, *172,* 1003–1007.

Block, J. "Some Enhancing and Consequential Structures of Personality." In A. I. Rubin (Ed.), *Further Explorations in Personality.* New York: Wiley-Interscience, 1981.

Bogen, J. E. "The Other Side of the Brain: An Appositional Mind." *Bulletin of the Los Angeles Neurological Societies,* 1969, *34*(3), 135–162.

Boland, R. J., and Pondy, L. R. "Accounting in Organizations: A Union of Natural and Rational Perspectives." *Accounting, Organizations, and Society,* 1983, forthcoming.

Boring, E. G. *A History of Experimental Psychology.* (2nd ed.) New York: Appleton-Century-Crofts, 1950.

Botkin, J. W., Elmandjra, M., and Malitza, M. *No Limits to Learning: Bridging the Human Gap.* New York: Pergamon Press, 1979.

Bowerman, W. R. "Subjective Competence: The Structure, Process, and Function of Self-Referent Causal Attributions." *Journal for the Theory of Social Behavior,* 1978, *8,* 45–57.

Braybrooke, D. "The Mystery of Executive Success Re-Examined." *Administrative Science Quarterly,* 1964, *8*(4), 533–560.

Braybrooke, D., and Lindblom, C. E. *A Strategy of Decision.* New York: Free Press, 1963.

Brentano, F. *Psychologie vom Empirischen Standpunkt.* Leipzig: Felix Meiner, 1924. (Originally published 1874.)

Bridges, W. *Making Sense of Life Transitions.* Reading, Mass.: Addison-Wesley, 1980.

Bridgman, P. W. *The Logic of Modern Physics.* New York: Macmillan, 1932.

Broverman, D. M., and others. "Roles of Activation and Inhibition in Sex Differences in Cognitive Abilities." *Psychological Review,* 1968, *75,* 23–50.

Bruner, J. "The Conditions of Creativity." In H. E. Gruber, G. Terrelli, and M. Wortheimer (Eds.), *Contemporary Approaches to Creative Thinking.* New York: Atherton, 1962a.

Bruner, J. *On Knowing: Essays for the Left Hand.* Cambridge, Mass.: Harvard University Press, 1962b.

Buhler, C. *Values in Psychotherapy.* New York: Free Press, 1962.

Buhler, C., and Massarik, F. (Eds.). *The Course of Human Life: A Study of Goals in the Humanistic Perspective.* New York: Springer, 1968.

Burns, T., and Stalker, G. M. *The Management of Innovation.* London: Tavistock, 1961.

Cangelosi, V., and Dill, W. "Organizational Learning: Observations Toward a Theory." *Administrative Science Quarterly,* 1965, *10,* 175-203.

Carlsson, B., Keane, P., and Martin, J. B. "R&D Organizations as Learning Systems." *Sloan Management Review,* Spring 1976, pp. 1-15.

Carter, E. E. "The Behavioral Theory of the Firm and Top Level Corporate Decisions." *Administrative Science Quarterly,* 1971, *16,* 413-428.

Carter, L. H. *The Limits of Order.* Lexington, Mass.: Lexington Books, 1974.

Chandler, A. D. *Strategy and Structure.* Cambridge, Mass.: M.I.T. Press, 1962.

Chickering, A. *Experience and Learning: An Introduction to Experiential Learning.* New York: Change Magazine Press, 1977.

Churchman, C. *The Design of Inquiring Systems.* New York: Basic Books, 1971.

Cohen, M. D., and March, J. G. *Leadership and Ambiguity: The American College President.* New York: McGraw-Hill, 1974.

Cohen, M. D., March, J. G., and Olsen, J. P. "A Garbage Can Model of Organizational Choice." *Administrative Science Quarterly,* 1972, *17,* 1-25.

Cohen, M. R., and Nagel, E. *An Introduction to Logic and Scientific Method.* New York: Harcourt Brace Jovanovich, 1934.

Cole, A. H. *Business Enterprise in Its Social Setting.* Cambridge, Mass.: Harvard University Press, 1959.

Combs, A. W., Richards, A. C., and Richards, F. *Perceptual Psychology.* New York: Harper & Row, 1976.

Conger, J. J. "Freedom and Commitment: Families, Youth, and

Social Change." *American Psychologist,* 1981, *36*(12), 1475–1484.

Cyert, R. M., and March, J. G. *A Behavioral Theory of the Firm.* Englewood Cliffs, N.J.: Prentice-Hall, 1963.

Dalton, G. W. "Influence and Organizational Change." In G. W. Dalton, P. R. Lawrence, and L. E. Greiner (Eds.), *Organizational Change and Development.* Homewood, Ill.: Irwin, 1970.

Dearborn, D. C., and Simon, H. "Selective Perception: A Note on the Departmental Identifications of Executives." *Sociometry,* 1958, *21,* 140–144.

"Delta: The World's Most Profitable Airline." *Business Week,* Aug. 31, 1981, pp. 68–72.

Dewey, J. *How We Think.* Lexington, Mass.: Heath, 1910.

Dewey, J. *The Quest for Certainty.* New York: Paragon, 1979. (Originally published 1929.)

Diekman, A. J. "Biomodal Consciousness." *Archives of General Psychiatry,* 1971, *25,* 481–489.

Dunckner, K. "On Problem Solving." (L. Slees, Trans.) *Psychological Monographs,* 1945, *58,* 20–21.

Edwards, B. *Drawing on the Right Side of the Brain.* Los Angeles: Tarcher Press, 1979.

Ellis, W. D. *A Source Book of Gestalt Psychology.* New York: Humanities Press, 1950.

Emery, F., and Trist, E. "The Causal Texture of Organizational Environments." *Human Relations,* 1965, *18,* 21–31.

Erikson, E. *Childhood and Society.* New York: Norton, 1950.

Fallaci, O. *Interview with History.* (J. Shepley, Trans.) Boston: Houghton Mifflin, 1977.

Fallaci, O. "Walesa Talks About His Position, Himself." *Boston Globe,* Mar. 15, 1981, pp. 1, 35ff.

Ferguson, M. *The Aquarian Conspiracy.* Los Angeles: Tarcher, 1980.

Fink, S., Beak, J., and Taddeo, K. "Organizational Crisis and Change." *Journal of Applied Behavioral Science,* 1971, 7(1), 15–37.

Fox, J. M. *Executive Qualities.* Reading, Mass.: Addison-Wesley, 1976.

Freire, F. *Pedagogy of the Opressed.* New York: Seabury Press, 1974.

Freud, S. "Dora: An Analysis of a Case of Hysteria." (A. Strachey and J. Strachey, Trans.) In S. Freud, *The Case of Dora and Other Papers.* New York: Norton, 1952. (Originally published 1905.)

Freud, S. *Das Ich und das Es* [The Ego and the Id]. New York: Norton, 1961. (Originally published 1923.)

Friedlander, F. "Behavioral Research as a Transactional Process." *Human Organization,* 1968, *27*(4), 369-379.

Friedlander, F. "Emerging Blackness in a White Research World." *Human Organization,* 1970, *29*(4), 239-250.

Friedlander, F., and Pickle, H. "Components of Effectiveness in Small Organizations." *Administrative Science Quarterly,* 1968, *13,* 289-304.

Friedlander, F., and Schott, B. "The Use of Task Groups and Task Forces in Organizational Change." In R. Payne and C. Cooper (Eds.), *Groups at Work.* New York: Wiley, 1981.

Fry, R., Rubin, I., and Plovnick, M. "Dynamics of Groups That Execute or Manage Policy." In R. Payne and C. Cooper (Eds.), *Groups at Work.* New York: Wiley, 1981.

Furth, H. T. *Piaget and Knowledge.* Englewood Cliffs, N.J.: Prentice-Hall, 1969.

Galbraith, J. *Organization Design.* Reading, Mass.: Addison-Wesley, 1977.

Garfinkel, H. "Common-Sense Knowledge of Social Structures: The Documentary Method of Interpretation." In J. Scher (Ed.), *Theories of the Mind.* New York: Free Press, 1962.

Gendlin, E. T. *Experiencing and the Creation of Meaning.* New York: Free Press, 1962.

Gibbard, G. S., Hartman, J. J., and Mann, R. D. (Eds.). *Analysis of Groups: Contributions to Theory, Research, and Practice.* San Francisco: Jossey-Bass, 1973.

Glaser, B. G., and Strauss, A. L. *The Discovery of Grounded Theory.* Chicago: Aldine, 1967.

Glasser, W. *Stations of the Mind.* New York: Harper & Row, 1981.

Goffman, E. *The Presentation of Self in Everyday Life.* Garden City, N.Y.: Doubleday Anchor, 1959.

Greenwald, A. G. "The Totalitarian Ego: Fabrication and Revision of Personal History." *American Psychologist,* 1980, *35* (7), 603–618.

Greiner, L. E. "Evolution and Revolution as Organizations Grow." *Harvard Business Review,* July-August 1972, pp. 55–64.

Grinyer, P. H., and Spender, J. C. *Turnaround—Managerial Recipes for Strategic Success.* New York: Associated Business Press, 1979.

Guilford, J. P., and Hoepfner, R. *The Analysis of Intelligence.* Toronto: McGraw-Hill, 1971.

Guth, W. D., and Taguri, R. "Personal Values and Corporate Strategies." *Harvard Business Review,* Sept.-Oct. 1965, *43,* 123–132.

Hampden-Turner, C. *Maps of the Mind.* New York: Macmillan, 1981.

Harding, M. *The I and the Not-I: A Study in the Development of Consciousness.* Princeton, N.J.: Princeton University Press, 1965.

Harris, T. A. *I'm OK—You're OK.* New York: Harper & Row, 1969.

Harrison, R. "Defense and the Need to Know." In R. T. Golembiewski and A. Blumberg (Eds.), *Sensitivity Training and the Laboratory Approach.* (3rd ed.) Itasca, Ill.: Peacock, 1977.

Hebb, D. O. *Essays on Mind.* Hillsdale, N.J.: Erlbaum, 1980.

Hedberg, B., Nystrom, P., and Starbuck, W. "Camping on Seasaws: Prescriptions for a Self-Designing Organization." *Administrative Science Quarterly,* 1976, *21,* 41–65.

Hegel, G. W. F. *System der Wissenschaft: Phänomenologie des Geistes* [Phenomenology of Mind]. Hamburg: Verlag von Felix Meiner, 1952. (Originally published 1807.)

Hilgard, E. R. "The Psychology of Consciousness." *Annual Review of Psychology,* 1979, *31,* 1–26.

Hillman, J. "The Fiction of Case History: A Round." In J. B. Wiggins (Ed.), *Religion as Story.* New York: Harper & Row, 1975a.

Hillman, J. *Revisioning Psychology.* New York: Harper & Row, 1975b.

Hirschman, A. O., and Lindblom, E. "Economic Development,

Research and Development, Policy Making: Some Converging Views." *Behavioral Science,* 1962, *8,* 211–222.

Husserl, E. *Cartesianische Meditationen* [Cartesian Meditations]. (D. Cairns, Trans.) The Hague: Martinus Nijhoff, 1960. (Originally published 1931.)

Husserl, E. *Ideen an einer reinen Phänomenologie und phänomenologischen Philosophie* [Ideas—General Introduction to Pure Phenomenology]. (W. R. B. Gibson, Trans.) New York: Collier, 1962. (Originally published 1913.)

Jackson, K. F. *The Art of Solving Problems.* New York: St. Martin's Press, 1975.

Jahoda, M. *Current Concepts of Mental Health.* New York: Basic Books, 1958.

James, W. *The Principles of Psychology.* New York: Holt, 1890.

James, W. "Is Life Worth Living?" In W. James (Ed.), *The Will to Believe.* New York: Dover, 1956. (Originally published 1895.)

Janis, I. L. "Group Think." *Psychology Today,* November 1971, pp. 43–46, 74–76.

Jaques, E. "Taking Time Seriously in Evaluating Jobs." *Harvard Business Review,* September-October 1979, pp. 124–132.

Jenkins, I. "Performance." In R. A. Smith (Ed.), *Aesthetic Concepts and Education.* Urbana: University of Illinois Press, 1970.

Jentz, B. (Ed.). *Entry: The Hiring, Training, and Supervision of Administrators.* New York: McGraw-Hill, 1981.

Jervis, R. *Perception and Misperception in International Policies.* Princeton, N.J.: Princeton University Press, 1976.

Jourard, S. M. "Healthy Personality and Self-Disclosure." In W. G. Bennis and others (Eds.), *Interpersonal Dynamics.* (3rd ed.) Homewood, Ill.: Dorsey, 1973.

Jung, C. G. *Psychological Types.* London: Routledge & Kegan Paul, 1923.

Jung, C. G. *Mysterium Coniunctionis: An Inquiry into the Separation and Synthesis of Psychic Opposites in Alchemy.* Princeton, N.J.: Princeton University Press, 1963.

Jung, C. G. *Analytical Psychology.* New York: Vintage, 1968.

Kadis, A. L., and others. *Practicum of Group Psychotherapy.* New York: Harper & Row, 1974.

Kanter, R., and Stein, B. A. (Eds.). *Life in Organizations.* New York: Basic Books, 1979.

Katz, D., and Kahn, R. *The Social Psychology of Organizations.* New York: Wiley, 1966.

Keeton, M. T., and Tate, P. J. (Eds.). *New Directions for Experiential Learning: Learning by Experience: What, Why, How,* no. 1. San Francisco: Jossey-Bass, 1978.

Kepner, J., and Trego, B. *The Rational Manager.* New York: McGraw-Hill, 1965.

Kilmann, R. "Problem Management: A Behavioral Science Approach." In G. Zaltman (Ed.), *Management Principles for Non-Profit Agencies and Organizations.* New York: American Management Association, 1979.

Klein, M. *Lives People Live: A Textbook of Transactional Analysis.* New York: Wiley, 1980.

Kohlberg, L. "State and Sequence: The Cognitive-Developmental Approach to Socialization." In D. A. Guslin (Ed.), *Handbook of Socialization Theory and Research.* Chicago: Rand McNally, 1969.

Köhler, W. *Gestalt Psychology.* New York: Liveright, 1947. (Originally published 1929.)

Kolb, D. A. *Experiential Learning: Experience as the Source of Learning and Development.* Englewood Cliffs, N.J.: Prentice-Hall, 1983.

Kolb, D. A., and Fry, R. "Toward an Applied Theory of Experiential Learning." In C. Cooper (Ed.), *Theories of Group Processes.* London: Wiley, 1975.

Kolb, D. A., Rubin, I., and McIntyre, J. *Organizational Psychology: An Experiential Approach.* Englewood Cliffs, N.J.: Prentice-Hall, 1979.

Kotter, J. P. *The General Managers.* New York: Free Press, 1982a.

Kotter, J. P. "What Effective General Managers Really Do." *Harvard Business Review,* November-December 1982b, pp. 156–167.

Kraft, J. "The Downsizing Decision." *New Yorker,* May 5, 1980, pp. 134–162.

Kübler-Ross, E. *On Death and Dying.* New York: Macmillan, 1969.

Kuhn, A. *The Logic of Social Systems: A Unified, Deductive, System-Based Approach to Social Science.* San Francisco: Jossey-Bass, 1974.

Kuhn, T. S. *The Structure of Scientific Revolutions.* (2nd ed.) Chicago: University of Chicago Press, 1970.

Lawrence, P. R., and Lorsch, J. W. *Developing Organizations: Diagnosis and Action.* Reading, Mass.: Addison-Wesley, 1969.

Leeper, R. W. *Lewin's Topological and Vector Psychology.* Eugene: University of Oregon Press, 1943.

Levinson, H. "Management by Whose Objectives?" *Harvard Business Review,* July-August 1970, pp. 125-134.

Lewin, K. *Field Theory in Social Science.* New York: Harper & Row, 1951.

Lindblom, C. E. "The Science of Muddling Through." *Public Administration Review,* 1959, *2,* 78-88.

Lindblom, C. E. *The Policy-Making Process.* Englewood Cliffs, N.J.: Prentice-Hall, 1968.

Lindner, R. *The Fifty-Minute Hour.* New York: Bantam Books, 1958.

Livingston, J. S. "Myth of the Well-Educated Manager." *Harvard Business Review,* January-February 1971, pp. 79-89.

Lofland, J. *Doing Social Work.* New York: Wiley, 1976.

Long, J. "By Trusting Intuition, Educated Guesses, Coke Capitalizes on Exchange-Rate Shifts." *Wall Street Journal,* September 3, 1982, p. 13.

Lord, J. *A Gicometti Portrait.* New York: Museum of Modern Art, 1965.

Luft, J. *Of Human Interaction.* Palo Alto, Calif.: National Press Books, 1969.

Lundberg, G. A. *Foundations of Sociology.* New York: Macmillan, 1939.

Lynn, L. E., and Whitman, D. de F. *The President as Policymaker: Jimmy Carter and Welfare Reform.* Philadelphia: Temple University Press, 1981.

Lyons, W. "Ryle's Three Accounts of Thinking." *International Philosophical Quarterly,* 1979, *19*(4), 443-450.

Lyons, W. *Gilbert Ryle: An Introduction to His Philosophy.* Atlantic Highlands, N.J.: Humanities Press, 1980.

McCall, M. W., Jr., Kaplan, R. W., and Gerlach, M. C. "Caught in the Act: Decision Makers at Work." Technical Report No. 20. Center for Creative Leadership, Greensboro, N.C., 1982.

McCall, M. W., Jr., Morrison, A. M., and Hannon, R. L. "Studies of Managerial Work: Results and Methods." Technical Report No. 9. Center for Creative Leadership, Greensboro, N.C., 1978.

Maccoby, M. *The Gamesman.* New York: Simon & Schuster, 1976.

McGrath, J. E. "Stress and Behavior in Organizations." In M. D. Dunnette (Ed.), *Handbook of Industrial and Organizational Psychology.* Chicago: Rand McNally, 1976.

McGuire, J. *Factors Affecting the Growth of Manufacturing Firms.* Seattle: Bureau of Business Research, University of Washington, 1963.

McHugh, P. *Defining the Situation.* Indianapolis: Bobbs-Merrill, 1968.

Mahrer, A. R. *Experiencing: A Humanistic Theory of Psychology and Psychiatry.* New York: Brunner/Mazel, 1978.

Maier, N. R. F. *Problem Solving and Creativity in Individuals and Groups.* Monterey, Calif.: Brooks/Cole, 1970.

Mangham, I. L., and Overington, M. A. "Dramatism and the Theatrical Metaphor." In G. Morgan (Ed.), *Beyond Method: Strategies for Social Research.* Beverly Hills, Calif.: Sage, 1983.

Manning, P. K. *The Narcs' Game.* Cambridge, Mass.: M.I.T. Press, 1980.

March, J. G., and Olsen, J. P. *Ambiguity and Choice in Organizations.* Bergen, Norway: Universitetsforlaget, 1976.

March, J. G., and Simon, H. A. *Organizations.* New York: Wiley, 1958.

Maslow, A. "A Theory of Human Motivation." *Psychological Review,* 1943, *50,* 370–396.

Mason, R. O., and Mitroff, I. I. *Challenging Strategic Planning Assumptions.* New York: Wiley, 1981.

Massarik, F. "The Science of Perceiving: Foundations for an Empirical Phenomenology." Working Paper. Graduate School of Management, University of California, Los Angeles, 1979.

Massarik, F. "The Interviewing Process Re-examined." In P.

Reuson and J. Rowan (Eds.), *Human Inquiry*. Chichester (U.K.) and New York: Wiley, 1981.

May, R. *The Courage to Create*. New York: Bantam Books, 1976.

Michael, D. N. *On Learning to Plan—and Planning to Learn: The Social Psychology of Changing Toward Future-Responsive Societal Learning*. San Francisco: Jossey-Bass, 1973.

Miles, R. H., and Randolph, W. A. "Influence of Organizational Learning Styles on Early Development." In J. R. Kimberly, R. H. Miles, and Associates (Eds.), *The Organizational Life Cycle: Issues in the Creation, Transformation, and Decline of Organizations*. San Francisco: Jossey-Bass, 1980.

Miller, D., and Friesen, P. H. "Momentum and Revolution in Organizational Adaptation." *Academy of Management Journal*, 1980, *23*(4), 591-614.

Miller, D. T., and Ross, M. "Self-Serving Biases in the Attribution of Causality: Fact or Fiction." *Psychological Bulletin*, 1975, *82*, 213-225.

Mills, T. *The Sociology of Small Groups*. Englewood Cliffs, N.J.: Prentice-Hall, 1965.

Mintzberg, H. *The Nature of Managerial Work*. New York: Harper & Row, 1973a.

Mintzberg, H. "Strategy Making in Three Modes." *California Management Review*, Winter 1973b, pp. 44-53.

Mintzberg, H. "Patterns in Strategy Formation." *Management Science*, 1978, *24*, 934-948.

Mintzberg, H. *The Structuring of Organizations: A Synthesis of the Research*. Englewood Cliffs, N.J.: Prentice-Hall, 1979.

Mintzberg, H. "What Is Planning Anyway?" *Strategic Management Journal*, 1981, *2*, 319-324.

Mintzberg, H., and Waters, J. A. "Tracking Strategy in an Entrepreneurial Firm." *Academy of Management Journal*, 1982, *25*, 465-499.

Mintzberg, H., and Waters, J. A. "Researching the Formation of Strategies: The History of Canadian Lady, 1939-1976." In R. Lamb (Ed.), *Strategic Management*. Englewood Cliffs, N.J.: Prentice-Hall, 1983.

Mitroff, I. I. "Is a Periodic Table of the Elements for Organization Behaviour Possible? Integrating Jung and TA for Organizational Analysis." *Human Systems Management,* 1981, *2,* 168-176.

Mitroff, I. I., and Kilmann, R. H. "Stories Managers Tell: A New Tool for Organizational Problem Solving." *Management Review,* 1975, pp. 18-28.

Mitroff, I. I., and Kilmann, R. H. "On Organizational Stories." In R. H. Kilmann, L. R. Pondy, and D. Slevin (Eds.), *Management of Organizational Design.* Vol. 1: *Strategies and Implementation.* New York: American Elsevier, 1976.

Mitroff, I. I., and Kilmann, R. H. *Methodological Approaches to Social Science: Integrating Divergent Concepts and Theories.* San Francisco: Jossey-Bass, 1978.

Mitroff, I. I., and Mason, R. O. *Creating a Dialectical Social Science.* Amsterdam: Reidel, 1981a.

Mitroff, I. I., and Mason, R. O. "On Dialectical Pragmatism: A Progress Report on an Interdisciplinary Program of Research on the Dialectical Inquiry System." *Synthese,* 1981b, *47,* 29-42.

Mitroff, I. I., and Mitroff, D. D. "Interpersonal Communication for Knowledge Utilization: Putting Freud and Jung Back Together again!" *Knowledge,* 1979, *1,* 203-218.

Mitroff, I. I., and Mitroff, D. D. "Personality and Problem Solving: Making the Link Visible." *Journal of Experiential Learning and Simulation,* 1980, *2*(2), 111-119.

Myers, I. B., and Briggs, K. C. *Myers-Briggs Type Indicator.* Princeton, N.J.: Educational Testing Service, 1962.

Neumann, E. *The Origins and History of Consciousness.* Princeton, N.J.: Princeton University Press, 1954.

Nisbett, R. E., and Ross, L. *Human Inference: Strategies and Shortcomings.* Englewood Cliffs, N.J.: Prentice-Hall, 1980.

Oldham, G. R., and Hackman, J. R. "Work Design in the Organizational Context." In B. M. Staw and L. L. Cummings (Eds.), *Research in Organizational Behavior.* Vol. 2. Greenwich, Conn.: JAI Press, 1980.

Orwell, G. *1984.* New York: Harcourt Brace Jovanovich, 1949.

Osborn, A. F. *Applied Imagination.* New York: Scribner's, 1953.

Ouchi, W. *Theory Z.* Reading, Mass.: Addison-Wesley, 1981.

Pascale, R., and Athos, A. *The Art of Japanese Management.* New York: Simon & Schuster, 1981.

Perkins, J. *College and University Presidents: Recommendations and Report of a Survey.* New York State Regents Advisory Committee on Educational Leadership, 1967.

Perls, F. S. "Four Lectures." In J. Fagan and L. Shepherd (Eds.), *Gestalt Therapy.* Palo Alto, Calif.: Science and Behavior Books, 1970.

Perls, F. S., Hefferline, R., and Goodman, P. *Gestalt Therapy.* New York: Julian Press, 1951.

Perrow, C. *Complex Organizations: A Critical Essay.* Glenview, Ill.: Scott, Foresman, 1972.

Peters, T. J. "A Style for All Seasons." *Executive,* Summer 1980, pp. 12–16.

Peters, T. J., and Waterman, R. H., Jr. *In Search of Excellence.* New York: Harper & Row, 1982.

Pettigrew, A. *The Politics of Organizational Decision Making.* London: Tavistock, 1973.

Pfeffer, J. "Management as Symbolic Action: The Creation and Maintenance of Organizational Paradigms." In L. L. Cummings and B. M. Staw (Eds.), *Research in Organizational Behavior.* Vol. 3. Greenwich, Conn.: JAI Press, 1981.

Pfeffer, J., and Salancik, G. R. *The External Control of Organizations: A Resource Dependence Perspective.* New York: Harper & Row, 1978.

Piaget, J. *Play, Dreams, and Imitation in Childhood.* New York: Norton, 1951.

Polster, E., and Polster, E. *Gestalt Therapy Integrated.* New York: Brunner/Mazel, 1973.

Powers, W. T. *Behavior: The Control of Perception.* Chicago: Aldine, 1973.

Prince, G. "Creative Meetings Through Power Sharing." *Harvard Business Review,* July-August 1972, pp. 47–54.

Prince, G. "The Mind Spring Theory: A New Development from Synectics Research." *Journal of Creative Behavior,* 1975, 9(3), 159–181.

Puglisi, M. "Franz Brentano: A Biographical Sketch." *American Journal of Psychology*, 1924, *35*, 414-419.

Quinn, J. B. "Managing Strategic Change." In M. L. Tushman and W. L. Moore (Eds.), *Readings in the Management of Innovation*. Boston: Pitman, 1982.

Rawls, J. *A Theory of Justice*. Cambridge, Mass.: Harvard University Press, 1971.

Reich, R. B. "Regulation by Confrontation or Negotiation." *Harvard Business Review*, May-June 1981, pp. 82-93.

Richards, M. D. "An Exploratory Study of Strategic Failure." *Academy of Management Proceedings*, 1973.

Roheim, G. *Psychoanalysis and Anthropology, Culture, Personality, and the Unconscious*. New York: International Universities Press, 1950.

Rosenthal, R. *Experimenter Effects in Behavioral Research*. New York: Wiley, 1976.

Ryle, G. "Some Problems About Thinking." In H. E. Kiefer and M. K. Munitz (Eds.), *Mind, Science, and History*. Albany, N.Y.: SUNY Press, 1970.

Ryle, G. *Collected Papers*. Vol. 2. New York: Barnes & Noble, 1971.

Sanderson, M. *Successful Problem Management*. New York: Wiley, 1979.

Sapir, E. *Language, Culture, and Personality*. Menasha, Wisc.: Sapir Memorial Publication Fund, 1941.

Schein, E. *Coercive Persuasion*. New York: Norton, 1961.

Schein, E. *Process Consultation: Its Role In Organizational Development*. Reading, Mass.: Addison-Wesley, 1969.

Schein, V. E., and Greiner, L. E. "Can Organization Development Be Fine Tuned to Bureaucracies?" *Organizational Dynamics*, 1977, *5*(3), 48-61.

Schmidt, R. (Ed.). *Die Philosophie der Gegenwart in Selbstdarstellungen* [Present-Day Philosophy in Biography]. Leipzig: Felix Meiner, 1924.

Sheldon, A. "Organizational Paradigms: A Theory of Organizational Change." *Organizational Dynamics*, Winter 1980, pp. 61-80.

Sherif, M., and Hovland, C. I. *Social Judgments*. New Haven, Conn.: Yale University Press, 1961.

Silverman, D. *The Theory of Organizations.* New York: Basic Books, 1971.

Slater, P. E. *The Glory of Hera: Greek Mythology and the Greek Family.* Boston: Beacon Press, 1968.

Slocum, J. "Does Cognitive Style Affect Diagnosis and Intervention Strategies of Change Agents?" *Group and Organizational Studies,* 1978, *3,* 199–210.

Smith, C. S. "Structural Hierarchy in Science, Art and History." In J. Wechsler (Ed.), *On Aesthetics in Science.* Cambridge, Mass.: M.I.T. Press, 1978.

Snow, C. C., and Hambrick, D. C. "Measuring Organizational Strategies." *Academy of Management Review,* 1980, *5*(4), 527–538.

Snyder, M. L., Stephen, W. G., and Rosenfeld, C. "Attributional Egotism." In J. H. Harvey, W. J. Ickes, and R. F. Kidd (Eds.), *New Dimensions in Attribution Research.* Hillsdale, N.J.: Erlbaum, 1978.

Snyder, M. L., Tanke, E. D., and Berscheid, E. "Social Perception and Interpersonal Behavior: On the Self-Fulfilling Nature of Social Stereotypes." *Journal of Personality and Social Psychology,* 1977, *35,* 656–666.

Snygg, D., and Combs, A. W. *Individual Behavior.* New York: Harper & Row, 1959.

Spiegelberg, H. *The Phenomenological Movement: A Historical Introduction.* The Hague: Martinus Nijhoff, 1965.

Sproull, L. S. "Beliefs in Organizations." In P. C. Nystrom and W. H. Starbuck (Eds.), *Handbook of Organizational Design.* Vol. 2. New York: Oxford University Press, 1981.

Srivastva, S., Obert, S., and Neilsen, E. "Organization Analysis Through Group Processes: A Theoretical Perspective for Organization Development." In C. Cooper (Ed.), *Organization Development in the UK and USA.* New York: Petrello, 1977.

Staw, B. M. "Rationality and Justification in Organizational Life." In B. M. Staw and L. L. Cummings (Eds.), *Research in Organizational Behavior.* Vol. 2. Greenwich, Conn.: JAI Press, 1980.

Staw, B. M. "The Escalation of Commitment to a Course of Action." *Academy of Management Review,* 1981, *6*(4), 577–588.

Steckroth, R. L., and others. "Organizational Roles, Cognitive Roles, and Problem Solving Styles." *Journal of Experiential Learning and Simulation,* 1980, *2,* 77–87.

Stewart, R. *Contrasts in Management.* New York: McGraw-Hill, 1976.

Strasser, S. *Phenomenology and the Human Sciences: A Contribution to a New Scientific Ideal.* Pittsburgh: Duquesne Studies, 1963.

Stumpf, C. *"Tonpsychologie."* Excerpted in B. Rund (Ed.), *Modern Classical Psychologists.* Boston: Houghton Mifflin, 1912.

Taggart, W., and Robby, D. "Minds and Managers: On the Dual Nature of Human Information Processing and Management." *Academy of Management Review,* 1981, *6*(2), 187–195.

Tannenbaum, R. "Some Matters of Life and Death." Working Paper 76-2. Human Systems Development Study Center, Graduate School of Management, University of California at Los Angeles, April 1976.

Teger, A. I. *Too Much Invested to Quit.* New York: Pergamon Press, 1980.

Terkel, S. *Working.* New York: Pantheon, 1972.

Terreberry, S. "The Evolution of Organizational Environments." *Administrative Science Quarterly,* 1968, *12,* 590–613.

Thomas, K. "Conflict and Conflict Management." In M. D. Dunnette (Ed.), *Handbook of Industrial and Organizational Psychology.* Chicago: Rand McNally, 1976.

Thompson, J. D. *Organizations in Action.* New York: McGraw-Hill, 1967.

Thompson, J. D. and Tuden, A. "Strategies, Structure, and Process of Organizational Decision." In J. D. Thompson, P. W. Hawkes, B. H. Junker, and A. Tuden (Eds.), *Comparative Studies in Administration.* Pittsburgh: University of Pittsburgh, 1959.

Toffler, A. *The Third Wave.* New York: Bantam, 1980.

Torbert, W. *Being for the Most Part Puppets: Interactions Among Men's Labor, Leisure, and Politics.* Cambridge, Mass.: Schenkman, 1972.

Torbert, W. *Learning from Experience.* New York: Columbia University Press, 1973.

Trist, E. "On Sociotechnical Systems." In W. Bennis, K. D. Benne, and R. Chin (Eds.), *The Planning of Change.* New York: Holt, Rinehart and Winston, 1969.

Truax, C. B., and Carkhuff, R. R. *Toward Effective Counseling and Psychotherapy: Training and Practice.* Chicago: Aldine, 1967.

Tuckman, B. W. "Developmental Sequence in Small Groups." *Psychological Bulletin,* 1965, *63,* 384-399.

Tuckman, B. W., and Jensen, M. A. C. "Stages of Small Group Developmental Revisited." *Group and Organizational Studies,* 1967, *2*(4), 419-427.

Vail, P. "Toward a Behavioral Description of High Performing Systems." In M. M. McCall and others (Eds.), *Leadership: Where Else Can We Go?* Durham, N.C.: Duke University Press, 1978.

Van de Ven, A. H. "The Three R's of Administrative Behavior: Rational, Random, and Reasonable." Paper presented at the Albany Conference on Organizational Theory and Public Policy, Albany, N.Y., April 1982.

Vickers, G. "Rationality and Intuition." In J. Wechsler (Ed.), *On Aesthetics in Science.* Cambridge, Mass.: M.I.T. Press, 1978.

Wallas, G. *The Art of Thought.* New York: Harcourt Brace Jovanovich, 1926.

Warwick, D. P. *A Theory of Public Bureaucracy: Politics, Personality, and Organization in the State Department.* Cambridge, Mass.: Harvard University Press, 1975.

Watzlawick, P., Beavin, J. H., and Jackson, D. D. *Pragmatics of Human Communication.* New York: Norton, 1967.

Weick, K. E. *The Social Psychology of Organizing.* (2nd ed.) Reading, Mass.: Addison-Wesley, 1979.

Weick, K. E. "Management of Organizational Change Among Loosely Coupled Elements." In P. S. Goodman and Associates, *Change in Organizations: New Perspectives on Theory, Research, and Practice.* San Francisco: Jossey-Bass, 1982.

Weick, K. E., Gilfillan, D. P., and Keith, T. "The Effect of Composer Credibility on Orchestra Performance." *Sociometry,* 1973, *36,* 435-462.

Weiss, C. H. "Knowledge Creep and Decision Accretion." *Knowledge*, 1980, *1*(3), 381–404.

Whorf, B. L. *Language, Thought, and Reality.* New York: Wiley, 1956.

Whyte, W. H. *The Organization Man.* New York: Simon & Schuster, 1956.

Wildavsky, A. "The Self-Evaluating Organization." *Public Administration Review*, 1972, *32*, 509–520.

Wildavsky, A. "If Planning Is Everything, Maybe It's Nothing." *Policy Sciences*, 1973, *4*, 127–155.

Wortman, C. B. "Causal Attributions and Personal Control." In J. H. Harvey, W. J. Ickes, and R. F. Kidd (Eds.), *New Dimensions in Attribution Research.* Vol. 1. Hillsdale, N.J.: Erlbaum, 1976.

Zand, D. "Collateral Organization: A New Change Strategy." *Journal of Applied Behavioral Sciences*, 1974, *10*(1), 63–89.

Index

A

Accommodation and assimilation, in learning, 196

Ackoff, R. L., 152, 164, 281-282, 311

Action: analysis of thinking in context of, 221-242; awareness of, and producing, 57; characteristics of, 235; as intensified by thinking, 224, 230-235; overview of, 12-13, 221-224; as provoked by thinking, 223-224, 228-230; as qualified by thinking, 223, 224-228; rationality and intuition in, 169-191; self-reinforcing linkages in, 233-235, 241; situation modified by, 232-233; symbolic, 185; thinking concurrent with, 222-224; thoughtful, conclusion on, 241-242; thoughtful, implications of, 235-241; timely, 84-108; watching, 239-240

Adaptation: adhocracy strategy formulation and, 76-82; characteristics of, 62, 76

Addressograph-Multigraph Corporation, personal vision at, 187

Adhocracy: concept of, 76; leadership of, 79-80; overview of, 5; strategist in, 82-83; strategy formulation in, 76-82

Adizes, I., 203, 311

Affirmation, in learning, 206-207

Air Canada, strategy of, 61, 70, 72-73

Alchemy, as projective psychology, 158

Alexander, 91

Alexander, C., 177, 311

Alignment, in transformative power, 18, 19

Ambiguity: in leadership environment, 17; as necessity of change, 183

Anomalies: amplification of, 183; concept of, 183; in rationality

331